THE POETRY READER'S TOOLKIT

THE POETRY READER'S TOOLKIT

*A Guide to Reading
and Understanding Poetry*

MARC POLONSKY

NTC Publishing Group
a division of NTC/CONTEMPORARY PUBLISHING COMPANY
Lincolnwood, Illinois USA

Executive Editor: Marisa L. L'Heureux
Editor: Lisa A. De Mol
Cover and interior design: Monica Baziuk
Project Editor: Dawn Barker

ISBN (student text): 0-8442-5988-8
ISBN (instructor's edition): 0-8442-5989-6

Library of Congress Cataloging-in-Publication Data

Polonsky, Marc, 1958–
    The poetry reader's toolkit ; a guide to reading and
understanding poetry / Marc Polonsky.
        p.   cm.
    Includes index.
    ISBN 0-8442-5988-8
    1. Poetics.   I. Title.
PN1042P58   1997
808.1—dc21
                                        97-347
                                        CIP
                                        AC

7 8 9 0 1 VL 0 9 8 7 6 5 4 3 2 1

CONTENTS

TO THE READER

This book has grown out of two strongly held convictions:

(1) POETRY IS IMPORTANT.

Poetry is the language of imagination, and imagination is the key to fulfillment. Our experience of life is largely determined by the ways in which we *imagine* our world. A great deal of our experience is mediated through words. Words can be—and often are—wielded in such a way as to *contract* the imagination, limiting its possibilities through advertising, political slogans, jargon, propaganda, and so on. But poetry uses words to open the doors of the mind, to light up new or neglected rooms of the imagination, *to enhance life*. Poetry points to imagination's infinite potential and reveals a world of unaccustomed sensations and thoughts.

(2) POETRY HAS BEEN NEEDLESSLY MYSTIFIED.

Most of my students come to my poetry classes convinced that they don't understand poetry, that poetry is necessarily obtuse, abstract, and removed from ordinary life, and that only extremely intellectual people can "interpret" it. This is a tragically mistaken perception. This book seeks to demystify poetry and to demonstrate that poetry is, in fact, accessible and relevant to everyone— given *patience*. It is my responsibility, as the author of this book, to convince you that this is true.

You do not have to like every poem. Indeed, you certainly will not. But you will undoubtedly like some poems, and you'll probably even *love* at least a few.

Reading poetry takes effort and practice; it certainly is not as straightforward as reading the newspaper. Poetry asks for a special kind of involvement, imaginative willingness, and even trust from you. Poetry also demands that you pay close attention to your own inner thoughts, feelings, images, and sensations as you read. A poem is not entirely up to your interpretation, but neither are you a passive recipient of a poem in the way that, for example, a television viewer passively absorbs a TV program. With poetry, you are required to participate with the poet in envisioning a distinctly unique perspective on some feature of life or some nuance of feeling. The role of the reader, as a *collaborator* in the poetic interaction, is of crucial importance. This is also why poetry is so remarkably valuable and healthy: It is an imagination exerciser.

This book is called *The Poetry Reader's Toolkit* because certain approaches to reading, along with some understanding of how various poetic techniques and devices work, can serve as tools for latching onto, and prying your way into, a poem.

In Chapter 1, "Why Poetry?" we will consider the question, Why poetry? If poetry is not relevant to your life or to your concerns, and if it does not interest you, then why should you bother with it? I certainly would not be so brazen as to assume that you should like poetry just because *I* do! So in this chapter we will discuss some reasons why poetry might be of value and interest to you, even if you never thought so before. We will also discuss *patience,* the first and most important tool you can use to appreciate poetry, and we will begin putting it into practice.

In Chapter 2, "Emotions," we will look closely at how words and images affect our internal universe of feeling. The names we give to our emotions—love, anger, joy, and so on—are rough and general. In this chapter we will see how poetry "fleshes out" emotions, how poetry can describe and evoke those hues and textures of emotional experience which are not so easily named. We will also talk about *connotation*, the ability of words to call to mind more than their literal meanings.

In Chapter 3, "Images," we will further explore the power of visual and sensual imagery. We will note the shapes that images take in our minds, as well as the sensations and thoughts that we associate with them. We will discuss the difference between *concrete* and *abstract* words, and we will see how concrete images can embody abstractions—that is, how an image may be at once tactile, emotional, and conceptual.

In Chapter 4, "Stories," we will look at some poems that tell stories, and we will examine the importance of stories in our lives. Stories are the *containers* of our lives, the shapes in which we perceive ourselves. We understand and explain ourselves by our stories. Poetry, as a literary form, has a uniquely versatile way of revealing how people hold their stories. Some details are emphasized and others obscured to keep stories pointed, coherent, personal, and specific to experience.

In Chapter 5, "Sound," we will begin to cultivate an awareness of how the sounds of the words in a poem play on our emotions as we read. We will look closely at sound-related elements such as rhyme, rhythm, assonance, and alliteration, with a view toward understanding *what they accomplish* within a poem.

In Chapter 6, "Metaphors, Similes, and Symbols," we will consider how thinking about things in terms of other things may broaden our perspective and understanding. That is why we make comparisons all the time, why we constantly speak in metaphor, simile, and symbol, often without realizing it. This chapter will demonstrate how poetry employs these tools in a particularly powerful manner. Also in this chapter, we will define what *symbols* are, what they do, why they are everywhere, and how we live by them.

In Chapter 7, "A Grab Bag of Devices," we will look briefly at several poetic devices: strategic line breaks, allusions, thematic recurrences or motifs, understatement, overstatement, synesthesia, synecdoche, and metonymy. These devices inspire the imagination in special ways, giving rise to colorful and unusual turns of thought. When we are aware of them and how they work, their impact is strengthened.

In Chapter 8, "Irrationality, Dreams, and Paradox," we will examine how poetry occasionally transcends rational meaning. We will acknowledge the rightful place that nonsense holds in all our lives and we will look at poetry that illustrates the dream dimension of our existence.

In Chapter 9, "Welding It Together," we will return to the question, Why Poetry? and see if we have uncovered some additional answers. We will explore ways of keeping poetry present in our lives, and we will discuss the difference, such as it is, between *meaning* and *being*.

So take a deep breath and get ready to use your imagination. Just like all your ligaments and muscles, your imagination requires toning and exercise to stay in shape. This book will give it a pretty good workout. It can also be seen as a series of conversations—between you and me, you and the poems, and you and yourself. You might even view it as a journey, an expedition into vibrant and exotic realms of feeling, thought, and perception. But first and foremost, consider this book a toolkit, a set of instruments to aid you in reading, understanding, and—most of all—enjoying poetry.

WHY POETRY?

Why Poetry?

Seriously—why poetry? It's a fair question.

Suppose I told you that poetry is important, not just to a few highbrow writers and readers, but important to you, to everyone, to the whole human race. Would you think I was exaggerating?

Because that *is* what I think. I think poetry is just about as essential as air. I believe that much of the violence and psychological illness and unease in our society is probably due to poetry deprivation.

In fact, bigotry and prejudice, being expressions of narrow-minded, unimaginative thinking, may not be curable by reason, but may wither away (I believe) from repeated exposure to poetry. Why? Simple. Poetry expands the mind; prejudice and bigotry contract it. Once a mind gets a taste of expansion, it resists contraction. It doesn't like to think in ways that cruelly limit and circumscribe its possibilities.

Poetry is a language that stretches the mind. Just as yoga and stretching exercises make the body more flexible, poetry limbers up the imagination, which is *at least* as important, maybe even more so, than limbering up the body.

But what *is* poetry? In one sense, everyone knows the answer to this question. I once watched a football game with my father and we saw quarterback Terry Bradshaw complete four quick passes, driving his team sixty yards for the touchdown. "That was poetry," my dad said.

What he meant was that Bradshaw's passing attack was graceful, unpredictable, and aesthetically satisfying. He didn't mean that it was *literally* poetry; he meant that this football game had taken on qualities that one normally associates with the poetry that is made of words. He was using the term *metaphorically*. He was making a comparison. My dad was not a poetry reader. He simply had an idea of what poetry is, or what poetry should be, as most of us do.

Here are two definitions of poetry from *Webster's New World Dictionary:*

> *an arrangement of words, especially a rhythmical composition, sometimes rhymed, in a style more imaginative than ordinary speech*

> *a composition, in verse, especially one characterized by a highly developed form and the use of heightened language and rhythm to express an imaginative interpretation of the subject*

A common, informal definition which I've heard from time to time is this: "Prose is words in the best order. Poetry is the best words in the best order." Here's what I would add: Poetry is words, chosen and arranged to inspire the imagination.

But, you say, your imagination is inspired enough. Your senses are open. You love life. You interact with people and with nature. Isn't that more important than puzzling out peculiar words on a page?

Of course it is, but why make the comparison? The purpose of poetry is not to fill a void or to compensate for something that may be missing. Poetry cannot replace walking in the forest, falling in love, or having stimulating conversations. It's not supposed to.

Nor is poetry there to improve you as a person, to increase your chances for success in the world, or even to make you more literate. It's just that there is nothing else in the world quite like reading a poem. It is an activity as unique and inimitable as listening to music.

Poetry, like music, contains *rhythms* which may affect your mood and your spirit. In fact, if you listen to music, chances are you've already had some experience of poetry. Most songs contain words, and these words cast little spells as they sing in your mind. Poetry does the same thing. Both poetry and music *engage your imagination*. Another way of looking at it is to say that you must *lend your imagination* to music or poetry to derive enjoyment and satisfaction.

In this text, I will occasionally quote poetry that comes from music I like. My favorite music, often being obscure or out-of-date, is probably different from yours. But no doubt there is poetry, compelling words that are especially meaningful or pleasing to you, in the music you enjoy. (If the music you like best contains no words, I would still say that it has a poetic effect on you if it moves you.)

Just as there is an infinite variety of musical forms, so too does the term *poetry* encompass an infinity of expressions and styles. If you have read one hundred poems in your life and you think you know what poetry is, that is like having heard only one hundred songs and believing you know what music is. In a sense you do, but only in a very limited sense. You have only a *base*, not a real *body*, of knowledge.

Learning to enjoy poetry is as natural as learning to swim. Even children can do it, though it takes practice, and the ability can be refined over time. Have you ever noticed how children experiment and play with words for fun, much as they play with, and within, water?

Some people think they don't understand poetry. This is because poetry has been needlessly mystified in our culture to the point where many people imagine that only extraordinarily educated persons with exquisitely developed perceptual powers can truly "interpret" it. They imagine that poetry is written by and for an elite group of lofty literary wizards.

Some people think a poem is like a piece of code to be deciphered. They think if they fail to "get" it, it's because they lack the cleverness required to puzzle out the secret message.

Well, a poem is neither a puzzle nor a secret code. A poem is not an obscure hieroglyph to be "interpreted." A poem, if it *works*, will *speak* to you. If it does not speak to you, then it simply *does not work*—for you. And that's not your problem. It's a matter of chemistry. You won't relate to every song you hear either, nor will you fall in love with every person you meet.

It takes time, though, to get to know a poem. You do have to give a poem, and yourself, a chance. A poem generally requires more than one exposure—just like a song or a person does. Reading a poem is not like reading the newspaper. Here's where many people get mixed up. They think: Words on a page, read 'em, that's it.

No. A poem requires patience. That is why the first and most essential tool in our toolkit is patience.

A poem shouldn't be cryptic or obscure. But it may require a third or fourth or sixth or seventh reading before it can unfold, full bloom, in your mind—at which point you might be happily surprised. The repeated readings should never feel like a chore, however. In a sense, that's the only "trick": cultivating the ease and patience—the suspension of urgency and anxiety—necessary to really feel and enjoy a poem.

You must suspend or, if possible, banish your impatience about getting on with the next thing you have to do. You cannot be in a hurry and read poetry at the same time. Honestly. That's like trying to sing opera while doing jumping jacks. It's like trying to hear your own heartbeat over the roar of a jet engine.

What Happens Next

In this book, we will read poems carefully, ask questions, do some thinking, and develop our poetry reading tools as a means of getting deeper into—or at least closer to—the life of the poems. This book is called a *toolkit* because certain ways of thinking about and looking at poems work like tools, or keys, for *getting inside* a poem. Understanding how an individual poetic device—such as a symbol or a rhythm—works within the poem and how it *informs your experience of the poem* is one such tool. We will often focus our attention on individual lines, words, phrases, or poetic devices such as specific images or metaphors.

But don't be fooled! Never think that this kind of clinical analysis can explain a poem any more than an examination of individual bodily organs or functions can explain a human being. The whole is always inexpressibly more than the sum of its parts. In employing our tools, we are by definition *dissecting* a poem. Keep in mind that the ultimate goal is not to take the poem apart, but rather to enter into it as wholly as possible, to inhabit it, or, better yet, to let *it* inhabit *you*.

Former United States poet laureate Rita Dove has said, "A poem should haunt you a little. Or, let's just say, it should *accompany* you."

Poet Victor Hernandez Cruz puts it this way: "Poetry gives us revelations, flashes, which illuminate those things which were mysterious to us."

An unread poem waits humbly yet potently on the doorstep of your imagination.

| *Wishes*   *by Ya-Ka-Nes (Patty L. Harjo)*

    Over the rainy day mountain
    Past the laughing blue rainbow
    Gliding in the cloudless ivory sky
    The young Happiness bird

| continued on page 6 |

In the freedom of the quiet solitude or   5
with a loved-one friend
Always follow the beauty road
Gliding in the cloudless ivory sky
Past the laughing blue rainbow
Over the rainy day mountain   10
Forever in happiness
Forever in beauty
Always ⊢—

DISCUSSION WORKSHOP

Devising a Question

One good tool for putting together a sense of what a poem might mean for you is to ask a question. Sometimes a good way to approach a poem is to read it once, twice, or even three times, and then see what questions you have.

Concerning the preceding poem, for example, I have the following question: What is a "cloudless ivory sky"? A cloudless sky is normally blue, but ivory is white. So why does this poem use such a curious phrase?

As I consider my question, different answers—and further questions—suggest themselves. Is this the sky of another planet? Somehow that doesn't feel right to me. Perhaps "ivory sky" represents a horizon that is absolutely clear and free of trouble or worry. After all, this poem is talking about a "Happiness bird." Then again, maybe "ivory sky" means that this sky is *shining* and *smooth* like ivory. Maybe "ivory" pertains more to the *texture* of the sky than to its color. Perhaps neither of my "answers" are precisely in line with what the author had in mind. Nonetheless, they bring me closer to the poem; they are a way of gathering the poem's essence into myself.

> Read the poem a few times and devise one or two questions of your own. Then, upon reflection, see if any answers present themselves. If not, that's okay too. Discuss these questions with a friend or classmate. Perhaps she can suggest answers to your questions, and in turn maybe you can provide possible answers to hers.

Patience

I know you're busy, so I'll try to keep this short.

A Buddhist monk once said, "The spiritual journey requires a cup of wisdom, a barrel of love, and an ocean of patience." This is also true about reading poetry. If you have patience the rest will follow. Guaranteed.

Make no mistake. You cannot read poetry like you read a newspaper. You can't read it like you read a novel. You can't even read it the way you would study technical information.

William Carlos Williams once called poetry "a machine made out of words." Well, what's a machine for? A machine *does something*, right? Otherwise it is not a machine. And a machine is only good if it *works*.

Some machines need electricity to work. These machines will not do anything unless they're plugged in or their batteries are charged. Other machines need a human operator to turn a crank or to pedal or push.

Poetry needs patience in order to work. Patience is to poetry as electricity is to the vacuum cleaner. But what does poetry *do* when it works? We know what a vacuum cleaner does. But if poetry is a machine, then what kind of machine is it?

Poetry is an imagination machine. Good poetry, given patience, lights up your imagination in some way. It surprises you, tickles you, gives you a nudge, or even awes you. It might reveal a new perspective, dazzle your mind's eye, or broaden your inner vision.

Go ahead and read the following two poems as quickly or as slowly as you like.

The Waking

by Theodore Roethke

I wake to sleep, and take my waking slow.
I feel my fate in what I cannot fear.
I learn by going where I have to go.

We think by feeling. What is there to know?
I hear my being dance from ear to ear.   5
I wake to sleep, and take my waking slow.

Of those so close beside me, which are you?
God bless the Ground! I shall walk softly there,
And learn by going where I have to go.

Light takes the Tree; but who can tell us how?   10
The lowly worm climbs up a winding stair;
I wake to sleep, and take my waking slow.

Great Nature has another thing to do
To you and me; so take the lively air,
And, lovely, learn by going where to go.   15

This shaking keeps me steady. I should know.
What falls away is always. And is near.
I wake to sleep, and take my waking slow.
I learn by going where I have to go.

Ka 'Ba

by Imamu Amiri Baraka (LeRoi Jones)

A closed window looks down
on a dirty courtyard, and black people
call across or scream across or walk across
defying physics in the stream of their will

| *continued on page 9* |

Our world is full of sound   5
Our world is more lovely than anyone's
tho we suffer, and kill each other
and sometimes fail to walk the air

We are beautiful people
with african imaginations   10
full of masks and dances and swelling chants
with african eyes, and noses, and arms,
though we sprawl in grey chains in a place
full of winters, when what we want is sun.

We have been captured,   15
brothers. And we labor
to make our getaway, into
the ancient image, into a new

correspondence with ourselves
and our black family. We need magic   20
now we need the spells, to raise up
return, destroy, and create. What will be

the sacred words? |—

Even at a glance, you will have noticed that these are most
definitely poems, not essays, not expositions, not prosaic statements of one sort or another. You may have been intrigued or
bewildered by them, but you were probably not bored.

Some poetry is more demanding of patience than other
poetry, but all poetry requires it.

WRITING WORKSHOP

Developing Patience

Read the poems again. This time, without "interpreting"
either poem, try and imagine *who* is speaking in each poem—

the **narrator** of the poem, if you will—and also try and imagine *to whom* each poem's narrator might be speaking.

This is an imaginative exercise. You are being asked to hear inside your mind the voice of each poem and perhaps even to picture the person behind that voice. It may help to read the poems aloud or at least to move your lips as you read.

When you are done, take a minute and jot down a few qualities that describe each poem's narrator. You can use adjectives like "friendly," "detached," "scary," or "jealous," or you can use phrases like "easy-to-please," "tight-lipped around strangers," or "likes animals."

Don't worry about being "correct." This exercise isn't about being right or wrong. It's about what you hear and see and feel as you read, and about paying attention to what you hear and see and feel. (If a poem works at all, given at least a little patience, it should make you hear or see or feel *something*.)

Qualities of the Narrator in "The Waking":

_____

_____

_____

Qualities of the Narrator in "Ka 'Ba":

_____

_____

_____

Now read each poem again and see if you can identify any thoughts or emotions that the poems stir in you. What do these poems make you think of? What do they make you feel? *How* do they make you feel?

Relax. Open your mind. There are no wrong answers. How could there be? Nobody but you knows what you think and feel; you are the authority here. The poem is just a machine, at your service.

Thoughts and Feelings about "The Waking":

_____

_____

_____

Thoughts and Feelings about "Ka 'Ba":

_____

_____

_____

Okay, let's do this one more time. Read the poems again. This time, read them slowly and pause at the end of each line or at the end of each complete sentence within the poems. (Sometimes sentences are broken between lines. This is called **enjambment.**)

Are you left with questions? If you're not sure, read the poems yet again and see if questions come up as you go along. After you read, write down your questions. This is optional. Perhaps you have no questions whatsoever. But you probably have at least a couple.

Questions about "The Waking":

_____

_____

_____

_____

Questions about "Ka 'Ba":

_____

_____

_____

_____

Still More Patience

Let's look at two more poems. But don't think that you are done with the first two. A poem is not a disposable machine, to be used only four or five times. A good poem keeps on working, and you can return to it over and over again. But, now and again, it's good to give any particular machine a rest.

The next poem is by American poet e. e. cummings (he seldom capitalized his name), who crafted sculpture as well as poetry. In his poems, cummings often employed unorthodox line breaks, spelling, and syntax. However, he was not random in his choices. When we read cummings, we can assume that he chose each word, each indentation, and each punctuation mark with the meticulous deliberation and exactitude of a sculptor wielding a chisel to render a precise image.

In fact, cummings sometimes _left out_ words with precision. When I read the following poem, it seems to me that one or two words are purposely omitted, and their absence creates a certain effect.

Go ahead, read this poem and see what you think. Read it several times; go through the same steps you went through with the previous poems. It takes patience. Don't worry about getting it right. Remember, that's not the point. Have fun. Don't worry.

if there are any heavens

by e. e. cummings

if there are any heavens my mother will (all by herself) have
one. It will not be a pansy heaven nor
a fragile heaven of lilies-of-the-valley but
it will be a heaven of blackred roses

my father will be (deep like a rose   5
tall like a rose)

standing near my

(swaying over her
silent)
with eyes which are really petals and see   10
nothing with the face of a poet really which
is a flower and not a face with
hands
which whisper
This is my beloved my   15

                    (suddenly in sunlight

he will bow,

& the whole garden will bow) ├—

Qualities of the Narrator in "if there are any heavens":

_____

_____

_____

Thoughts, Feelings, and Associations about "if there are any heavens":

_____

_____

_____

Questions about "if there are any heavens":

_____

_____

_____

_____

    Now consider a poem written by the great Spanish poet Federico García Lorca.

Song of the Barren Orange Tree

by Federico García Lorca

Woodcutter.
Cut my shadow from me.
Free me from the torment
of seeing myself without fruit.

Why was I born among mirrors?   5
The day walks in circles around me,
and the night copies me
in all its stars.

I want to live without seeing myself.
And I will dream that ants   10
and thistleburrs are my
leaves and my birds.

| *continued on page 15* |

Woodcutter.
Cut my shadow from me.
Free me from the torment   15
of seeing myself without fruit. ⊢

translated by W. S. Merwin

Qualities of the Narrator in "Song of the Barren Orange Tree":

_____

_____

_____

Thoughts, Feelings, and Associations about "Song of the Barren Orange Tree":

_____

_____

_____

Questions about "Song of the Barren Orange Tree":

_____

_____

_____

_____

DISCUSSION WORKSHOP

Sharing Perceptions

Bouncing ideas around in small groups, comparing thoughts and perceptions, is an excellent tool for deepening your appreciation of a poem.

In a small group, compare responses to the two preceding poems.

Unearthing More Poems

Occasionally this book will ask you to find more poems on your own. Where can you look for them?

Perhaps you own or have access to an anthology of poems. If not, you can easily find poetry collections in your school or city library. Poems are also found in popular magazines such as *The New Yorker* and *The Atlantic Monthly* as well as in literary journals.

Also, the book you're holding contains a lot of poems. It is perfectly acceptable to leaf through the pages of this book to find the poem that you need, even if it's a poem you have examined in a previous chapter. There are, after all, many ways to look at a poem. In one chapter we will focus on poetic *images*, while in another chapter we will place more attention on *sounds*. But poems generally contain both images *and* sounds as well as many other elements. So feel free to "recycle" the poems in this book as we move along. This is a fine and legitimate way of forging further into the poems. In fact, this toolkit will also utilize several poems more than once.

Right now, your task is to find another poem, preferably one that you have never read before. Transcribe or photocopy the poem, and go through the same steps that you did with the poems we have just discussed. Read the poem at least three times, write down your impressions of the poem's narrator, write down any thoughts, feelings, or associations that the poem calls forth, and write down any questions you are left with.

I recommend you select a poem that:

- intrigues you,

- puzzles you at first reading, at least in some way, and

- speaks to you somehow—that is, it's for *you* in some fashion; it *resonates* with something in you. (This doesn't mean that it has to be about something you've experienced, though it could be.)

Okay. Don't hurry. Have fun. Take your time. Enjoy your discovery.

EMOTIONS

2

Our Emotional Life

We've defined poetry as an imagination machine. Imagination is very important because imagination is what determines the quality of our inner lives.

Our internal experience consists of thoughts, imaginings, and *feelings,* which are also known as *emotions.* The feeling we get when we are in physical contact with something—say, a warm wool sweater—is called a *sensation* rather than an emotion. But even sensations, such as the touch of a warm sweater, always evoke emotions.

Thoughts, too, evoke emotions. Always. There is no thought distinct from emotion. Remember, even apathy and boredom are emotions. The fact is, if you are alive, you are having emotions, even right now. You are swimming in a sea of emotions, of feelings. And the words you are now reading are affecting your emotions too. Watch closely and you will see that anything you do or read or watch or think influences your emotional state. It is a good and healthy thing to be aware of this.

One very unhealthy result of being bombarded by the media with images of violence and gratuitous sex is that we become desensitized. We don't feel our feelings. But these images do affect our emotional life even if we are not consciously aware of it. Once in a while, a person doesn't seem to feel his or her emotions at all. The clinical term for this condition is depression and it is very dangerous.

The more *sensitive* we are to our emotions, the more we allow our emotions into our awareness, the healthier we are and the more fully we live. Poetry knows that emotions are real, that human life is a constantly shifting, fluid emotional reality. Strangely enough, though some view poetry as a frivolous form of communication, poetry understands that the mind is nothing to play with (at least not in a careless or ungraceful way) and that the imagination is a volatile arena of emotions.

Propaganda, advertisements, pornography, and ultraviolent movies . . . all of these do violence to our imaginative and emotional capacity; they affront our psyches with the brute, blunt, callous impact of a sledgehammer (ouch!). Poetry, by contrast, dances carefully in our minds. It teases us, prods us, invites our involvement in a respectful way, a way that befits the subtlety and majesty of our rich, complex emotional life. Poetry does not take us, or our imaginations, for granted.

Emily Dickinson, born in 1830, lived a quiet, secluded life. She died in the house where she was born, and she rarely left her hometown of Amherst, Massachusetts. But though she did not travel far geographically, Dickinson knew her emotions very intensely, as is evidenced by this poem.

| Poem #249   *by Emily Dickinson*

Wild Nights—Wild Nights!
Were I with thee
Wild Nights should be
Our luxury!

Futile—the Winds—   5
To a Heart in port—
Done with the Compass—
Done with the Chart!

Rowing in Eden—
Ah, the Sea!   10
Might I but moor—Tonight—
In Thee! |—

It's a short poem, so patiently read it again a few times. Pay attention to your feelings as you read.

Connotation and Denotation

You might note that Dickinson capitalizes words which would not normally be capitalized in prose or discourse. She also uses an unusual number of dashes, a jagged and dramatic punctuation. In fact, this poem contains no commas or periods—just dashes and exclamation marks. Does her punctuation have any emotional effect on you?

Let's look at her capitalization for a moment. Conventionally speaking, the first word in each line of a poem is capitalized (though this is not always the case), so we may, for our purposes, ignore the capital letters that begin lines in this poem, as well as the capital *I*.

The remaining capitalized words are:

Wild	Chart
Nights	Eden
Winds	Sea
Heart	Tonight
Compass	Thee

Each of these words has a meaning that we know and can easily agree upon. If I look up *wild* in my dictionary, for example, I find definitions such as "living or growing in its original, natural state" and "fantastically impractical; reckless." It is worth noting that the "Wild" in "Wild Nights" conveys both of these meanings to some degree, as well as a few others that my dictionary offers such as "not easily controlled," "lacking social or moral restraint," and "turbulent; stormy."

Dictionary definitions of words are called **denotative** meanings. These are the "straight" meanings, the obvious, literal meanings of words. Sea means sea: a great big body of water such as a giant lake or an ocean. Night, of course, is the dark period that alternates with day, and so on.

But in addition to their denotative meanings, many (or possibly even *all*) words also have multiple connotative meanings. **Connotations** are simply the *associative meanings* of a word, the meanings that a word *points to*. When I say the word *mother* for example, you might automatically picture your own mother, or perhaps you might envision some mythic mother goddess or earth mother. You might be reminded of nurture, of babies at the breast, of deep unconditional love, and so on. You may think of the Virgin Mary. These are but a few of the connotations associated with the word *mother.*

Of course everyone has (at least slightly) differing sets of associations with various words, which is but one important reason why you should never believe anyone who tells you that there is a single correct way to read a poem. Still, most of us have certain feelings and experiences in common. "Night" for most of us is associated with darkness, and darkness is associated with mystery, the unknown, the dangerous, the fertile, . . . the wild. Both the womb and the tomb exist in darkness, literally and figuratively. In a literal, physical sense, no sunlight shines in the womb or in the tomb. And in a figurative sense, if the womb stands for what is before life, and the tomb stands for what is after death, they are both mysteries, and the light of our knowledge and understanding cannot penetrate either of them.

So this poem is about "Wild Nights." Just those two words evoke a host of connotations, don't they? They could mean excitement, they could mean adventure, they could mean deadly danger. For the moment, in the first line, we are at sea, just like the poem, because we don't know what kind of Wild Nights we're in for. But given that everything is capitalized, we may assume that whatever kind of Wild Night it is, it is going to be a very big one. The capital letters amplify the connotations.

We read on and find that the narrator of the poem is addressing someone in particular: "Were I with thee." Then, "Wild Nights should be / Our luxury!" lets us know that these Wild Nights are desirable indeed, and here we might infer that this is a passionate love poem, a poem of desire.

Many of the words that follow—*Winds, port, Compass, Chart, rowing, Sea, moor*—are associated with the image of a sea-faring vessel. On a real Wild Night, when it is pitch dark and the waters are turbulent, such a vessel is in danger of losing its bearings or even being shipwrecked. Perhaps the same can be said of a heart that is deeply adrift in love.

Consider the connotations of the other capitalized words in their respective contexts.

Winds are more than gusts of air; they have a distinctive force, like the personality of some fateful god. The word is used figuratively in everyday expressions such as "winds of change" and "whichever way the wind blows." The word has powerful emotional connotations for most of us. The "winds" of our lives move us in different directions. When I think of wind, I also think of something that can knock me off of my feet and rip away my self-control.

The word "heart," of course, does not simply denote a physical organ, but also refers to the seat of our emotions, particularly love. To speak of "a Heart in port" implicitly likens the heart itself to a kind of boat or ship. For the heart to do what a heart is built to do then, it must be out on the (wild?) waters, precarious as that may sometimes be. "A Heart in port," we gather, is a stranded heart; hence the winds are "futile" to a heart in this position. A heart, by definition, is made to be moved.

"Done with the Compass— / Done with the Chart!" A compass is a directional device. A chart could be a map, or anything that shows graphically where things lie in relation to one another. We all have various direction finders and orientation mechanisms in our lives. To throw out the compass and the chart—as this speaker apparently desires to do with great vehemence—might be to cast oneself recklessly to the winds, or it might be to literally lose oneself in something one deems worthy, exalted, desirable, or simply too compelling to resist. It's an extreme statement, isn't it? How often, in love or no, do we actually say, "Done with the Compass— / Done with the Chart!" and what are the consequences of such moments, such times? What are the emotions like?

"Eden," of course, represents paradise. What do you think of when you see or hear this word? I think of a lush, green, natural beauty; I see images of great sweeping trees, peaceful animals, and, now that I come to think of it, there was some issue concerning nakedness in the Garden of Eden, wasn't there? Consider the different connotations that might have arisen here had Dickinson used the word *heaven* instead.

A word like "Sea" has connotations so immense, so numerous, and so universal that we call it an **archetype.** An archetype is an image or idea that has been encoded somehow into the human race's unconscious and carries with it profound emotional charges and associations. (Other archetypal words and images include *mother, fire, death, earth,* and *marriage.*) Everyone has feelings about the sea, including people who have never seen it.

To understand how the archetype "Sea" works in the context of this particular poem, you need only pay careful attention to your own feelings, thoughts, and internal images. The sea at night will probably mean something different to your emotional imagination than the sea in daylight. We know that the sea has many qualities: It covers more than three-fourths of the earth's surface, it is powerful, it contains an infinite variety of life forms, it can *consume* you. . . . Some scientists say that all earthly life began, eons ago, in the sea. Enough said!

The word "Tonight" is capitalized. Why? Tonight simply means this evening, doesn't it? Or, rather, *this night*. What is the effect of giving it a capital *T* here? Does the capital letter serve to emphasize anything about this night? I leave this for you to say.

A small word of warning seems appropriate here. In allowing me to "pick apart" a poem for you in this manner, you run the risk of also allowing me to *dictate your experience* of the poem, which is just about the same thing as allowing me to destroy your experience of the poem. A dictated experience is a secondhand experience, and a secondhand experience is not authentically an experience at all. So I'm warning you, just to be fair. Be careful. Don't trust me instead of your feelings. Don't take my word casually. Trust your own experience first and foremost.

Now that you have been amply warned, consider with me the word "Thee." In addition to rhyming with "Sea," the word "Thee" has some distinctly different connotations from its synonym, the word *you* (even if *you* is also capitalized). I leave these connotations to your own ample, energetic, well-practiced imagination. But it is also worth noting that "thee" is *not* capitalized in the first stanza. Has a change occurred? Is the narrator now talking to a different "Thee"? Or has "thee" been reconceived somehow? "Thee" is a word often found in the Bible, and when it is capitalized, it may refer to God, the Creator of the Universe. So perhaps the narrator's longing is for a transcendent union with her Creator, as opposed to, or in addition to, an earthly longing for a human beloved. Or have the two longings been confused here? Or have they *fused?*

Note the prepositions: In the first stanza she says "Were I *with* thee" as in keeping company with someone, but at the end she says, "*In* Thee!" as if to be ecstatically *immersed* in, or consumed by, this "Thee." Of course, one could feel immersed in the arms of an earthly lover as well. Then again, the sea itself can immerse and swallow one. Do lover, sea, and God merge here?

The poem is, to a certain extent, ambiguous. Many poems are ambiguous, which means that they can be read to have two or more different meanings. Ambiguity is not a bad thing; life itself is generally rather ambiguous. Most life events tend to have more than a single significance, and most of the time our feelings about things and about people are somewhat mixed. (Right? Check it out.) *Ambiguous* should not be confused with *vague,* which means unclear or indistinct. Something that is ambiguous is not necessarily unclear, and poetry in particular is anything but indistinct, ambiguous or no.

Most of us will probably agree that "Wild Nights" is a very emotionally charged poem, a very passionate poem. The words and images all speak strongly of passion. Concerning my earlier point about poetry as a form of language that respects imagination, compare words such as "Were I with thee / Wild Nights should be our luxury!" and "Done with the Compass— / Done with the Chart!" to phrases like "red hot sex" and "pining for true love." Are you saying, "Yuck!"? Well, good. Do you see how trite, unimaginative, and manipulative language dulls, deadens, and shrinks the imagination and the emotional life? Can you see how poetry enhances, dignifies, and expands the imagination and emotional life?

WRITING WORKSHOP

Examining Connotations

Departure

by Genny Lim

Please tell me you are not afraid
While I cover your shoulder, big sister
I'll pretend it's morning and
the fog has lifted

| *continued on page 27* |

Please open your eyes 5
Let me hear you yawn like a child
Let me see your smile
Talk about the old days
in your Chinatown accent

If there is an odor of stale incense 10
withered roses with antiseptic spray
You can criticize my house-cleaning
I won't mind
if you scold
the way you did when I borrowed 15
your white satin cheongsam without asking
and spilled sweet and sour sauce on it
fifteen years ago

I won't avoid your eyes
staring out of their sockets like glass 20
When I ask how you are
I won't hear you choking
When I rise to leave you
I won't notice your hands trembling
reaching for me 25
from your bed
across the TV tray
fumbling with cotton gauze, syringe
3 cc's of morphine
shot thru your brain 30

I won't flinch
I won't cry ├─

    This poem is not quite as ambiguous as "Wild Nights." Clearly, the narrator is speaking to a dying older sister whom she is caring for in her sister's waning days. Yet, like

Dickinson's poem, this poem contains several words and phrases that are laden with significance beyond their straightforward denotative meanings. Even a simple phrase like "fifteen years ago," by itself in a single line at the end of a stanza, assumes a connotative weight in a context such as this. It calls to mind the fact that much time has passed, that some happier era is now lost, and that, in the end, all things are lost and all happiness and sorrow are undone by time.

Paying attention to the subtle emotional impact of connotations is yet another tool for wedging your way into the life of a poem. Identify one or two other words or phrases that carry connotations in this poem and describe those connotations.

Tone

As we read the poem "Departure," we can hear the narrator's voice as she speaks lovingly and sadly to the sister she is losing. She says, "Please tell me you are not afraid" and "Please open your eyes," and she promises, "I won't . . ." several times. All these *please*s and *I won't*s (and, for that matter, *let me*s) convey an attitude, a tone. **Tone,** in poetry, is the *attitude* of the poem's speaker as conveyed by the words and rhythms in the poem. In this case, the narrator's tone is *plaintively pleading* with her sister to not go away, even as she tacitly acknowledges that the departure is inevitable.

The tone of Dickinson's "Wild Nights" is quite different. That poem's word choices, jagged punctuation, and rhythm all communicate tremendous passion and urgency.

In the poem "Song of the Barren Orange Tree" by Federico García Lorca (from Chapter 1), the tone is *lamenting, yearning.* This is conveyed by phrases such as "Free me . . . ," "Why was I born . . . ?," "I want to live . . . ," and "I will dream . . . ." What the speaker in this poem is longing for, apparently, is a proper death. In beseeching the woodcutter to "Cut my shadow from me," the tree is asking the woodcutter to chop the tree down. The melancholy tone of this poem underscores its content.

Tone is inextricably entwined with emotion. We communicate our attitudes and emotions in our tone of voice when we speak. Likewise, poetry conveys emotion and attitude with tone. Attitude and emotion are very closely related, but they are not quite the same thing. In a sense, one could say that attitude is the *result* of emotion or the *chosen means of expressing* an emotion. For example, let's say that a friend has let you down or lied to you. You are hurt and angry and disappointed, but your means of expressing these feelings could take any of several tones. You might yell and curse, you might be cold and curt, or you might even employ sarcasm. All of these *attitudes* are communicated through your words and, even more so, through your tone of voice.

In the two poems which follow, both narrators take a clear attitudinal stance towards their respective situations. These poems have distinctive tones.

When I Think about Myself

by Maya Angelou

When I think about myself,
I almost laugh myself to death,
My life has been one great big joke,
A dance that's walked
A song that's spoke,   5
I laugh so hard I almost choke
When I think about myself.

Sixty years in these folks' world
The child I work for calls me girl
I say "Yes ma'am" for working's sake.   10
Too proud to bend
Too poor to break,
I laugh until my stomach ache,
When I think about myself.

| *continued on page 30* |

My folks can make me split my side,   15
I laughed so hard I nearly died,
The tales they tell, sound just like lying,
They grow the fruit,
But eat the rind,
I laugh until I start to crying,   20
When I think about my folks. ⊢

Warning

by Jenny Joseph

When I am old I shall wear purple
With a red hat which doesn't go, and doesn't suit me.
And I shall spend my pension on brandy and summer gloves
And satin sandals, and say we've no money for butter.
I shall sit down on the pavement when I'm tired   5
And gobble up samples in shops and press alarm bells
And make up for the sobriety of my youth.
I shall go out in my slippers in the rain
And pick up the flowers in other people's gardens
And learn to spit.   10

You can wear terrible shirts and grow more fat
And eat three pounds of sausages at a go
Or only bread and pickle for a week
And hoard pens and pencils and beermats and things in boxes.

But now we must have clothes that keep us dry   15
And pay our rent and not swear in the street
And set a good example for the children.
We must have friends to dinner and read the papers.

But maybe I ought to practice a little now?
So people who know me are not too shocked and surprised 20
When suddenly I am old and start to wear purple. ⊢

Name That Tone

> How would you characterize the tones of the preceding poems? What particular words or phrases convey the attitudes you perceive? Discuss your ideas with a classmate.

The Names of Our Emotions

Grief, joy, anger, love, fear, sadness, elation, amusement, annoyance, hope, despair, pity, and pride. We know that by giving names to emotions we do not pin them down. Words naming emotions are merely devices for talking about that which cannot truly be named. Emotional weather is nuanced and fluid. That's why we often try and describe emotions figuratively with terms like "feeling high," "feeling down in the dumps," or "feeling blue." Even these expressions are, at best, approximations.

Poetry takes a different tack to get at the essence of emotional experience. In the next poem, Emily Dickinson describes the emotion called "hope" as a kind of bird. In the song-poem that follows this one, folk singer/songwriter Joules Graves offers a portrait of "sorrow" as a lonely woman. Don't forget to read both of these poems more than once.

Poem #254

by Emily Dickinson

"Hope" is the thing with feathers—
That perches in the soul—
And sings the tune without the words—
And never stops—at all—

And sweetest—in the Gale—is heard   5
And sore must be the storm—
That could abash the little Bird
That kept so many warm—

| *continued on page 32* |

I've heard it in the chillest land—
And on the strangest Sea—   10
Yet, never, in Extremity,
It asked a crumb—of Me. ├─

Sorrow

by Joules Graves

Sorrow lifts her melancholy eyes
Gazing longingly towards grey and cloudy skies
She sits in a wooden chair at the corner of the room
She wears scented tears as her only perfume
Waiting endlessly by the silent phone   5
Wondering wordlessly, how did she get to be so alone?

Sorrow wanders somber through the daze
Fading formlessly in shades of stormy greys
She dwells in attic realms with dust as thick as years
She stores ancient woes as lonely souvenirs   10
Weeping endlessly, sadness to the bone
Wondering wordlessly, how did she get to be so alone?

Sorrow cries her prayer into the rain
Will she ever know happiness again?
She spins cobweb threads upon her spinning wheel   15
She's afraid loneliness is all she'll ever feel
Raining endlessly, dripping to the drone
Wondering wordlessly, how did she get to be so alone?
So alone, so alone ├─

Poetry renders a specific, intuitive, and imaginatively risk-taking description of emotional experience. The problem with words like *hope* or *despair* is that sometimes we hear these words and thought stops: We think we know what they mean, and that's the end of the issue. Poetry takes us further into emotional reality than do the simple words which name emotions.

To take us deeper and further into emotional experience, poetry employs images and words with potent connotations. (As we will see later, even rhythm, rhyme, and sound have connotations.) In doing so, poetry's goal is not to "nail" the emotion once and for all, but rather to reveal the less visible textures of emotion in some of—if not all of—their glory. It's interesting to realize that, in serving this function, poetry is the closest expression we have of the thing itself—it's the most precise emotional language available.

WRITING WORKSHOP

The Textures of Emotion

In Emily Dickinson's "Poem #254," qualities are ascribed to the emotion known as "Hope." It has "feathers" like a bird and it "sings" without stopping, sweet and strong above the worst of storms and in the coldest of lands. Hope is *humble*— it never asks even a crumb for all that it gives. In Joules Graves's song, "sorrow" is represented as a woman with "melancholy eyes" and "scented tears," who "spins cobweb threads" and "stores ancient woes" in "attic realms with dust as thick as years." These poets have given body, soul, and character to emotions.

Think of an emotion you feel strongly or have felt strongly recently. In a journal entry, go ahead and name your emotion in the conventional way—affection, relief, frustration, whatever. Now give your emotion some qualities. What does it look like? What is its shape? How much does it weigh? What color is it? If it's a person or an animal, where does it live? What else can you say about this entity/emotion? Be as specific as possible.

Connotation Revisited

Take a good, patient look at these three poems.

i carry your heart with me

by e. e. cummings

i carry your heart with me(i carry it in
my heart)i am never without it(anywhere
i go you go,my dear;and whatever is done
by only me is your doing,my darling)
                                        i fear   5
no fate(for you are my fate,my sweet)i want
no world(for beautiful you are my world,my true)
and it's you are whatever a moon has always meant
and whatever a sun will always sing is you

here is the deepest secret nobody knows   10
(here is the root of the root and the bud of the bud
and the sky of the sky of a tree called life;which grows
higher than soul can hope or mind can hide)
and this is the wonder that's keeping the stars apart

i carry your heart(i carry it in my heart)   15

The Snow Man

by Wallace Stevens

One must have a mind of winter
To regard the frost and the boughs
Of the pine-trees crusted with snow;

And have been cold a long time
To behold the junipers shagged with ice,   5
The spruces rough in the distant glitter

| continued on page 35 |

Of the January sun; and not to think
Of any misery in the sound of the wind,
In the sound of a few leaves,

Which is the sound of the land   10
Full of the same wind
That is blowing in the same bare place

For the listener, who listens in the snow,
And, nothing himself, beholds
Nothing that is not there and the nothing that is. ├─   15

| My People

by Langston Hughes

The night is beautiful,
So the faces of my people.

The stars are beautiful,
So the eyes of my people.

Beautiful, also, is the sun.   5
Beautiful, also, are the souls of my people. ├─

Do these poems touch your emotions?

That's an interesting expression, isn't it—"touch your emotions"? As if the emotions are all there inside you somewhere, just waiting to be activated or touched, like a set of piano keys. That idea may not be entirely accurate. But all the same, a poem can compel us to a sense of *emotional recognition*. As in, "Yes! I *know*. I *understand* that feeling!"

Sometimes you don't even have to understand all of the words in the poem, let alone all of the ideas. And you don't even necessarily have to remember having had that particular feeling; it may seem like something brand new, or only dimly recalled, or just barely glimpsed before.

This is one of the truly amazing and important gifts of poetry. It can inspire empathy for others' experiences. Remarkably, it allows us not just to feel *for*, but also to feel *with*. Poetry connects our lives with lives entirely unlike our own through the universal currency of emotion.

Connotation Dissection

Taking apart a poem and looking at its individual components is not the same thing as "appreciating" a poem. But it can be interesting nonetheless and can occasionally afford us insight. Consider these words from the preceding poems:

fate	winter	faces
world	frost	stars
secret	time	eyes
root	glitter	souls
	nothing	

Select one of these sets of words. Write each word down on a separate sheet of paper. Spend five to ten minutes with each one and write down some of the connotations that the word has for you: some of the associated thoughts, images, and feelings.

Relax. Let your mind wander. Don't worry about completing this task. To do it thoroughly would take much longer than ten minutes for each word! "Getting it all down" is not important here. It might even be impossible.

Have fun. Chances are you may surprise yourself at some point in this process. Feel free to "go off on a tangent" or even to be irrational. See what you come up with.

When you are done, compare notes with a friend or a small group.

Unearth a Poem

Find a poem (not from this chapter) that stirs something in you emotionally. It doesn't have to be a poem you understand, just one that moves you to feel something, even if you're not sure what it is you feel. Transcribe or photocopy the poem. Read it again to yourself, patiently.

Find one word, phrase, or line in the poem that is particularly powerful for you. Write down that word, phrase, or line separately and list some of its connotations.

Then, in a paragraph or two (or more, if you wish), describe your overall feeling about the poem and how some of the connotations you listed contribute to or reflect that overall feeling. In listing the connotations, did you find that your overall feeling changed at all?

Unearth Another Poem

Find a poem (not from this chapter) that has a clear and distinctive tone. (*All* poems have a tone, but some have a more palpable tone than others.) Transcribe or photocopy the poem. Describe the tone that you hear in this poem and identify words or phrases that convey this tone to you most strongly.

Share and Tell

In a small group, share one of the poems that you have found and talk about why you picked this poem, what intrigued you about it, and the tone or connotations you perceive in it.

Strike Your Own Tone

Write a short poem concerning an emotion. Think of a strong feeling you have or have had. Then think of someone or something (yourself, another person, the whole world, God, a tree, a pet) that you might address your feelings to. Adopt an attitude and start writing.

IMAGES

3

Concrete and Abstract

A visual image is the most direct route to the imagination. Compare the line "Love is a many-splendored thing" to this poem.

| *Autumn*
by Jacques Prevert

A horse collapses in the middle of an alley
Leaves fall on him
Our love trembles
And the sun too. ⊢

translated by Lawrence Ferlinghetti

Which of the two is more interesting? Chances are you chose the poem. While the sentiment expressed in "Love is a many-splendored thing" may be wise and even vaguely poetic, there is nothing *concrete* for us latch onto. Most poetry relies greatly on concreteness. Words that are **concrete** denote things we can actually see or feel in some way: *horse, alley, leaves, sun.*

In contrast, words that are **abstract** denote things we understand the meanings of, but cannot see or feel: *love, justice, knowledge, meaning.* The saying "Love is a many-splendored thing" contains not one single concrete word. It is entirely abstract. We know what the words mean, but they do not compel any specific images.

Prevert's little poem, on the other hand, with its four short lines, is replete with concrete imagery. We *see* a horse collapsing in the middle of an alley, and then we *see* leaves falling on the collapsed horse. The subject of the third line, the pivotal line of the poem, is love—which, as we noted before, is an abstract word, not concrete. But the action of *trembling* is very tangible, and therefore we might envision something nonetheless. The final line, which tells us succinctly that the sun, like "our love," trembles, conjures an image in our mind's eye that is simple, direct, powerful, and quite strange.

So here we have one abstract statement amongst three very clear, concrete images. What is the relationship between them?

Let's look at what they all have in common. A horse collapsing is not something we see too often. We may presume that the horse was overwhelmed by some great force, perhaps fatigue, perhaps . . . , who knows? In any case, the horse, being a horse, must have hit the ground with a certain force as well, the impact of a mighty, massive thing in free fall.

When leaves fall, however, they fall softly. They waver and float on the air before they come to rest. So by the second line, we already have an imagistic contrast of things that fall hard and fast with a terrible thump and things that descend gradually, gently, with something like a sigh.

Nonetheless, both the horse and the leaves have *fallen.* They have both been *overcome,* perhaps by death (certainly death, in the case of the leaves). Powerful, irresistible forces have come to bear on both life forms.

When something or someone "trembles," we may presume that this thing or this being cannot control or resist the force causing the trembling (at least not for the moment). To say that "our love trembles" is to say, possibly, that these feelings of love are extremely strong, maybe even overwhelming, perhaps even somewhat fearsome.

Then, of course, we see the sun itself trembling in the sky, a fantasy image, but one that brings home the power of the forces in this poem. Something is at work here that is overwhelming all things, that is making all things tremble or fall. If one is romantically inclined, one may assume that this is a romantic poem and that the powerful force in question is the romantic love between the narrator of the poem and his sweetheart. (Prevert was male, so I am assuming a male narrator, though this is not always a reliable policy.)

Note the leap that was made through imagery here. We began with two images that made simple rational sense, though one of the images was slightly uncommon. Then an abstract statement was made, challenging and stretching our visual imaginations, and then followed another very concrete, but thoroughly impossible, image. Who has seen the sun tremble? Unless, of course, one is trembling so profoundly that absolutely everything else, including the sun, must be seen as trembling too. In any case, we can see that the simple imagery of the first two lines brought us into the poem, prepared the ground of the poem, acquired our confidence, and then, with the abstract third line, catapulted us unsuspecting into the final fantastic image.

There are two important points to note here. The first is that concrete images in a poem engage us immediately. They bring us along and lay the groundwork for the introduction of further images.

The second, more important, point is that a good concrete image is an object *on which to hang an abstraction*. Figuratively speaking, if an abstract idea or phenomenon, such as love, can be thought of as a living spirit or soul, then the concrete image to which the abstraction is joined in a poem, such as a trembling sun, is the *body* housing and giving expression to the soul.

Imagine that Prevert had simply stated, "Our love is an awesome thing which sets me to trembling. Our love is sensationally, enormously, overwhelmingly powerful." Would this have said as much as his images? *A concrete image is the most direct, economical, and effective avenue to symbolic or emotional understanding.* This is why most poetry employs a dynamic *interplay* between abstract and concrete elements. These elements illumine and enliven each other.

There may also be, of course, other important things going on in Prevert's poem besides strong romantic feeling. The poem is entitled "Autumn" and he may be evoking the mood of the season, which is when things fall and shake in the wind. There may be inherent symbolic implications of the force and movement and spirit of the time of year, but that is another discussion.

WRITING WORKSHOP

A Quick Question

You will notice that Prevert's poem is centered on the page, not justified with the left margin. Thus the words on the page meet your eye in an unusual way. Does this affect your experience of the poem at all? Does it alter the way you read it? If so, how? Why do you suppose the poem was constructed in this fashion? Describe your reactions to this poem in a journal entry.

Just Images?

William Carlos Williams once declared: "No ideas but in things." His own poetry was starkly visual, with little abstract or discursive commentary. Consider the following poem.

| *The Young Housewife*　　　*by William Carlos Williams*

At ten A.M. the young housewife
moves about in negligee behind
the wooden walls of her husband's house.
I pass solitary in my car.

Then again she comes to the curb　　　　　　　　　　5
to call the ice-man, fish-man, and stands
shy, uncorseted, tucking in
stray ends of hair, and I compare her
to a fallen leaf.

The noiseless wheels of my car　　　　　　　　　　　10
rush with a crackling sound over
dried leaves as I bow and pass smiling. |—

If there is an idea in this poem, it is not highlighted in any dramatic fashion and it is certainly of no greater significance than the images themselves. (We can speculate as to why the speaker compares the housewife to a fallen leaf, but there is no reason to think that this simile embodies a central idea on which the poem turns.)

Our first apprehension of the world is through sensations and images. It is possible, even likely, that we perceive coherent images before we can think coherent thoughts. So while it is nice to hang an abstraction on an image, an image by itself, with no particular attendant ideas or abstractions, is also nice. That is to say, ideas and emotions in poetry normally require the enlivening power of images, but images do not necessarily require ideas to give them life.

It is most common, however, even in the simplest poetry, for an image to contain or correspond to a thought or a feeling. The following poems are almost entirely concrete, yet the closer we look at them, the more we may sense ideas and emotions brimming within, and below the surfaces of, the images.

The Bean Eaters

by Gwendolyn Brooks

They eat beans mostly, this old yellow pair.
Dinner is a casual affair.
Plain chipware on a plain and creaking wood,
Tin flatware.

Two who are Mostly Good.   5
Two who have lived their day,
But keep on putting on their clothes
And putting things away.

And remembering . . .
Remembering, with twinklings and twinges,   10
As they lean over the beans in their rented back room that is full of
      beads and receipts and dolls and cloths, tobacco crumbs,
      vases and fringes. ⊢

Alaskan Mountain Poem #1

by Leslie Marmon Silko

Dark branches
dark leaves
snow deep,
in sky
that encloses the mountain.   5
The sun is hidden
in green moss feathers
that cling to
the gray alder branches.

| continued on page 45 |

On the mountain 10
within the endless
white sky
spruce trees entangle the snow
and only the silence
dances free. 15

————

By the time
I wrote the spruce tree poem
the snow winds came
And the mountain
was gone. |— 20

Early in the Morning

by Li-Young Lee

While the long grain is softening
in the water, gurgling
over a low stove flame, before
the salted Winter Vegetable is sliced
for breakfast, before the birds, 5
my mother glides an ivory comb
through her hair, heavy
and black as calligrapher's ink.

She sits at the foot of the bed.
My father watches, listens for 10
the music of the comb
against hair.

| *continued on page 46* |

My mother combs,
pulls her hair back
tight, rolls it   15
around two fingers, pins it
in a bun to the back of her head.
For half a hundred years she has done this.
My father likes to see it like this.
He says it is kempt.   20

But I know
it is because of the way
my mother's hair falls
when he pulls the pins out.
Easily, like the curtains   25
when they untie them in the evening. ⊢—

In the first poem, Gwendolyn Brooks offers a simple portrait of an old couple ("this old yellow pair"), sketches an image of them at dinner, and, in the poem's last line—its longest—names a series of items which populate this couple's "rented back room." Clearly, this list is important, as Brooks devotes the poem's most conspicuous line to it. Up until this moment, she has rendered a vague, summary account of these two people's lives: "Two who have lived their day / But keep on putting on their clothes / And putting things away." But it is the tangibles—the visible, concrete things that fill the room—that contain, preserve, and transmit the flavor of this couple's story. Taken by itself, a bead is just a bead, a doll is just a doll, a crumb is merely a crumb. But in this particular room, in relationship and proximity to each other, all of these acquire a distinct *character* which belies their status as "mere objects."

In the second poem, Leslie Marmon Silko describes a natural setting: a mountain in Alaska, partially and then completely covered by snow. She also describes the trees on the mountain and the "white sky" above. Every line, every statement in this poem is plain, concrete, and straightforward—except for one:

"and only the silence / dances free." Here, against a background of striking but simple images, she slips in a completely fanciful idea. How can *silence dance?* Does it make sense? Can you somehow imagine it? Do the images which surround this provide the backdrop required to bring it *alive?*

As for the images themselves, perhaps they are not as stark and simple as we may have deemed them to be at first glance. The sky "encloses" the mountain, green moss feathers "cling to" branches, trees "entangle" the snow. And though, in the end, the snow has completely submerged the mountain, the mountain is not really, as the narrator asserts, "gone." Calling it "gone" is far more dramatic—and subjective—than simply stating that it has disappeared from sight. So this poem, which initially seems to contain only images, actually *suffuses* its natural setting with character and connotation.

Li-Young Lee, a Chinese-American poet born in Indonesia, also presents us with a series of apparently simple, uncomplicated images. In the first stanza we see the grain in the boiling water, the stove flame, his mother's comb, and his mother's hair "black as calligrapher's ink." Then we see Lee's mother sit down to comb her hair as his father watches. In the next stanza, we see the hair combed and pinned into a bun, as she has arranged it for "half a hundred years." Finally, we are presented with the image of her hair falling: "Easily, like the curtains / when they untie them in the evening." This will occur, we know, when Lee's father removes the pins.

Nothing more needs to be said. We know that this poem isn't simply about hair or about breakfast time in Lee's childhood home. It is the father who watches the combing of the hair, who "listens for the music" of the combing, and who bears in mind what the hair looks and feels like when it is loosened and falling free after he pulls out the pins in the evening. The connotations are subtle yet unmistakable. This poem is about, among other things, the intimacy of a long-standing marriage in a discreet and dignified culture.

Prying Open the Images—
Looking within and beyond

In the following poem, the image of the moon is invested with tremendous character and power.

The Window Frames the Moon

by Laureen Mar

Some nights the moon is the curve of a comb,
tumble of night held casually;
other nights, a plate broken perfectly in half,
box of night coveting the smooth edge.

The window frames the moon, places it   5
to the left of the world, to the right,
decides if it floats, hurtles, suspends,
glances, antagonizes, surrenders.

By eleven the moon is as certain and fixed
as the clock on the dresser,   10
the chink in the wall,
the black tablecloth with silver dots of glitter.

Every night is the opportunity to rearrange the world!
With the window, I push the moon into place
as if it were a vase of flowers.   15
Oh, the glory of the night contained!

But there are nights the moon looms large,
so large it refuses to fit in the frame,
so large it refuses to splinter,
and when I push the moon, it pushes back   20

| continued on page 49 |

and fills my house, and I am forced to abandon
the clock and the dresser
to stand with the trees, leaves, grass,
taking my place among the small things of the world. ⊢

This narrator seems to have a peculiar relationship with the moon and its image. Whether the image of the moon can fit within the frame of her window is apparently a matter of no small significance to her. She defines herself, somehow, by the moon and its phases. In a journal entry, describe how you would characterize her feelings about the moon. Which images, in particular, connote the character of her sentiments regarding the moon?

There are other objects named in this poem that the narrator imbues with special importance in relation to herself. What are they? What function do they fulfill in this poem? How do they serve as points of reference for the narrator?

Sensory Imagery

Imagery, by definition, is *sensual,* but not all imagery is necessarily *visual.* Sight is but one of our five senses. Good poetry may make use of the other four senses as well. In the poem "Departure," for example, from Chapter 2, there is the ". . . odor of stale incense / withered roses mingled with antiseptic spray." By these olfactory images we are vividly introduced into the atmosphere of the dying sister's room.

In "The Young Housewife," seen earlier in this chapter, the wheels of the narrator's car "rush with a crackling sound over / dried leaves. . . ." This is a *sound* we can all recognize, drawing us palpably into the scene.

The following poem by Pablo Neruda relies greatly on the senses of taste and smell and touch, as well as on sight, to achieve its delectable effect.

Ode to Tomatoes

by Pablo Neruda

The street
filled with tomatoes,
midday,
summer,
light is   5
halved
like
a
tomato,
its juice   10
runs
through the streets.
In December,
unabated
the tomato   15
invades
the kitchen,
it enters at lunchtime,
takes
its ease   20
on countertops,
among glasses,
butter dishes,
blue saltcellars.
It sheds   25
its own light,
benign majesty.
Unfortunately, we must
murder it:
the knife   30
sinks
into living flesh,
red
viscera

| continued on page 51 |

a cool   35
sun,
profound,
inexhaustible,
populates the salads
of Chile,   40
happily,
it is wed
to the clear onion,
and to celebrate the union
we   45
pour
oil,
essential
child of the olive,
onto its halved hemispheres,   50
pepper
adds
its fragrance,
salt, its magnetism;
it is the wedding   55
of the day,
parsley
hoists
its flag,
potatoes   60
bubble vigorously,
the aroma
of the roast
knocks
at the door,   65
it's time!
come on!
and, on
the table, at the midpoint
of summer,   70
the tomato,

| *continued on page 52* |

star of earth, recurrent
and fertile
star,
displays   75
its convolutions,
its canals,
its remarkable amplitude
and abundance,
no pit,   80
no husk,
no leaves or thorns,
the tomato offers
its gift
of fiery color   85
and cool completeness. |—

translated by Margaret Sayers Peden

How many instances of nonvisual imagery do you see in this poem? Or are you too hungry now to look?

Sense Data and Images

Another good tool for increasing your sensitivity to poetry—as well as your sensitivity in general—is taking notice of your internal impressions. Think of something you like to touch. It could be a warm pillow, a comfortable sweater, somebody's hair, the steering wheel of a car, grass, a tree, a pet, a favorite drinking mug, anything at all.

In a journal entry, describe what it feels like to touch this being or thing. Go ahead and use plain adjectives at first (such as *fuzzy, hot, soft,* and *thrilling*), but then allow your imagination to wander. What other images arise, as you experience the sensations of touching what you enjoy touching? What visions, smells, tastes, sounds, or textures come to mind? Describe them.

Emotion into Image

In some poems there are images which evoke feelings and thoughts, and these feelings and thoughts in turn give rise to subsequent images. Such is the case in the following story-poem by Elizabeth Bishop, a quiet-living twentieth-century American poet whose work has been described as "controlled and restrained," yet who often slyly combined reality with fantasy.

| *The Fish*

by Elizabeth Bishop

I caught a tremendous fish
and held him beside the boat
half out of water, with my hook
fast in a corner of his mouth.
He didn't fight.   5
He hadn't fought at all.
He hung a grunting weight,
battered and venerable
and homely. Here and there
his brown skin hung in strips   10
like ancient wallpaper,
and its pattern of darker brown
was like wallpaper:
shapes like full-blown roses
stained and lost through age.   15
He was speckled with barnacles,
fine rosettes of lime,
and infested
with tiny white sea-lice,
and underneath two or three   20
rags of green weed hung down.
While his gills were breathing in
the terrible oxygen

| *continued on page 54* |

—the frightening gills,
fresh and crisp with blood,   25
that can cut so badly—
I thought of the coarse white flesh
packed in like feathers,
the big bones and the little bones,
the dramatic reds and blacks   30
of his shiny entrails,
the pink swim-bladder
like a big peony.
I looked into his eyes
which were larger than mine   35
but shallower, and yellowed,
the irises backed and packed
with tarnished tinfoil
seen through the lenses
of old scratched isinglass.   40
They shift a little, but not
to return my stare.
—It was more like the tipping
of an object toward the light.
I admired his sullen face,   45
the mechanism of his jaw,
and then I saw
that from his lower lip
—if you could call it a lip—
grim, wet, and weaponlike,   50
hung five old pieces of fish-line,
or four and a wire leader
with the swivel still attached,
with all their five big hooks
grown firmly in his mouth.   55
A green line, frayed at the end
where he broke it, two heavier lines,
and a fine black thread
still crimped from the strain and snap
when it broke and he got away.   60

| continued on page 55 |

Like medals with their ribbons
frayed and wavering,
a five-haired beard of wisdom
trailing from his aching jaw.
I stared and stared   65
and victory filled up
the little rented boat,
from the pool of bilge
where oil had spread a rainbow
around the rusted engine   70
to the bailer rusted orange,
the sun-cracked thwarts,
the oarlocks on their strings,
the gunnels—until everything
was rainbow, rainbow, rainbow!   75
And I let the fish go. ├—

Bishop begins her story with very simple, unadorned images: a tremendous fish, hook in mouth, not fighting. Then her emotion-driven perceptions come into play: She sees the fish as "battered and venerable / and homely." "Battered" we might imagine to be a straightforward description of the fish's condition, since the fish is, after all, caught on a hook. But "venerable," which means dignified and worthy of respect, is a **personification.** The speaker projects a personality, or a set of human character traits, onto the fish. "Homely," of course, is an aesthetic value judgment.

Once the speaker's feelings and ideas have been mixed into the brew of perception, the images also become more striking. Sharp details and colorful comparisons abound. The fish's skin "hung in strips like ancient wallpaper." He was "speckled with barnacles" and "infested with tiny white sea-lice." His "coarse white flesh" is "packed in like feathers," his irises "backed and packed / with tarnished tinfoil / seen through the lenses / of old scratched isinglass."

Within and throughout all this vivid imagery, Bishop's narrator continually *feels for* the fish. This is evidenced when she describes "his gills breathing in the terrible oxygen" and when she "looked into his eyes" and "admired his sullen face."

Then she sees that there are already five old hooks in this fish's mouth, remnants of past battles with other fishers. These are described objectively, dispassionately, and meticulously.

And then, upon their literal image, the poet superimposes the analogous images of "medals with their ribbons / frayed and wavering" and "a five-haired beard of wisdom." These imaginary images are as vivid and finely rendered as the real images that come before, but they are clearly products of feeling and judgment rather than actual sight. Thus image and idea/emotion are fused.

Now the ground has been laid for the only abstract statement in the poem: "victory filled up the little rented boat." "Victory" is an abstraction; one cannot see or touch victory. We don't normally think of victory *filling* anything. But we have now, along with Bishop's narrator, come to see this fish as a hero of sorts, and heroes, so to speak, radiate victory.

Then she sees the tiny pool of oil in the boat reflecting rainbow colors. She sees that the "rainbow" spill has spread all over the little boat (she dutifully names every object the spill has touched) "until everything / was rainbow, rainbow, rainbow!" The sun is playing tricks on her; the light has dazzled her eyes. But more than this, she is imbued with the spirit of victory which has filled the boat. Also, the rainbow, traditionally, is a symbol of hope, renewal, and victory or redemption from adversity. So the rainbow she sees, and that we see, is another wedding of idea with image.

In the presence of such glory, how could she *not* let the fish go?

Ambiguous Imagery

Bishop's poem is a story of literal events that caused feelings and ideas to arise. The events were rendered in images, and the feelings and ideas were also rendered in images.

In the following poem Emily Dickinson begins with abstract considerations: the soul and its extreme states—anguish and despair on the one hand, joy and release on the other. In describing these she personifies the soul, gives it a body, and does the same for other abstract qualities such as fright.

She blends concrete and abstract elements in such a way as to conjure fantastical and occasionally ambiguous images. Precisely detailed imagery, as we have seen, can be extremely effective. But ambiguity too, in the hands of a master like Dickinson, can be remarkably powerful.

| Poem #512

by Emily Dickinson

The Soul has Bandaged moments—
When too appalled to stir—
She feels some ghastly Fright come up
And stop to look at her—

Salute her—with long fingers— 5
Caress her freezing hair—
Sip, Goblin, from the very lips
The Lover—hovered—o'er
Unworthy, that a thought so mean
Accost a Theme—so—fair— 10

The soul has moments of Escape—
When bursting all the doors—
She dances like a Bomb, abroad,
And swings upon the Hours,

As do the Bee—delirious borne— 15
Long Dungeoned from his Rose—
Touch Liberty—then know no more,
But Noon, and Paradise—

| *continued on page 58* |

The Soul's retaken moments—
When, Felon led along,   20
With shackles on the plumed feet,
And staples, in the Song,

The Horror welcomes her, again
These, are not brayed of Tongue— ├—

We normally think of the soul as invisible, beyond substance. But bandages we see. So with this poem's first line, something takes shape. Since we know that bandages are for covering bruises and injuries, we may assume that whatever is hidden from our sight by the bandages is what is causing the Soul to be "too appalled to stir."

Next comes a "ghastly Fright" that salutes the Soul with long fingers and caresses her freezing hair. So now both Soul and Fright are personified: the Fright has fingers, the Soul has hair. Furthermore, the Soul is female, a "her."

"Ghastly Fright" is neither specific nor concrete. It is abstract, yet most of us can probably conjure up a corresponding image, whatever our own version of a "ghastly Fright" may be. In the lines that follow, this self-same "ghastly Fright" is recast as "Goblin" and "a thought so mean," respectively. All of these, then, are different names for the same thing, which we see shifting shape, as it were, as we read along. The Fright becomes a Goblin (the only concrete designation) and "sips" from the Soul's lips, a horrible, disgusting image of violation and defilement. Both Soul and Fright then fade into abstraction as "Goblin" becomes "a thought so mean" and Soul becomes "Theme."

It is as if the horrific images have resolved back into an ethereal realm. In much of Dickinson's poetry, abstractions such as fear, death, love, and doubt are the sources from which concrete images proceed. In Dickinson, the abstract gives birth to the concrete.

The next stanza skips and slides recklessly between the poles of concreteness and abstraction. Just as the soul has momentarily escaped, so has the poet found the freedom to dissolve distinctions between physical and nonphysical, visible and invisible, tangible and intangible.

"Bursting all the doors" is powerful, clear, and concrete. Next, "dances like a Bomb" is even more furiously exuberant. As an *image*, however, it pushes the edge of rationality. Bombs do not dance; they explode. So what image or images flash across your mind's eye when you read "She dances like a Bomb, abroad"?

The exultation of "swings upon the Hours" is infectious, and now we are outside the bounds of rationality altogether. How does one "swing" upon units of time? Does it matter? Do ambiguous images arise all the same? Does your heart respond?

The next stanza proceeds along similar lines. The Bee has been "Dungeoned" or kept away from "his Rose." This is all quite clear and concrete (and symbolic). To "Touch Liberty" we understand to mean escape. But "know no more, / But Noon, and Paradise" stretches our rational image-making capacity. Noon, of course, is the brightest moment of the day, when the sun is directly overhead and there is absolute daylight. To "know no more / But Noon" is to be enveloped in an enormous, unending brightness, and the bee itself is very small, almost too small to be seen within such a powerful light.

In the final two stanzas, the Soul is, sadly, "retaken" and shackled like a "Felon," led along like a beaten prisoner with "plumed feet." And again, "staples, in the Song" blends concreteness (staples) with abstraction (Song) in such a way that we are bound to envision *something*, though it may well be different to different readers. But the similarity will reside in the *character* of the image, which will be one of gruesome misery.

Symbolically speaking, a staple is something that fixes something shut, and a song, normally, is something that proceeds from an open mouth and an open heart. A song which is stapled shut cannot be sung. Imagistically speaking, it may be hard to envision what a song looks like; perhaps your image-making imagination may default to a rational image associated with song, such as the singer's tongue. In any case, whatever you envision, you will certainly agree that staples don't belong in the picture and that they hurt.

Then "The Horror welcomes her, again—." The Horror, of course, is but still another name for the Fright, the Goblin, the thought so mean. It "welcomes" her, we may assume, in a most sinister fashion. "These, are not brayed of Tongue—": a bray is a harsh, loud, fearful cry of a donkey. Perhaps the Horror which receives back the imprisoned Soul could cause such a sound, if the Soul could but utter it. But then, perhaps the Horror is so overwhelming that the bray of a Tongue could not even begin to voice the terror and revulsion which this Horror inspires. This, then, is mortification so profound that the Tongue is silenced, stapled, struck dumb.

WRITING WORKSHOP

Unearth a Poem

Find a poem, other than the last two, that contains emotion-laden imagery. Write a paragraph or two describing the emotion contained or expressed in a specific image or images.

The Image on the Page Itself

We have seen how concrete images spark emotions and vice-versa. We have also seen how abstract and concrete elements may be combined in ways that inspire images which are nonspecific but tremendously powerful.

Images are also sometimes suggested by the arrangement of the words and letters on the page itself. Look again at this poem by e. e. cummings.

i carry your heart with me

by e. e. cummings

i carry your heart with me(i carry it in
my heart)i am never without it(anywhere
i go you go,my dear;and whatever is done
by only me is your doing,my darling)
                    i fear   5

no fate(for you are my fate,my sweet)i want
no world(for beautiful you are my world,my true)
and it's you are whatever a moon has always meant
and whatever a sun will always sing is you

here is the deepest secret nobody knows   10
(here is the root of the root and the bud of the bud
and the sky of the sky of a tree called life;which grows
higher than soul can hope or mind can hide)
and this is the wonder that's keeping the stars apart

i carry your heart(i carry it in my heart) ├─   15

Two things about this poem's punctuation are a little odd: the abundant usage of parentheses and the lack of spaces separating the parentheses from adjoining letters. (These peculiarities are actually common to many of cummings's poems. But for our purposes, we'll note the effect they achieve in this particular poem.)

The statement with which the poem begins and ends—"i carry your heart with me(i carry it in my heart)"—describes something precious being carried *inside* the speaker. Similarly, parentheses *enclose* the words within. Also, the speaker is presumably holding that other heart very closely, just as letters surround the parentheses closely. In this way, the poem's punctuation graphically illustrates the poem's theme.

Here is an even more dramatic example of a poem that arranges words in an image-like fashion. Read carefully. (Ignore the title's instruction.)

Beware: Do Not Read This Poem

by Ishmael Reed

tonite , thriller was
abt an ol woman, so vain she
surrounded herself w/
    many mirrors

it got so bad that finally she   5
locked herself indoors & her
whole life became the
    mirrors

one day the villagers broke
into her house , but she was too   10
swift for them . she disappeared
    into a mirror
each tenant who bought the house
after that , lost a loved one to
    the old woman in the mirror :   15
    first a little girl
    then a young woman
    then the young woman/s husband

the hunger of this poem is legendary
it has taken in many victims   20
back off from this poem
it has drawn in yr feet
back off from this poem
it has drawn in yr legs
back off from this poem   25
it is a greedy mirror

| *continued on page 63* |

you are into this poem . from
    the waist down
nobody can hear you can they ?
this poem has had you up to here   30
     belch
this poem aint got no manners
you cant call out frm this poem
relax now & go w/ this poem
move & roll on to this poem   35
do not resist this poem
this poem has yr eyes
this poem has his head
this poem has his arms
this poem has his arms   40
this poem has his fingers
this poem has his fingertips

this poem is the reader & the
reader this poem

statistic: the us bureau of missing persons reports   45
    that in 1968 over 100,000 people disappeared
    leaving no solid clues
       nor trace   only
  a space   in the lives of their friends ├─

Instances of unconventional punctuation and spelling abound in this poem. (In fact, Reed, like cummings with his parentheses, employs many of these strange conventions—such as contracted words—in a lot of his poems.) We can itemize them in a series of questions:

- Why are there no capital letters?

- Why is *tonight* spelled "tonite"?

- Why is there so much space surrounding the comma in the first line?

- Why is *about* abbreviated to "abt" in the second line?

- Why is *old* abbreviated to "ol"?

- Why is *with* abbreviated to "w/"?

- Why is line 4 indented?

- Why is "&" used instead of the word *and?*

- Why is line 8 indented?

- Why is there so much space surrounding the comma in line 10?

- Why is there so much space surrounding the period in line 11?

- Why is line 12 indented?

- Why is there so much space surrounding the comma in line 14?

- Why are the last four lines of the third stanza indented?

- Why is there a space between the word *mirror* and the colon in line 15?

- Why is *woman's* spelled "woman/s" in line 18?

- Why is *your* spelled "yr"?

- In line 27, why is there a period in the middle of a sentence, and why is there so much space around the period?

- Why are lines 28 and 31 indented?

- Why are the apostrophes missing in "aint" and "cant"?

- Again: why use "&" instead of *and,* why have "w/" instead of *with,* and why employ "yr" instead of *your?*

- Why is the last section of the poem indented to the left and why is there so much odd spacing between some of the words?

- Why is *U.S.* spelled "us"?

Ultimately, the answers to these questions reside in your own experience as a reader. The question is not so much, What is the author trying to do?, but rather, How is this affecting my perception as I read? No one else can give you the answers. Still, we may explore possible answers together. In the discussion that follows, you can go along with what matches your perceptions and leave the rest.

When something is pushed up against a mirror, part of the image is lost on both ends. There is a contraction of the image; the inside, the part touching the edge of the mirror, cannot be seen. Perhaps the abbreviation of certain words reflects (no pun intended) this phenomenon. The slash in "w/" looks, to me, a little bit like a mirror.

This is a poem about things getting sucked into a mirror and disappearing. It seems appropriate, therefore, that there are inexplicable spaces in the poem as well, places where things should be but aren't.

The first four indented lines in the poem all contain either the word "mirrors" or the word "mirror." It is as if every time a mirror is mentioned, we have to fall forward a little bit into the line, much as the poem's victims have fallen into mirrors.

In the line "you are into this poem . from" I see the period as a kind of threshold, perhaps the threshold of the mirror itself. The sentence could have reasonably ended with the word "poem" but, crossing the threshold of the period, the sentence continues. Then, next thing I know, I'm into it from (falling forward again) the waist down.

The "us bureau of statistics" signified momentarily, as I first read it, *our* bureau of statistics, or, more succinctly, *our statistics—* the statistics on *us*. This was a little scary; I did not want to be part of any such statistics. (Or worse yet, become a statistic myself.)

But, all in all, I find this poem more playful than frightening. What do you think?

Images and Indentations

The following poem employs uneven and unconventional line indentation. How would you describe the effect of these unorthodox indentations as you read? What, if anything, do they emphasize or illustrate? Discuss your reactions with a friend.

Where Mountain Lion Lay Down with Deer

by Leslie Marmon Silko

I climb the black rock mountain
   stepping from day to day
          silently.
I smell the wind for my ancestors
      pale blue leaves   5
      crushed wild mountain smell.
Returning
  up the gray stone cliff
  where I descended
          a thousand years ago.   10
Returning to faded black stone
  where mountain lion lay down with deer.
It is better to stay up here
        watching wind's reflection
        in tall yellow flowers.   15
The old ones who remember me are gone
     the old songs are all forgotten
and the story of my birth.

| *continued on page 67* |

How I danced in snow-frost moonlight
>>>distant stars to the end of the Earth   20
How I swam away
>>in freezing mountain water
>>narrow mossy canyon tumbling down
>>>out of the mountain
>>>>out of the deep canyon stone   25
>down
>>the memory
>>>spilling out
>>>into the world. ⊢

Moods and Images

In the final line of this next poem, the narrator likens himself to a ghost. Do any of the preceding images contribute
to a ghostlike mood in this poem? If so, how?

Summer Night

by Antonio Machado

A beautiful summer night.
The tall houses
their balcony shutters open
to the wide plaza of the old village.
In the large deserted square,   5
stone benches, burning bush and acacias
trace their black shadows
symmetrically on the white sand.
In its zenith, the moon; in the tower,
the clock's illuminated globe.   10
I walk through the ancient village,
alone, like a ghost. ⊢

The next poem is somewhat similar in that its images culminate in a mood articulated at the poem's end. What is the mood, and how do the images contribute to it?

Looking for a Monk and Not Finding Him

by Li Po

I took a small path leading
up a hill valley, finding there
a temple, its gate covered
with moss, and in front of
the door but tracks of birds;   5
in the room of the old monk
no one was living, and I
staring through the window
saw but a hair duster hanging
on the wall, itself covered   10
with dust; emptily I sighed
thinking to go, but then
a light rain fell as if it
were flowers falling from
the sky, making a music of   15
its own; away in the distance
came the cry of a monkey, and
for me the cares of the world
slipped away, and I was filled
with the beauty around me. ├─   20

translated by Rewi Alley

In a small group discussion, examine the preceding two poems and address the question of how the images define the mood.

Contrasting Images

Read the following poem very carefully.

Eating Together

by Li-Young Lee

In the steamer is the trout
seasoned with slivers of ginger,
two sprigs of green onion, and sesame oil.
We shall eat it with rice for lunch,
brothers, sister, my mother who will   5
taste the sweetest meat of the head,
holding it between her fingers
deftly, the way my father did
weeks ago. Then he lay down
to sleep like a snow-covered road   10
winding through pines older than him,
without any travelers, and lonely for no one.

Examine this poem with your classmates in a small group. There are two distinct scenes—or sets of images—in this poem. What are they? Describe them. How do they differ in mood? Why does one flow into the other with no discernible break? What is the impact of this abrupt change of imagery? What has happened? What is the narrator thinking about?

Constructing Vibrant Imagery

Picture a scene or a striking visual image—preferably one that you are quite familiar with. Describe it as meticulously as you can. Be objective and concrete and use as much detail as you can possibly call to mind. Fill up at least a page.

Now go over what you've written. What is there in your description that carries connotations? What suggests feelings, judgments, concepts, or ideas?

STORIES

4

Stories Are Us

The novelist Barbara Kingsolver once said, "In the end, stories are all we have, and all we are." Was she exaggerating?

Well, what else are we? Impulses? Appetites? Desires? Bodily organisms? We certainly are every one of these things, but perhaps what Kingsolver meant is that, whereas animals may have impulses, desires, emotions, and perhaps even thoughts, only humans have stories. Stories *connect* all the rest. Stories are the patterns we make of our lives, the order we impose on events.

We tend to think of ourselves *in terms* of our stories: where we've been, what we've done, where we're going, and what we have yet to do. And of course, somewhere in there, there's also the present moment. We orient ourselves in this world by stories, and we generally plan what we're going to do next on the basis of some story or another.

This is not to say that our life stories are *fictional*. But we do have to believe in them, we have to follow the plot lines, and to a certain extent we have to make them up.

We all know what a story is. Formal definitions aside, a story is simply a bunch of events that make sense together, that have a point. The story is the glue that binds events together, without which the events would be random and there'd be no meaning to any of it.

Humans like meaning. We have a natural tendency, a biological imperative, in fact, to create meaning and to set things in order. We are constantly selecting and ordering our perceptions. Every moment we are bombarded with sensory data, only a small fraction of which we can allow in and incorporate into our experience. The data is then "understood," and then (sometimes) "remembered."

What is memory, after all, but a story we make of our lives? How could we keep the train of memory coherent without an intelligible story line?

So stories are us, we are stories, we tell them, we hear them, we think them, we need them. And every so often, we read them. It's no wonder that we like different kinds of stories, being made of stories ourselves. Organic matter must consume organic matter to live. We are stories that consume stories. Have you ever felt, as you were reading or listening to a story, that the words were kind of . . . *delicious?*

A Tasty One

Speaking of food, look at this:

| *Zen and the Art of Peanut Butter*   *by W. G. McDonald*

First, seek the most direct path
leading to the pantry.
Focus on the jar itself.

| *continued on page 73* |

Reveal the contents
with a reverse spiral motion.   5
Delicately insert the knife.
Delicately withdraw the knife.
As if applying salve
to the infinite being himself,
spread the contents   10
on the leavened slice.
Attentively lick the remainder
from the blade,
and throw the sandwich away. ├─

Does this poem tell a story? It describes an event, certainly: a rather mundane event—preparing a sandwich. For our purposes, we will consider this a story. And now the question arises: Is any story, any event, perception, or experience worthy of a poem? Can anything be *made into* a poem? Perhaps.

Maybe it depends on how we look at life. Perhaps every moment contains a story. Perhaps every story could be a poem. What does it mean to make a story into a poem?

Well, let's start with this. If somebody says to you, "When I make a peanut butter sandwich, my favorite part of the meal is licking the extra peanut butter off of the knife before I even take my first bite," you might chuckle. And if this person added, "Sometimes I'm so satisfied then that I just throw the sandwich away," you'd laugh some more. It could even be a memorable story. But poetry puts the words to this story in a particularly tasty order.

Every story, whether it's told aloud or in print, has a particular *voice*. By the voice we perceive the storyteller's *attitude*, which is part and parcel of the story itself. The attitude of "Zen and the Art of Peanut Butter" could be described as tongue-in-cheek. The gentle irony conveyed in this poem would be difficult to match in straightforward prose or speech.

Consider the title. We are tipped off immediately, by the connotations of the words "Zen" and "art," that peanut butter sandwiches are about to be exalted above their accustomed status. We may also already infer a sense of humor about all this.

Then, through the skillful use of carefully chosen words and line breaks, the author invokes a facetious religious mood.

> *First, seek the most direct path*
> *leading to the pantry.*

"Seeking the direct path" is often used to connote spiritual discipline, as in "seek the most direct path to God" or "seek the most direct path to enlightenment." Particularly in the Eastern spiritual traditions, of which Zen Buddhism is one, the term *path* often refers to spiritual practices. Zen is most "direct" in that it is based on the premise that enlightenment is available *now,* this very moment, and all that is required to realize enlightenment is the right stimulus, the right push.

So the first line of this poem calls forth associations with the sublime, the divine, the greatest of mysteries.

Then the second line takes us to the pantry, which is hardly a mystery, and only divine if we know we're going to find something there that's *really good.* Even then, it's not the kind of divinity we might have been led to expect by the connotations in the preceding line. (Although, of course, having read the title, we might not be *too* surprised.) Part of what makes this poem effective is the tension it continuously employs between the mundane and the transcendent, the sublime and the ridiculous.

The author continues: "Focus on the jar. . . ." *Focus* is a word often used in association with meditative practices.

"Reveal the contents. . . ." *Reveal* and *revelation* are often used in religious contexts, such as "all will be revealed" or "when God reveals Himself." Revealed truth is a kind of knowledge that comes perfectly clearly, all in one piece, beyond analysis, a "pure knowing."

"Delicately insert" and "Delicately withdraw" again imply carefulness, reverence, respect, and sublimity. Similarly, in line 12, "Attentively lick" also connotes an attitude of respect.

"As if applying salve to the infinite being himself" is an explicitly religious reference and it also contains an irony. "Applying salve" can be a kind of anointment or consecration, yet how can one possibly apply salve to an "infinite being"? Though there are references to anointment in the Bible and other religious texts, God Himself is never anointed; the idea is absurd. For one thing, God is not physical, and for another, God is just too big! (You'd need an infinite amount of salve.)

Finally, the "leavened slice." Where but in religious texts do you find references to leavened bread? Have you ever seen leavened bread for sale in the supermarket? Do you know what *leavened* means?

Now, of course, the irony is that we know he's talking about peanut butter, and even the hungriest amongst us seldom confuse peanut butter with God. But note how every line, every action he prescribes, contains some intimation of awe and reverence and worship—until the very end. The last injunction, "Throw the sandwich away," is something of a shock not only because of its actual meaning, but also because it does not come qualified by a reverent adverb such as "thoughtfully," "attentively," "carefully," or "delicately." In its blunt, unapologetic, unadorned simplicity, it contrasts to every other statement and instruction in the poem. This is truly the Zen moment, the one that momentarily startles us out of our habitual way of thinking by violating our expectations. It's the poetic equivalent of a cold shower or the proverbial rap on the shoulder of a meditator by a Zen master's stick. It's the line that "wakes us up."

It is also worth noting that this poem exquisitely uses *parallel structure*, which is a technique that is employed as much in prose as in poetry. **Parallel structure** means structuring a passage so that similar grammatical constructs follow one another in a series, creating a certain rhythm and resonance. In this case, note that every statement (or sentence) in the poem is a *command*, and thus the verbs "seek," "focus," "reveal," "insert," "withdraw," "spread," "lick," and "throw" stand *parallel* to each other.

How does this parallel structure influence our experience of the poem? Ultimately only you, the reader, can say. But you have to look and feel carefully. I, as a reader, might say that the parallel structure of command sentences gives this poem a certain flow and force as well as an emphasis which helps maintain the pseudo-lofty tone. The no-nonsense consistency of the poem's syntactic structure makes for a *posture* that lends a manner of credibility to the poem's mock solemnity.

So, as a reader, I walk away from this poem tickled, bemused, entertained, and provoked. I perceive multiple ironies, smiles within smiles. Could such a complexity have been rendered from the same raw material in a form other than a poem? Perhaps. It's conceivable. But the point is that a poem, as a form, lends itself to this complexity, this economy.

WRITING WORKSHOP

A First Date Story

Paying attention to idiosyncracies of structure, detail, emphasis, and word choice in a story-poem (or any poem) is a good tool for grasping some of the less obvious layers of significance. Here is a poem about a most memorable occasion.

Oranges

by Gary Soto

The first time I walked
With a girl, I was twelve,
Cold, and weighted down
With two oranges in my jacket.
December. Frost cracking   5
Beneath my steps, my breath
Before me, then gone,
As I walked toward
Her house, the one whose
Porch light burned yellow   10
Night and day, in any weather.

| *continued on page 77* |

A dog barked at me, until
She came out pulling
At her gloves, face bright
With rouge. I smiled,   15
Touched her shoulder, and led
Her down the street, across
A used car lot and a line
Of newly planted trees,
Until we were breathing   20
Before a drugstore. We
Entered, the tiny bell
Bringing a saleslady
Down a narrow aisle of goods.
I turned to the candies   25
Tiered like bleachers,
And asked what she wanted—
Light in her eyes, a smile
Starting at the corners
Of her mouth. I fingered   30
A nickel in my pocket,
And when she lifted a chocolate
That cost a dime,
I didn't say anything.
I took the nickel from   35
My pocket, then an orange,
And set them quietly on
The counter. When I looked up,
The lady's eyes met mine,
And held them, knowing   40
Very well what it was all
About.

    Outside,
A few cars hissing past,
Fog hanging like old   45
Coats between the trees.

| *continued on page 78* |

I took my girl's hand
In mine for two blocks,
Then released it to let
Her unwrap the chocolate. 50
I peeled my orange
That was so bright against
The gray of December
That, from some distance,
Someone might have thought 55
I was making a fire in my hands. ⊢

Note the details this narrator recalls about the first time he "walked with a girl." He remembers, among other things, the weather, the porch light of the girl's house, the newly planted trees by the used car lot, the candy bars in the drugstore "tiered like bleachers," the girl's smile, and the light in her eyes. He also vividly remembers peeling his orange as the girl unwrapped her chocolate.

Write a journal entry describing your reactions to this poem. What other specific visual and tactile details does he recall about this day? How do these details draw us into his point of view? How do they color the experience?

Furthermore, what transpired in the store between the narrator and the lady behind the counter?

What is significant about oranges? The title of the poem is "Oranges" and the final statement in the poem is about an orange. Why?

The Tales We Tell, the Tapestries We Weave

We have stated that memory itself is a story which we spin from our lives. It is no accident that a tale, or story, is sometimes referred to as a *yarn*, something composed of small fibers, tied together into a coherence.

When we spin the tales of our own lives, we do so from our own unique perspectives. We have all had the experience of being with someone, witnessing or taking part in some event together (perhaps even a simple event like a conversation), and then coming back with strikingly different stories about what transpired.

Native Americans have a term: the **Medicine Wheel.** The Medicine Wheel is the world, or the entire universe, understood as a great Mirror that constantly reflects ourselves back to ourselves. All the objects and beings in the universe are also Medicine Wheels, smaller Medicine Wheels, which can act as Mirrors.

If the entire universe can be imagined, for a moment, as a big circle, then every one of us sits at some point on the perimeter of the circle, at the edge of the great Medicine Wheel, looking within at the universe. What we see, our perspective, depends entirely upon where we are sitting. Where we are sitting, in turn, depends upon who and what we are, our innate qualities and dispositions, as well as our biases and our conditioning. As we live, however, we can also move around the wheel. We can take a different seat and a different view of life if we choose. It's up to us.

It's up to us. Living is a matter of imagination and so is constructing the tale of our lives. Whether we are aware of it, we are constantly, actively, *imagining* our lives as they happen and as they have happened.

This is not to say that nothing has an independent reality outside our minds. Nor is it to say that if something traumatic or unjust has occurred, it's only because you are "making it up." It might be more accurate to say that life, as we experience it, is a kind of *collaboration* between what we imagine and the phenomena/events bearing on us that we don't actively imagine. It's an absolutely constant collaboration that goes on every second, including this one. We take what life gives us, or we take from life what we desire, and we spin our lives out of this raw material. This is known as "being human."

Sometimes we paint portraits in our memories of past events which represent important turning points, transitions, new understandings, or a new awareness. Many of us like to keep and occasionally tell stories which we have inscribed inside ourselves about our first romantic experiences, or the first time someone close to us died, or our proudest or most embarrassing moments.

In keeping and telling these stories, we must necessarily build them up each time we use them, each time we speak them or refer to them in the privacy of our own memories. These stories do not merely exist, static, unchanging, immutable, on their own. These stories require the power of imagination to maintain them, and to—yes—embellish them.

These stories do not stay exactly the same. Or at least they shouldn't. Of course, they should not become totally different or opposite from their original versions either; that's called "rewriting history." But if the stories don't change at least slightly over time, then they also start to become less true. See for yourself. Feel this for yourself. Perhaps forgotten details are recalled, perhaps a few slightly new ones are added; it doesn't matter. Perhaps some of the old details are renewed, replaced, reconstructed, done over in more vibrant colors. This is fine and right; this is the way memories are kept alive and vital.

Have you ever heard anyone tell the same story over and over again in exactly the same way, and have you noticed how tired and rickety the story starts to seem? Have you ever heard yourself tell such stale, worn-out stories?

Memories require maintenance. It is not simply a question of accuracy. Accuracy is certainly desirable, but perfect accuracy, we must realize and accept, is perfectly impossible. Life is too full of details, too full of subtleties; we can only select and recount a mere fraction of them.

So as we continually, semiconsciously, slowly, and subtly recondition our stories over time, we occasionally choose different details to emphasize or fill in, to stay as faithful as we can to the truth, spirit, and significance of our stories. That's as real as we can get. And this is not a bad thing. To a certain extent, reality *is* creative, though not simply fabricated. This distinction may be a dangerous line to walk, but walk it we must, and we do.

In this light, consider the following two poems.

| *In the Waiting Room*   by *Elizabeth Bishop*

In Worcester, Massachusetts,
I went with Aunt Consuelo
to keep her dentist's appointment
and sat and waited for her
in the dentist's waiting room.   5
It was winter. It got dark
early. The waiting room
was full of grown-up people,
arctics and overcoats,
lamps and magazines.   10
My aunt was inside
what seemed like a long time
and while I waited I read
the *National Geographic*
(I could read) and carefully   15
studied the photographs:
the inside of a volcano,
black, and full of ashes;
then it was spilling over
in rivulets of fire.   20
Osa and Martin Johnson
dressed in riding breeches,
laced boots, and pith helmets.
A dead man slung on a pole
—"Long Pig," the caption said.   25
Babies with pointed heads
wound round and round with string;
black, naked women with necks
wound round and round with wire
like the necks of light bulbs.   30
Their breasts were horrifying.
I read it right straight through.
I was too shy to stop.

| *continued on page 82* |

And then I looked at the cover:
the yellow margins, the date.   35

Suddenly, from inside,
came an *oh!* of pain
—Aunt Consuelo's voice—
not very loud or long.
I wasn't at all surprised;   40
even then I knew she was
a foolish, timid woman.
I might have been embarrassed,
but wasn't. What took me
completely by surprise   45
was that it was *me:*
my voice, in my mouth.
Without thinking at all
I was my foolish aunt,
I—we—were falling, falling,   50
our eyes glued to the cover
of the *National Geographic,*
February, 1918.

I said to myself: three days
and you'll be seven years old.   55
I was saying it to stop
the sensation of falling off
the round, turning world
into cold, blue-black space.
But I felt: you are an *I,*   60
you are an *Elizabeth,*
you are one of *them.*
Why should you be one, too?
I scarcely dared to look
to see what it was I was.   65
I gave a sidelong glance
—I couldn't look any higher—

| *continued on page 83* |

at shadowy gray knees,
trousers and skirts and boots
and different pairs of hands   70
lying under the lamps.
I knew that nothing stranger
had ever happened, that nothing
stranger could ever happen.
Why should I be my aunt,   75
or me, or anyone?
What similarities—
boots, hands, the family voice
I felt in my throat, or even
the *National Geographic*   80
and those awful hanging breasts—
held us all together
or made us all just one?
How—I didn't know any
word for it—how "unlikely" . . .   85
How had I come to be here,
like them, and overhear
a cry of pain that could have
got loud and worse but hadn't?

The waiting room was bright   90
and too hot. It was sliding
beneath a big black wave,
another, and another.

Then I was back in it.
The War was on. Outside,   95
in Worcester, Massachusetts,
were night and slush and cold,
and it was still the fifth
of February, 1918. ├─

The Premonition

by Theodore Roethke

Walking this field I remember
Days of another summer
Oh that was long ago! I kept
Close to the heels of my father,
Matching his stride with half-steps   5
Until we came to a river.
He dipped his hand in the shallow:
Water ran over and under
Hair on a narrow wrist bone;
His image kept following after,—   10
Flashed with the sun in the ripple.
But when he stood up, that face
Was lost in a maze of water. ⊢

Read each poem at least twice, carefully, slowly, unhurriedly.

Both of these poems tell stories. These stories describe events that took place, years before the writers wrote them, events that happened during the writers' respective childhoods. Childhood is, of course, when we learn how to make memories and when we develop most of our own unique ways of viewing the world.

Bishop's poem takes place in the waiting room of a dentist's office, where she is waiting for her Aunt Consuelo. It is three days before her seventh birthday. In Roethke's poem, he is walking with his father through a field to a river. We do not know just how old he is, only that "Oh that was long ago!"

There are many things to see and hear, smell and think about, and focus on or ignore in a field, by a river, or in a dentist's waiting room. These poets have selectively presented us with certain details and not others. The details which they have chosen to recall and relate (as well as, in a different sense, the details which they have chosen to leave unmentioned or forgotten) give us the full flavor of their distinctive stories.

If we were to paraphrase these stories, to summarize each one briefly in pedestrian "objective" language, how might we do it? We might say, "Elizabeth Bishop was in the dentist's waiting room three days before her seventh birthday, having accompanied her aunt to an appointment. As she sat there, young Bishop thumbed through a magazine and observed the other people in the waiting room. She heard a noise, a cry of some sort, that startled her."

We could say, "Theodore Roethke once walked through a field with his father. They came to a riverbank and Roethke's father dipped his hand in the water, while Roethke watched. Even after his father withdrew the hand, Roethke continued to look at the water."

The above descriptions are the bare bones. They are no more the stories than the skeleton is the human being.

Bishop's memories are very particular. She offers us many tangible images. There are the overcoats and "arctics" (which my dictionary defines as "warm, waterproof overshoes") on the "grown-up people," lamps, *National Geographic,* a volcano spewing "rivulets of fire," and more, which you can see. Somehow all these images are bound up in her memory of this event. And what *was* the event? Why did Elizabeth Bishop write about this particular visit to the dentist's office? What made it a story worth telling? Something happened. What happened?

This story-poem is told in five stanzas. There are two very short ones at the beginning and end, and three longer (two *very* long) ones in the middle. Since the stanzas are not uniform in length, we might assume that they are organized according to some other logic.

Looking closer, we see that this is clearly so. The stanzas are essentially episodic. The first stanza sets the scene, telling us where this poem takes place and what the occasion was.

The second stanza gives us images: of the season, the room, the people in the room, the pictures in the magazine. There is no editorial comment here, no description of feeling or sensation. Bishop is simply reporting in this stanza, giving us raw data which is, of course, inevitably, selected data, particular data.

Next comes the pivotal moment, the cry of pain from inside the office. Now the focus shifts to the girl's inner experience as she describes her curious and profound reaction to the sound.

The fourth stanza consists almost entirely of a description of young Bishop's internal sensations, which have *apparently* been set in motion by the sound she described in the third stanza. There is also, of course, mention of a few external details—"shadowy knees," "trousers and skirts and boots," "different pairs of hands lying under the lamps." But even these outer perceptions (the results of a "sidelong glance") are *obviously* subjective, as opposed to merely necessarily subjective as all perceptions are. In this stanza we are distinctly aware not only that these things exist in the room, but that it is our speaker Elizabeth Bishop who sees them, and it is her perspective that we share. Even so, this stanza, the longest by far, is devoted primarily to inner perceptions, complexes of thought and emotion. These internal events are the essence of the story. They are why the story is being rendered in the first place, we sense. And somehow we also know that these inner events would not have transpired as they did without the outer events which preceded and perhaps precipitated them.

We should consider what exactly the nature of Bishop's experience was in the fourth stanza, what it is she is describing, and why it was important. But first, note that the fifth and final stanza steps back, bringing us back into the world, the outer context, the stage. It echoes the first stanza in its brevity, its matter-of-fact description of contextual data, and its usage of the orienting words "Worcester, Massachusetts."

Moving back to the fourth stanza, we find (among other things) a few very odd questions. "But I felt: you are an *I*, / you are an *Elizabeth*, you are one of *them*. / *Why* should you be one too?" "Why should I be my aunt, / or me, or anyone?" "What similarities . . . held us all together or made us all just one?" Attendant to these questions are sensations of "falling off / the round, turning world / into cold, blue-black space" and feeling the room "bright / and too hot" and "sliding / beneath a big black wave."

What do we make of all this? Clearly, her questions have something to do with her perception of herself as a human being among other human beings, as well as her amazement and perhaps ambivalence ("those awful hanging breasts") about this. The dramatic physical sensations she describes could be a result of some overwhelming emotion, such as shock.

Why should she be shocked to find out that she is human, just like everybody else? Surely she didn't think, up until then, that she was *not* human. And yet, a subtle but profound perceptual shift has occurred in a not-quite-seven-year-old girl, to whom the time, the place, the people, the clothes, and the pictures all seem so odd and peculiar and unlikely. She is a part of it too, and this is the revelation. She is contained within the same matrix as all these beings and things. Just as fate has defined each of them, so it has defined her.

This is not the kind of perception that would shock most adults. In fact, if it were described in ordinary language, it would probably be difficult for most adults to understand exactly what is so impressive about it. In a sense, it's perfectly obvious: we are human; we are part of the human race in a particular place at a particular time. This is not headline news. It isn't even an insight, by normal standards.

And yet, we see again how a poem can render nuances of feeling and perception that are far more elusive in straightforward prose. Elizabeth Bishop has used stanzas, line breaks, and specific images in such a way as to distinctly *frame* the pivotal perception so that we are right in it with her, so that we too feel it as strange, remarkable, even life-changing. Or, even if we are not right inside it with her, we are intrigued and it somehow makes intuitive sense that this could have been a turning point in her life and in her understanding of self.

Bishop has constructed a story for us from the raw material of her life and her memories, and she has constructed it in a distinctly poetic fashion. She introduces us to a very young girl (herself) and gives us this girl's perceptions of visual phenomena about her. We can easily accept and understand these concrete and unsurprising visual details. They bring us quickly and smoothly into her point of view and thus serve as a kind of scaffolding for what follows: the internal phenomena that Bishop really wants to point our attention to, wants us to relate to, and wants us to understand.

In Roethke's poem, we are also oriented with a few well-chosen, accessible images: the field, the heels of his father, the stride and the half-steps. When we get to the river, Roethke directs our vision (along with his own) to the surface of the water and just below, where his father's hand rests momentarily. Roethke lingers here, looking in this direction, gazing within and upon the water. We see the "hair on a narrow wristbone" and the reflected image of his father's face which "kept following after" the flowing water and which "flashed with the sun in the ripple" and was ultimately "lost in a maze of water." And this is what we are left with: the image of a face dissolving in water.

The title of this poem is "The Premonition." A premonition is a foreboding, a hunch about something to come, usually something ominous, something dangerous or tragic. This poem, we may assume before we even read it, might describe the actual premonition or feeling. It might even tell us what the premonition actually forewarned. As it turns out, the poem does neither of these things explicitly.

Instead we are given a simple story, a story that, on the face of it, seems to begin and end somewhere in the middle. We don't know why Roethke and his father went to the river, we don't know why Roethke's father put his hand in the water, and we don't know what happens after Roethke's father stands up again.

But we do have a title. The title indicates something about the story. It indicates that the point, perhaps, is not why they went to the river or even what happened there. The point is that, somewhere in the story, a premonition set in for the narrator.

Of the poem's thirteen lines, the last seven speak about what took place upon their reaching the river. While the first six lines set the stage and then describe a length of time we may assume to have been at least several minutes, the last seven describe a series of events that occurred over a span of mere moments. Given that the narrator lavishes so much attention on these moments, we might assume that this is where the premonition occurred.

In fact, the final image is portentous indeed: a face lost in a maze. So what was foreshadowed? His father's death, perhaps? An accident of some sort? A disappearance? An emotional dissolution due to trauma? We don't know. We can only speculate and feel the emotional tenor of the moment in the images of the rippling water, the flashing sunlight, and the dissolving face.

Again, the poetic form here—the peculiar structure of the penultimate sentence, the idiosyncratic points of beginning and ending, the line breaks, the compactness, and the lack of explanatory commentary which induces us to look again at the title— all contribute to the effect and frame this story in a very distinctive light.

Both of the foregoing poems concern external *and* internal events, as do all stories. But poems generally give more credence and attention to the internal universe—the realm of imagination—than do other forms of reportage.

DISCUSSION WORKSHOP

How the Story's Told

Discuss the three following story-poems in a small group.

The first poem by Rita Dove relates the story of a terrible day, a day she realized that she was pregnant, and then, hours later, received news of her husband's death. The next poem describes her experience of the wake that took place days later in the home she had shared with the father of her yet-unborn child.

Your Death

by Rita Dove

On the day that will always belong to you,
lunar clockwork faltered
and I was certain. Walking
the streets of Manhattan I thought:
Remember this day. I felt already   5
like an urn, filling with wine.

To celebrate, your son and I
took a stroll through Bloomingdale's
where he developed a headache
among the copper skillets and   10
tiers of collapsible baskets.
Pain tracked us through
the china, driving us
finally to the subway
and home,   15

where the phone was ringing
with bad news. Even now,
my new daughter
asleep in the crib, I can't shake
the moment his headache stopped   20
and the day changed ownership.
I felt robbed. Even the first
bite of the tuna fish sandwich
I had bought at the corner
became yours. ├—   25

The Wake

by Rita Dove

Your absence distributed itself
like an invitation.
Friends and relatives
kept coming, trying
to fill up the house.   5
But the rooms still gaped—
the green hangar swang empty, and
the head of the table
demanded an empty plate.

When I sat down in the armchair   10
your warm breath fell
over my shoulder.
When I climbed to bed I walked
through your blind departure.
The others stayed downstairs,   15
trying to cover
the silence with weeping.

When I lay down between the sheets
I lay down in the cool waters
of my own womb   20
and became the child
inside, innocuous
as a button, helplessly growing.
I slept because it was the only
thing I could do. I even dreamed.   25
I couldn't stop myself. ⊢

These poems express feelings of grief and injustice. In both poems she addresses her words to her beloved who has passed away. Look closely at her phrases.

In the first poem, "Your Death," she speaks of the day "belonging to" the deceased man, of it "changing ownership" at some point. She says she "felt robbed." Who *should* the day have belonged to, and why? Does she seem angry? Resentful? Is she confused?

Why is the last statement in the poem about a tuna fish sandwich? Does this strike you as silly, irreverent, or even disrespectful? Or does it communicate something sharp, vivid, and painful?

Consider some of the other language she employs and the details she remembers. What does she mean by "lunar clockwork faltered" and what is the effect of her stating it in this way, as opposed to a more prosaic fashion? What is the significance of her stepson's headache?

In "Your Wake," the tone is slightly different, isn't it? How would you characterize the difference in tone? How is she feeling in this poem? What are the words and phrases that most strongly communicate her state of mind?

The following poem by Li-Young Lee is told from the point of view of a young man who, while removing a splinter from his wife's hand, recalls a time when he was a child and his father performed the same service for him.

The Gift

by Li-Young Lee

To pull the metal splinter from my palm
my father recited a story in a low voice.
I watched his lovely face and not the blade.
Before the story ended, he'd removed
the iron sliver I thought I'd die from.   5

| *continued on page 93* |

I can't remember the tale,
but hear his voice still, a well
of dark water, a prayer.
And I recall his hands,
two measures of tenderness   10
he laid against my face,
the flames of discipline
he raised above my head.

Had you entered that afternoon
you would have thought you saw a man   15
planting something in a boy's palm,
a silver tear, a tiny flame.
Had you followed that boy
you would have arrived here,
where I bend over my wife's right hand.   20

Look how I shave her thumbnail down
so carefully she feels no pain.
Watch as I lift the splinter out.
I was seven when my father
took my hand like this,   25
and I did not hold that shard
between my fingers and think,
Metal that will bury me,
christen it Little Assassin,
Ore Going Deep for My Heart.   30
And I did not lift up my wound and cry,
Death visited here!
I did what a child does
when he's given something to keep.
I kissed my father. ├─   35

   This poem begins in the past, when the narrator was
seven years old, then shoots forward briefly into the present
where the narrator is with his wife, and then it rushes back
into the past again. Why is this "rubber band" effect

appropriate for this poem? How are the two incidents, past and present, related? How does one splinter removal episode bear on the other? How are they similar? How are they different?

Why does the narrator use such melodramatic language—"Metal that will bury me / christen it Little Assassin / Ore Going Deep for My Heart," and "Death visited here!"—in the final stanza? After all, he is telling us that he did *not* think or speak these phrases at the time, so why is he articulating them now?

The poem is entitled "The Gift." Why? What *was* the gift, and why does the narrator appreciate it now?

The Ballad: A Different Story

There is another kind of story-poem very different in nature, tone, and purpose from the ones we have looked at thus far. A **ballad** is a poem that tells a story not of personal experience but of events, usually historical ones. Sometimes ballads relate folktales or myths. In ballads the word *I* does not appear (unless it is contained in dialogue, as in "Lord Randal" on page 95) and the narrator's point of view is neither distinctive nor important. Here are two examples of ballads:

Harriet Tubman

by Eloise Greenfield

Harriet Tubman didn't take no stuff
Wasn't scared of nothing neither
Didn't come in this world to be no slave
And wasn't going to stay one either

"Farewell!" she sang to her friends one night   5
She was might sad to leave 'em
But she ran away that dark, hot night
Ran looking for her freedom

| continued on page 95 |

She ran to the woods and she ran through the woods
With the slave catchers right behind her   10
And she kept on going till she got to the North
Where those mean men couldn't find her

Nineteen times she went back South
To get three hundred others
She ran for her freedom nineteen times   15
To save black sisters and brothers
Harriet Tubman didn't take no stuff
Wasn't scared of nothing neither
Didn't come in this world to be no slave
And didn't stay one either   20

And didn't stay one either ├─

Lord Randal

by Anonymous, 16th century (?)

"Oh, where have you been, Lord Randal, my son?
Oh, where have you been, my handsome young man?"
"Oh, I've been to the wildwood; mother, make my bed soon,
I'm weary of hunting and I fain would lie down."

"And whom did you meet there, Lord Randal, my son?   5
And whom did you meet there, my handsome young man?"
"Oh, I met with my true love; mother, make my bed soon
I'm weary of hunting and I fain would lie down."

"What got you for supper, Lord Randal, my son?
What got you for supper, my handsome young man?"   10
"I got eels boiled in broth; mother, make my bed soon
I'm weary of hunting and I fain would lie down."

| *continued on page 96* |

"And who got your leavings, Lord Randal, my son?
And who got your leavings, my handsome young man?"
"I gave them to my dogs; mother, make my bed soon   15
I'm weary of hunting and I fain would lie down."

"And what did your dogs do, Lord Randal, my son?
And what did your dogs do, my handsome young man?"
"Oh, they stretched out and died; mother, make my bed soon
I'm weary of hunting and I fain would lie down."   20

"Oh, I fear you are poisoned, Lord Randal, my son.
Oh, I fear you are poisoned, my handsome young man."
"Oh, yes, I am poisoned; mother, make my bed soon
For I'm sick at the heart and I fain would lie down."

"What will you leave your mother, Lord Randal, my son?   25
What will you leave your mother, my handsome young man?"
"My house and my lands; mother, make my bed soon
For I'm sick at the heart and I fain would lie down."

"What will you leave your sister, Lord Randal, my son?
What will you leave your sister, my handsome young man?"   30
"My gold and my silver; mother, make my bed soon
For I'm sick at the heart and I fain would lie down."

"What will you leave your brother, Lord Randal, my son?
What will you leave your brother, my handsome young man?"
"My horse and my saddle; mother, make my bed soon   35
For I'm sick at the heart and I fain would lie down."

"What will you leave your true-love, Lord Randal, my son?
What will you leave your true-love, my handsome young man?"
"A halter to hang her; mother, make my bed soon
For I'm sick at the heart and I want to lie down." ⊢   40

What's the Difference?

Aside from the fact that these two ballads were composed centuries apart, there are other noticeable differences between them as well. One is a story told in dialogue; the other is a story told in narration. One repeats the same refrain in each verse; the other does not repeat anything until the last five lines of the poem. The rhythms are different, the voices are different, the stories told are quite different, and yet these are both ballads.

As ballads they have certain features *in common* that are not found in personal-story poems. Personal-story poems have in common other qualities not found in ballads. Which kind of poem do you prefer? How would you characterize the essential difference between the experience of reading a ballad poem and the experience of reading a personal-story poem? Write a paragraph or two responding to these questions.

Beginnings, Middles, and Endings

Stories begin and end where we say they do.

Where I choose to begin and end a story depends on my sense of the story's meaning. We frame our stories within schemas and patterns of meaning that we determine. When we feel that a certain meaning has been thoroughly revealed or rendered, then we feel our story is complete and may conclude. This completion may not necessarily have to do with outcomes or results of events. It may have to do with small epiphanies or revelations, magical moments, heightened perceptions, or other things. So, at times, to you, my stories might seem to end in the middle. To me, your stories might seem to begin at the end, and so on.

Ultimately, the structure of a story is dictated by the logic of overall meaning, not the logic of chronology. This is especially apparent in poems such as "In the Waiting Room," "The Premonition," and "The Gift."

In the following poem by Sylvia Plath, nothing much actually happens. This poem tells a story which begins and ends in a hospital room. It describes objects that are in the room and the patient's relationship with her nurses. It also describes, in greater detail, the patient's relationship with the flowers someone has left for her.

Although events past and future are intimated, practically no time transpires within the poem itself. But perhaps, in the time it takes to read the poem, something transpires within us, the readers.

Take your time and read this poem slowly and carefully.

Tulips

by Sylvia Plath

The tulips are too excitable, it is winter here.
Look how white everything is, how quiet, how snowed-in.
I am learning peacefulness, lying by myself quietly
As the light lies on these white walls, this bed, these hands.
I am nobody; I have nothing to do with explosions.   5
I have given my name and my day-clothes up to the nurses
And my history to the anaesthetist and my body to surgeons.

They have propped my head between the pillow and the sheet-cuff
Like an eye between two white lids that will not shut.
Stupid pupil, it has to take everything in.   10
The nurses pass and pass, they are no trouble,
They pass the way gulls pass inland in their white caps,
Doing things with their hands, one just the same as another,
So it is impossible to tell how many there are.

| *continued on page 99* |

My body is a pebble to them, they tend it as water   15
Tends to the pebbles it must run over, smoothing them gently.
They bring me numbness in their bright needles, they bring me
    sleep.
Now I have lost myself I am sick of baggage—
My patent leather overnight case like a black pillbox,
My husband and child smiling out of the family photo;   20
Their smiles catch onto my skin, little smiling hooks.

I have let things slip, a thirty-year-old cargo boat
Stubbornly hanging on to my name and address.
They have swabbed me clear of my loving associations.
Scared and bare on the green plastic-pillowed trolley   25
I watched my tea-set, my bureaus of linen, my books
Sink out of sight, and the water went over my head.
I am a nun now, I have never been so pure.

I didn't want any flowers, I only wanted
To lie with my hands turned up and be utterly empty.   30
How free it is, you have no idea how free—
The peacefulness is so big it dazes you,
And it asks nothing, a name tag, a few trinkets.
It is what the dead close on, finally; I imagine them
Shutting their mouths on it, like a Communion tablet.   35

The tulips are too red in the first place, they hurt me.
Even through the gift paper I could hear them breathe
Lightly, through their white swaddlings, like an awful baby.
Their redness talks to my wound, it corresponds.
They are subtle: they seem to float, though they weigh me down, 40
Upsetting me with their sudden tongues and their color,
A dozen red lead sinkers around my neck.

| *continued on page 100* |

Nobody watched me before, now I am watched.
The tulips turn to me, and the window behind me
Where once a day the light slowly widens and slowly thins,   45
And I see myself, flat, ridiculous, a cut-paper shadow
Between the eye of the sun and the eyes of the tulips,
And I have no face, I have wanted to efface myself.
The vivid tulips eat my oxygen.

Before they came the air was calm enough,   50
Coming and going, breath by breath, without any fuss.
Then the tulips filled it up like a loud noise.
Now the air snags and eddies round them the way a river
Snags and eddies round a sunken rust-red engine.
They concentrate my attention, that was happy   55
Playing and resting without committing itself.

They are opening like the mouth of some great African cat,
And I am aware of my heart: it opens and closes
Its bowl of red blooms out of sheer love for me.
The water I taste is warm and salt, like the sea,   60
And comes from a country as far away as health. ⊢

We will return to this powerful poem later, looking more closely at the devices Plath employs to communicate the precise emotional experience of the narrator in the poem (herself, perhaps?). But for now, since we are talking about stories, consider the following: There is a story that took place before the story in this poem. What story is that, and what clues are we given about it?

This story—the story this poem actually tells—happens in the present tense: "it is winter," "I am learning," "I am . . . lying," "My body is," and "The tulips are." There are references, mostly vague, to the past. But the poem's focus is on the present.

In the first stanza, the narrator states, "I have given my name and my day-clothes up to the nurses / And my history to the anaesthetist. . . ." If she has given away her name and her history, what can remain other than the present moment and its conditions? The present moment, then, contains the entire story. The present moment is pregnant with all the meaning necessary to make this story the story that it is.

Why is this so? In this story, why are the beginning, the middle, and the ending implicit right there in that room, in that bed, vis-à-vis those tulips? What is this story *about?*

WRITING WORKSHOP

Why This Story?

Patiently read the following poem by Robert Frost.

The Wood-Pile

by Robert Frost

Out walking in the frozen swamp one gray day,
I paused and said, "I will turn back from here.
No, I will go farther—and we shall see."
The hard snow held me, save where now and then
One foot went through. The view was all in lines   5
Straight up and down of tall slim trees
Too much alike to mark or name a place by
So as to say for certain I was here
Or somewhere else: I was just far from home.
A small bird flew before me. He was careful   10
To put a tree between us when he lighted,
And say no word to tell me who *he* was
Who was so foolish as to think what he thought.
He thought that I was after him for a feather—
The white one in his tail; like one who takes   15
Everything said as personal to himself.
One flight out sideways would have undeceived him.

| *continued on page 102* |

And then there was a pile of wood for which
I forgot him and let his little fear
Carry him off the way I might have gone,   20
Without so much as wishing him goodnight.
He went behind it to make his last stand.
It was a cord of maple, cut and split
And piled—and measured, four by four by eight.
And not another like it could I see.   25
No runner tracks in this year's snow looped near it.
And it was older than this year's cutting,
Or even last year's or the year's before.
The wood was gray the bark warping off it
And the pile somewhat sunken. Clematis   30
Had wound strings round and round it like a bundle.
What held it though on one side was a tree
Still growing, and on one a stake and prop,
These latter about to fall. I thought that only
Someone who lived in turning to fresh tasks   35
Could so forget his handiwork on which
He spent himself, the labor of his ax,
And leave it there far from a useful fireplace
To warm the frozen swamp as best it could
With the slow smokeless burning of decay. ├─   40

This poem relates a fairly straightforward story of one
man's walk in the woods. In the second line he thinks about
turning back, but he decides to explore further. He observes
the snow, the trees, and a small bird. He imagines a fanciful
relationship between the bird and himself. He assumes, or
pretends to assume, that he is aware of what the bird is
thinking and why the bird alights where it does.

But then his attention is distracted by the woodpile and
he forgets entirely about the little bird "Without so much as
wishing him goodnight." He contemplates this pile of wood
for the remainder of the poem, about half of the poem's forty

lines. Thus the woodpile looms with a larger significance than the bird, the trees, the snow, or even the swamp.

He notes concrete physical details about the woodpile and makes inferences about the person who left it there and how long ago it was cut. Perhaps it was intended to be firewood long ago, but forgotten, and is now, so to speak, warming the swamp itself "With the slow smokeless burning of decay." Frost leaves us right here, focused on the woodpile and its "smokeless burning."

In a journal entry, describe what you think is the point of this story. What is it *about?*

Do you feel it ended at a natural point? Or did it end in the middle?

How might this story be different if it were told in prose, not poetry?

A Mother-Daughter Story

In the following poem, the speaker addresses her mother and describes the spiritual and emotional legacy her mother has bequeathed her.

Black Mother Woman

by Audre Lorde

I cannot recall you gentle
yet through your heavy love
I have become
an image of your once delicate flesh
split with deceitful longings.   5

| continued on page 104 |

When strangers come and compliment me
your aged spirit takes a bow
jingling with pride
but once you hid that secret
in the center of furies   10
hanging me
with deep breasts and wiry hair
with your own split flesh
and long suffering eyes
buried in myths of little worth.   15

But I have peeled away your anger
down to the core of love
and look mother
I Am
a dark temple where your true spirit rises   20
beautiful
and tough as chestnut
stanchion against your nightmares of weakness
and if my eyes conceal
a squadron of conflicting rebellions   25
I learned from you
to define myself
through your denials. ⊢

   Address the following questions in a small group: How
does this daughter feel toward her mother? Grateful? Angry?
Affectionate? Sad? What words or phrases signal her feelings,
and how do they work? How does this daughter feel about
herself? How do her feelings about her mother and her
mother's image bear on her feelings about herself? What is
she saying to her mother? What has she learned from her
mother? Is her mother physically present with her in this
poem? What makes you think that her mother is or is not
physically present?

Unraveling the Yarn

Take a look at this poem by e. e. cummings.

nor woman

by e. e. cummings

nor woman
        (just as it be

             gan to snow he dis
              a
                ppeare   5
                d leavi
                  ng on its

                  elf pro
                  pped uprigh
                  t that in this o   10
                  ther w

                ise how e
              mpty park bundl
              e of what man can

            't hurt any more h   15

         u
      sh
nor child) ⊢

The words of this poem form a kind of image on the page. Many of the words in the poem are broken into pieces by the line breaks. The syntax of the poem's one sentence is highly unorthodox. Let's see how far we can get by unraveling it into a straight line:

nor woman (just as it began to snow he disappeared leaving on itself propped upright that in this other wise how empty park bundle of what man can't hurt anymore hush nor child)

We note, among other things, that the words "nor woman" are outside the parentheses which contain the rest of the poem.

Taking further liberties, let's rearrange the order of the words, add articles and a punctuation mark or two, and dispense with the parentheses. Let's add, subtract, and slightly change just a few words to get what might be, at first blush, a clearer statement.

Just as it began to snow, he disappeared, leaving in this otherwise empty park, propped upright on itself, a bundle of what neither man, nor child, nor woman can hurt anymore.

Now it makes sense. We have, of course, for the moment, broken the poem down, but it does make sense. Perhaps it is worth looking at the poem in dismantled form for a moment before returning to the original, as some pertinent questions now suggest themselves:

• What is in the bundle, or rather, what *is* the bundle?

• Why has the bundle been left?

• Why can't the bundle be hurt anymore?

• What's the story?

Now let's go back to the original poem and deem it restored. Further questions arise:

• What image or images come to mind just by looking at the poem and not reading it? (Try turning the page at different angles to see if it changes the image.)

- How does the imagery of the poem's physical shape relate to its words?

- What might have been different if this story were told in prose rather than in poetry? Would it have been shorter or longer? What might have been lost or gained?

- Why is "nor woman" separated from the rest of the poem?

- Why are the line breaks and placement of words on the page so bizarre and unconventional? What is their effect?

- Why is the word "disappeared" spread out over four lines? What is the effect of this?

- Why is the word "hush" spread out over four lines (including blanks)? What is the effect of this?

- Why don't any of the lines, save the first and last, end with an entire word? (Why are so many words *broken?*)

- There are words within words in this poem, such as *be* in "began," *a* in "disappeared," *can* in "can't," *pro* in "propped," *its* and *elf* in "itself," and the exclamation *o* in "other." Why are they set apart in such a way as to mislead us at first glance?

- What is the emotional tenor of this poem and how is it reinforced by the poem's highly stylized form?

In a small group, speculate on the answers to some of these questions.

WRITING WORKSHOP

Unearth a Story

Find another poem (not from this chapter, and not a ballad) that tells a story. Paraphrase the poem into prose.

What, if anything, is lost or gained by changing this story from poetry to prose? How is the story different?

Look at the poem again. Identify words or phrases with potent connotations. Describe the impact of these powerful or suggestive words and phrases.

Look at how the poem is arranged in terms of line breaks and stanzas. In what ways does the poem's form *direct* your attention and your focus?

WRITING WORKSHOP

What's Your Story?

Recall an event or story from your life and recast it as a poem.

Think about what you want to emphasize and how you want to do it. What is most important about the story? Why is it worth telling? What details do you recall most vividly? What feeling or feelings do you most strongly associate with this memory? How can you communicate and draw attention to these feelings? What do you want to leave uppermost in your reader's mind after he reads your poem?

SOUND

Sounds Everywhere

According to surveys, most people, if they had to choose, would rather go blind than deaf. Why?

Arguably, sound is more intimate than sight. Beautiful sights can thrill us, but beautiful sounds can fulfill us. Horrible sights can disturb us; horrible sounds can literally hurt us. Sound, like touch or taste, is much closer to the bone than sight.

For many people, the enjoyment of music is one of life's primary pleasures. But all sound, in one sense, is music. Sound touches us in a deep sensual province of our minds. The sound of a voice is a kind of music and it can move us emotionally.

Sound goes on and on. Sometimes, when we close our eyes, the images stop, and we experience the absence of sight. But the *sound* inside our heads does *not* stop. Even right now, the words you are reading are being "sounded out" in your mind. If you were to put this page down now and be still, even if you are in a silent place, you would still hear sounds in your mind, perhaps music, perhaps voices. Try it and see.

It's as if we each have radio stations in our heads, playing twenty-four hours a day, 365 days a year, broadcasting a variety of material that has either glued itself into our brains (advertising jingles are designed to do this, for example, as are some pop songs) or that our minds generate spontaneously, without (apparently) the slightest effort on our part. In fact, the ultimate goal of most meditation practices is to still this "voice inside the head." The result is said to be a transcendent state of consciousness: *samadhi,* bliss, enlightenment, an attainment of a most advanced spiritual condition. Silencing the mind completely is a psycho-spiritual feat equivalent to swimming the English Channel. There are very few people who *claim* to have done it for more than a few minutes at a time.

The aim of poetry, therefore, is more modest. While a totally quiet mind may be a profoundly marvelous thing, and even a relatively quiet mind may be a good and desirable thing, it is not poetry's business to adjust the volume. Rather, poetry's job is to borrow the internal sound apparatus and harness it for interesting and enlivening purposes. Just as music imposes a certain order and pleasurable coherence on sounds which we hear with our ears, so poetry takes words and arranges them in such a way as to evoke something like music inside our minds.

One of poetry's favorite techniques is creating sounds that match images. Here is an example from a story-poem/song by Robin Williamson (formerly of the Incredible String Band) entitled "Darling Belle":

> *holding his hand to see the swans*
> *hissing louder than rustling dresses of gracious ladies*
> > *bustling by.*

The *s* sounds—including the *shh* in "gracious" and the soft *s* in "ladies"—hiss in your mind's ear while you see the swans and the gracious ladies in your mind's eye. Even if you don't consciously notice what you're *hearing* as you read, the effect is coherent and tactile. The mind is subtly arrested and focused by the combination of image and sound offered to your imagination.

The Sounds in Your Mind

Close your eyes for a minute and listen to the sounds that go through your mind. What are they? Describe them in a journal entry. Are they pleasant sounds? Are they music? Are they chatter? Are they coherent? Discordant? Soothing? Irritating? Clear? All mixed-up? Loud? Soft? Where do you suppose they come from?

Alliteration

The preceding Robin Williamson lines use a technique known as **alliteration.** This simply means that a particular consonant sound—in this case, the *s* sound—is repeated in a line. Here are a few other examples:

Western wind, when will thou blow?

—Anonymous

To leap large lengths of miles when thou art gone . . .

—William Shakespeare

The fair breeze blew, the white foam flew,
The furrow followed free . . .

—Samuel Taylor Coleridge

O sweet spontaneous
earth how often have
the
doting

    fingers of
prurient philosophers pinched
and

    poked

  thee . . .

—e. e. cummings

What is the purpose of alliteration? As you read the lines carefully, how do the repeated sounds affect *you?*

Different consonant sounds have different characters. The *p* sounds in the preceding cummings excerpt fall upon the inner ear a bit more harshly than do the *w* sounds in the line from "Western Wind." In fact, the *w*s have an airy quality, like the wind, while the *p*s are more imposing, more physical, more blunt, like a pinch or a poke. The *l* sounds in the Shakespeare quote roll off the tongue with a fluid momentum, as if to leap the long miles. Alliteration does not always lend itself to this kind of blithe explication, but the consonant sounds always carry emotional resonance.

Assonance

Vowel sounds also convey emotional resonance. Sylvia Plath begins her famous poem "Daddy" with the lines:

You do not do, you do not do
Any more, black shoe.

The *oo* sound is a low vowel sound, originating deep in the throat. It is not a light or high sound, like *ah* or *ee*. When we speak the *oo* sound, we purse our lips slightly, which is also the face of remonstration and disapproval. Thus the sound of the vowels themselves in "You do not do" underscores the actual meaning of the words. (Of course, *ooh* is also sometimes an expression of amazement, and pursed lips are also the shape of a kiss. Sounds signify different things in different contexts.)

The repetition of a vowel sound in lines of poetry is known as **assonance.** Assonance, like alliteration, has emotional impact which we may or may not be consciously aware of as we read. The more carefully we read, the more likely we are to notice both the presence of these devices and how they affect us internally.

Rhyme

Another very common configuration of sound in poetry is **rhyme,** a device most of us are familiar with. Rhyming words, or rhyming lines, end in identical sounds. Rhyme has many functions, including making poems musical, catchy, pleasing, and easy to remember.

> *Whose woods these are I think I know*
> *His house is in the village, though . . .*

—Robert Frost

Rhymes have a way of fixing words in our minds and capturing our attention. Here are examples of rhyming stanzas from two poems which we have already seen.

> *Harriet Tubman didn't take no stuff*
> *Wasn't scared of nothing neither*
> *Didn't come in this world to be no slave*
> *And wasn't going to stay one either.*

—Eloise Greenfield

When I think about myself,
I almost laugh myself to death,
My life has been one great big joke,
A dance that's walked
A song that's spoke,
I laugh so hard I almost choke
When I think about myself.

—Maya Angelou

Sometimes people talk about stanzas of poetry in terms of **rhyme scheme.** This refers to the *pattern of rhyming sounds* in a poetic stanza. We arrive at a rhyme scheme by assigning a letter of the alphabet to each sound that ends a line. So in the preceding Eloise Greenfield stanza, the rhyme scheme is *abcb* because *neither* and *either* end in the same sound (they *rhyme*), and hence they are represented by the same letter. In the Angelou stanza, the rhyme scheme is *abcdcca*. In this verse, the third, fifth, and sixth lines all end in *-oke* and thus are assigned the same letter. The first and last lines, of course, end in the same word and are therefore given the same letter in the rhyme scheme.

Sometimes rhyming occurs *within* single lines of poetry. This is known as **internal rhyme.**

I wake *to sleep, and* take *my* wak*ing slow* . . .

—Theodore Roethke

*To the s*winging *and the* ringing . . .

—Edgar Allan Poe

Internal rhyme is yet another method of catching the mind's ear and creating an inner music.

Unearth a Poem

Yet another tool for divining the less-than-obvious emotional connotations of poetry is listening closely to its sounds.

Find a poem (not from this chapter) that employs alliteration, assonance, or internal rhyme. Write a paragraph describing how this technique enhances the poem's impact as you read.

Does the use of sound reinforce or emphasize a mood, idea, or emotion in the poem? Does it have an effect on the poem's tone? Does it influence the way you understand the semantic content of the words or the way you picture the images? Does it please your inner ear? Or does it do none of these things?

The Emotional Impact of Sounds

The following poem by Edgar Allan Poe employs all of the sound devices we have noted so far: alliteration, assonance, and both external and internal rhyme. Read this poem carefully with a few things in mind.

Observe, on the one hand, Poe's usage of the above-mentioned techniques. Then, perhaps on a second or third reading, see if you can *feel* how his use of sound reinforces the actual meaning of his words and pay attention to how the sounds play on your emotions as you read.

The Bells

by Edgar Allan Poe

I
Hear the sledges with the bells—
    Silver bells!
What a world of merriment their melody foretells!
How they tinkle, tinkle, tinkle,
   In the icy air of night!   5
While the stars that oversprinkle
All the heavens, seem to twinkle
  With a crystalline delight;
    Keeping time, time, time,
    In a sort of Runic rhyme,   10
To the tintinnabulation that so musically wells
    From the bells, bells, bells, bells, bells,
      Bells, bells, bells—
From the jingling and the tinkling of the bells.

II
Hear the mellow wedding bells—   15
    Golden bells!
What a world of happiness their harmony foretells!
  Through the balmy air of night
  How they ring out with delight!—
    From the molten-golden notes,   20
    And all in tune,
  What a liquid ditty floats
To the turtle-dove that listens, while she gloats
    On the moon!
    Oh, from out the sounding cells,   25
What a gush of euphony voluminously wells!
    How it swells!
    How it dwells
   On the Future!—how it tells
   Of the rapture that impels   30

| *continued on page 117* |

To the swinging and the ringing
    Of the bells, bells, bells—
Of the bells, bells, bells, bells,
      Bells, bells, bells—
To the rhyming and the chiming of the bells!   35

III

Hear the loud alarum bells—
    Brazen bells!
What a tale of terror, now, their turbulency tells!
  In the startled ear of night
  How they scream out with affright!   40
    Too much horrified to speak,
    They can only shriek, shriek,
      Out of tune,
In a clamorous appealing to the mercy of the fire,
In a mad expostulation with the deaf and frantic fire,   45
      Leaping higher, higher, higher,
    With a desperate desire,
    And a resolute endeavor
    Now—now to sit, or never,
By the side of the pale-faced moon,   50
    Oh, the bells, bells, bells!
    What a tale their terror tells
      Of Despair!
    How they clang, and clash, and roar!
    What a horror they outpour   55
  On the bosom of the palpitating air!
    Yet the ear, it fully knows,
      By the twanging
      And the clanging,
    How the danger ebbs and flows;   60
Yet the ear distinctly tells,
    In the jangling
    And the wrangling,
How the danger sinks and swells,

| *continued on page 118* |

By the sinking or the swelling in the anger of the bells— 65
    Of the bells—
  Of the bells, bells, bells, bells,
    Bells, bells, bells—
In the clamor and the clangor of the bells!

IV
Hear the tolling of the bells— 70
    Iron bells!
What a world of solemn thought their monody compels!
   In the silence of the night,
   How we shiver with affright
At the melancholy menace in their tone! 75
   For every sound that floats
   From the rust within their throats
     Is a groan.
    And the people—ah, the people—
    They that dwell up in the steeple, 80
     All alone,
   And who tolling, tolling, tolling,
    In that muffled monotone,
  Feel a glory in so rolling
     On the human heart a stone— 85
They are neither man nor woman—
They are neither brute nor human—
    They are Ghouls:—
   And their king it is who tolls:—
   And he rolls, rolls, rolls, 90
     Rolls
   A paean from the bells!
  And his merry bosom swells
     With the paean of the bells!
  And he dances, and he yells; 95
Keeping time, time, time,
In a sort of Runic rhyme,
    To the paean of the bells—
    Of the bells:

| *continued on page 119* |

Keeping time, time, time, 100
In a sort of Runic rhyme,
    To the throbbing of the bells—
  Of the bells, bells, bells—
    To the sobbing of the bells:
Keeping time, time, time, 105
   As he knells, knells, knells,
  In a happy Runic rhyme,
    To the rolling of the bells
  Of the bells, bells, bells—
    To the tolling of the bells 110
  Of the bells, bells, bells—
    Bells, bells, bells—
To the moaning and the groaning of the bells. ⊢

The first section of the poem describes the silver bells which are light and merry. "What a world of merriment their melody foretells." Here the repetition of the *m* sound could suggest the expression *Mmmm* as when one savors something pleasurable.

The rest of the verse is replete with repetitions of the *in* vowel-consonant combination: "tinkle," "In," "oversprinkle," "twinkle," "crystalline," "tintinnabulation," "jingling," and "tinkling." The short *i* coupled with the *n* makes a thin, vibrating sound, perhaps much like the silver bells themselves. It is a simple, small, light, and unthreatening sound.

The other vowel sound most prevalent in this verse is the long *i* sound, as in "delight," "night," "time," and "rhyme." This *i* sound is more emotive and dramatic than its short *i* counterpart. It is a kind of a cry; it involves opening the mouth wide and putting some strength into one's voice. Here, it seems, the exclamation it signifies is one of exultation.

Then there is the *ells* sound, as in "foretells," "wells," and, of course, the oft-repeated "bells." These sounds appear throughout the poem, and their emotional weight and significance evolve from verse to verse. (They are, perhaps, suggestive of *ringing*, the *reverberating* quality that all bells have when they are rung.)

The golden bells of the next verse are more serious and their sound has more gravity. "What a world of happiness their harmony foretells." Whereas the silver bells express merriment, the golden bells foretell happiness. Though happiness and merriment are related, they are different. Merriment is a light and intoxicated condition, borne of the moment. Happiness is a more general feeling of well-being, often quite sober, borne of a deeper relationship to circumstances and one's apprehension of the present and future. In the repetition of the breathy *h*s in "harmony" and "happiness," there is more awe and reverence than in the simple gratification of *Mmmmm*.

There is a greater variety of repeated vowel sounds in this verse than in the first one. We have the long *i* again, with "night" and "delight." We also have, of course, plenty of *ell*s. In addition, there is the long *o* sound of "golden," "notes," "floats," and "gloats," as well as the *oo* sound of "tune" and "moon." These sounds are rounder, fuller than the wispy *in* of the silver bells. They have, in essence, more body. They are more earthy, more substantial.

The brass alarm bells of verse three are coarser and denser yet. They are also more *shrill* than even the silver bells. "What a tale of terror now, their turbulency tells." The *t* sound is hard-edged, sharp, bringing tongue and teeth together, momentarily stopping the air flow in the mouth.

Now the long *i* sound is a cry of "affright" rather than exultation, and the *eek* sound is a "shriek."

A number of vowel combinations with the ending consonant *r* ensue, beginning with *ire,* moving through *er,* coming at last to *air* and *oar.* The *r* sound, like the *n* sound, has a vibrating quality; it seems to never quite stop. Unlike the *n,* the *r* sound is open-mouthed, louder, more—conceivably—desperate.

Finally, we get repetitions of *ang* and, relatedly, *am:* "twanging," "clanging," "jangling," "wrangling," "anger," "clamor," and "clangor." This is a most unsubtle sound, a broad and ungraceful sound. This is the sound of an inner chaos, of terror in the face of terrible danger.

The iron bells in the final verse are the weightiest of all, both literally and figuratively. They compel "solemn thought" and they "groan" with "melancholy menace." Note the alliteration of *m*s in this verse is more a dreadful grunt than a murmur of satisfaction. This verse concerns the dark endless misery of "Ghouls," or ghosts.

The long *o* figures prominently in this verse, particularly in combination with *n* (as in "tone," "groan," "alone," "stone," "monotone," "moaning," and "groaning") and with *l* (as in the repeated "tolling," "rolling," "tolls," and "rolls"). Over and over then, we hear the plaintive groan, *Ohhh . . .* as we read. The ceaseless quality of this moan of the dead, as it were, is accentuated by the vibrating consonants *l, r,* and *n,* which never come to a full stop.

Thus the sounds that these vowel-consonant combinations create are like the vibrations emanating from the bells. As a bell loses momentum and stops swinging, its sounds lessen until they become almost imperceptible, and then entirely imperceptible. But they continue to reverberate nonetheless.

Slant Rhyme

One more type of poetic sound is the so-called **slant rhyme,** a rhyme which is deliberately inexact. In slant rhyme, or **approximate rhyme** as it is sometimes called, the rhyming sounds are similar but not precisely alike, so we hear them in a different way from exact rhymes. Emily Dickinson used slant rhyme a great deal.

| *Poem 1078*
by Emily Dickinson

The Bustle in a House
The Morning after Death
Is solemnest of industries
Enacted upon Earth—

The Sweeping up the Heart
And putting Love away
We shall not want to use again
Until Eternity. ├─

5

The second and fourth lines in both verses of the above poem are "slantedly" rhymed. "Death" and "Earth" have the same ending consonant sound (*th*) and a similar internal vowel sound (short *e*), but the *r* in "Earth" alters the syllable, and hence skews the rhyme. Similarly, "away" and "Eternity" end in long vowel sounds that are similar but not identical.

What does slant rhyme accomplish? Again, it's up to your imagination, and the answer is different in each instance.

Here is my view of this particular case. Although Dickinson used slant rhyme in many of her poems, it seems particularly appropriate here. This poem is about the spiritual, emotional, and practical activity in a house the morning after a loved one has died therein. This is an extraordinary time—a time in which, briefly, the door between two worlds is necessarily opened, so that a certain invisible commerce may be accomplished. There is a shift in perspective; all things appear a bit differently.

In the same way, the phonetic shift from "Death" to "Earth" and from "away" to "Eternity" imparts a slight shock, a turning of a corner, a nudge into a strange, unknown territory where the survivors must spend a little time—attending to the deceased, releasing that which has been lost, and consolidating what remains—before resuming their business.

WRITING WORKSHOP

The Emotional Weight of Sounds

Here is a poem that you've seen in the first chapter of this book.

The Waking

by Theodore Roethke

I wake to sleep, and take my waking slow.
I feel my fate in what I cannot fear.
I learn by going where I have to go.

We think by feeling. What is there to know?
I hear my being dance from ear to ear.   5
I wake to sleep, and take my waking slow.

Of those so close beside me, which are you?
God bless the Ground! I shall walk softly there,
And learn by going where I have to go.

Light takes the Tree; but who can tell us how?   10
The lowly worm climbs up a winding stair;
I wake to sleep, and take my waking slow.

Great Nature has another thing to do
To you and me; so take the lively air,
And, lovely, learn by going where to go.   15

This shaking keeps me steady. I should know.
What falls away is always. And is near.
I wake to sleep, and take my waking slow.
I learn by going where I have to go.

Note Roethke's use of alliteration, assonance, and rhyme. Where, and to what effect, does he employ these techniques? Write your response in a paragraph or two.

Rhythm and Meter

It would be improper to devote a chapter to the uses of sound in poetry without discussing the element of **rhythm.** You know what a rhythm is. You hear rhythms in music, and sometimes these rhythms compel you to move your body in various ways. Should you ever stop to notice it, you'd find that there is also a certain rhythm to your thoughts. Speech, too, has rhythms.

Rhythm is not to be confused with *meter*. **Meter** is the formal structure of a line of poetry in terms of its *stressed* and *unstressed* syllables. The most common poetic meter is called *iambic meter*, in which unstressed syllables alternate with stressed syllables like this:

> *Whose* woods *these* are *I* think *I* know
> *His* house *is* in *the* vil*lage* though . . .

>   —Robert Frost

or:

> *I* can*not* dance *up*on *my* toes . . .

>   —Emily Dickinson

Another way to represent iambic meter is simply

> *daDUM daDUM daDUM daDUM.*

The line, as seen in this fashion, may be divided into even units of syllables. Each such unit is called a **foot**. So, "I *can-*" is a foot and "-not *dance*" is the next foot. "I cannot dance upon my toes" contains four metrical feet.

A line of *five* feet in iambic meter has a special name: **iambic pentameter.** This is a classic and very common metrical pattern:

> *daDUM daDUM daDUM daDUM daDUM.*

> *She hears, upon that water without sound,*
> *A voice that cries, "The Tomb in Palestine*
> *Is not the porch of spirits lingering*
> *It is the grave of Jesus, where he lay."*
> *We live in an old chaos of the sun,*
> *Or old dependency of day and night,*
> *Or island solitude, unsponsored, free,*
> *Of that wide water, inescapable."*

>   —Wallace Stevens

When iambic pentameter is unrhymed, as in the preceding verse, it is referred to as **blank verse.**

Although iambic meter is the most common and well-known meter, there are other meters as well, such as

- the **spondee,** which is a foot of two stressed syllables, as in:
  dead beat
  first kiss
  DUM-DUM

- the **trochee,** which reverses iambic meter, putting the stressed syllable first:
  whether
  heaven
  person
  DUM-da

- the **anapest,** which is a foot of three syllables, stressing only the last one:
  to the woods
  at a glance
  for a change
  da-da-DUM

- the **dactyl,** which reverses the anapest, placing one stressed syllable in front of two unstressed syllables:
  carefully
  adjective
  afterlife
  DUM-da-da

- and many others.

It is unnecessary to study or memorize these different meters to appreciate poetry. What is important is to notice rhythms.

Rhythm is to meter as melody is to musical notes. Meter is a part of what rhythm consists of, but it is not the only determining factor. Rhythm also consists of the natural speed with which the syllables flow, as well as the character of how sound moves and is interpreted by the reader. To this reader, for example, "I cannot dance upon my toes" has a much quicker rhythm than "Whose woods these are I think I know" even though both lines are in iambic meter and they are both eight syllables long.

Meter is a (more or less) objective *measure* of the way sound is constructed in terms of stresses and accents. But the rhythm is the musical *mood* of the word flow.

Some rhythms exist apart from meter altogether. Any *repetition,* for example, has a kind of rhythm.

> *Of the bells, bells, bells, bells,*
> *Bells, bells, bells—*
> *To the rhyming and the chiming of the bells!*

WRITING WORKSHOP

The Emotional Weight of Rhythms

One more time, carefully read Theodore Roethke's "The Waking."

The Waking

by Theodore Roethke

I wake to sleep, and take my waking slow.
I feel my fate in what I cannot fear.
I learn by going where I have to go.

We think by feeling. What is there to know?
I hear my being dance from ear to ear.   5
I wake to sleep, and take my waking slow.

| continued on page 127 |

Of those so close beside me, which are you?
God bless the Ground! I shall walk softly there,
And learn by going where I have to go.

Light takes the Tree; but who can tell us how?   10
The lowly worm climbs up a winding stair;
I wake to sleep, and take my waking slow.

Great Nature has another thing to do
To you and me; so take the lively air,
And, lovely, learn by going where to go.   15

This shaking keeps me steady. I should know.
What falls away is always. And is near.
I wake to sleep, and take my waking slow.
I learn by going where I have to go. ⊢

Write a paragraph or two responding to these questions. Are there rhythms in this poem? Are they fast or slow? Steady or uneven? Choppy or smooth? Is there, by any chance, a recognizable meter? How does Roethke's employment of rhythm and repetition affect the mood, tone, and meaning of this poem?

Free Verse

There are **free verse** poems written entirely without regard for any semblance of a uniform meter. This does not mean, however, that these poems have no rhythm.

Consider the following two poems (the first poem, by Whitman, includes only the first two stanzas).

There Was a Child Went Forth

by Walt Whitman

There was a child went forth every day,
And the first object he looked upon and received with wonder or
    pity or love or dread, that object he became,
And that object became part of him for the day or a certain part of
    the day . . . or for many years or stretching cycles of years.

The early lilacs became part of this child,
And grass, and white and red morning-glories, and white and red
    clover, and the song of the phoebe-bird,   5
And the March-born lambs, and the sow's pink-faint litter, and the
    mare's foal, and the cow's calf, and the noisy brood of the
    barnyard or by the mire of the pondside . . . and the fish
    suspending themselves so curiously below there . . . and the
    beautiful curious liquid . . . and the water-plants with their
    graceful flat heads . . . all became part of him. |—

Any Man's Advice to His Son

by Kenneth Fearing

If you have lost the radio beam, then guide yourself by
    the sun or the stars.
(By the North Star at night, and in daytime by the compass
    and the sun.)
Should the sky be overcast and there are neither stars nor a sun,
    then steer by dead reckoning.
If the wind and direction and speed are not known, then trust to
    your wits and your luck.

Do you follow me? Do you understand? Or is this
    too difficult to learn?   5
But you must and you will, it is important that you do,
Because there may be troubles even greater than these
    that I have said.

| *continued on page 129* |

Because, remember this: Trust no man fully.
Remember: If you must shoot at another man squeeze,
    do not jerk the trigger. Otherwise you may miss and die,
    yourself, at the hand of some other man's son.
And remember: In all this world there is nothing so easily
    squandered, or once gone, so completely lost as life.   10

I tell you this because I remember when you were small,
And because I remember all your monstrous infant boasts and lies,
And the way you smiled, and how you ran and climbed, as no one
    else quite did, and how you fell and were bruised,
And because there is no other person, anywhere on earth, who
    remembers these things as clearly as I do now. ⊢

These poems would be difficult, if not impossible, to break into meter, line by line. Yet they have rhythm, don't they? As you read them silently, or even read them aloud to yourself or others, do you perceive a cadence, a music in the flow of the words?

Fearing's poem approximates the rhythms of speech in some instances, but it is more smooth, more balanced than normal speech. Note how the rhythms change from stanza to stanza, but within stanzas the rhythms are quite similar line by line. Note his use of repetition: "If . . . then . . ." in the first stanza, "remember" in the third stanza, and "because" in the fourth stanza. What is the *mood* of these rhythms? How do they reinforce or color the meaning of the words?

Whitman's poem is also somewhat speech-like, but very different from Fearing's. The lines are long and expansive, sweeping buoyantly from phrase to phrase, with many repetitions of "and," as well as "and the." How do Whitman's rhythms reinforce his theme? As you read these verses, how is your mood affected?

Other Common Verse Forms

A poem's structure directly bears on the way that the words play in your inner ear. There are several formal poetic structures that have stood the test of time because they are elegant and evocative, and, in the right hands, they can render a colorful and finely nuanced array of poetic sensation. Here are four of the most commonly used and widely known poetic forms.

QUATRAIN

A rhyming four-line stanza is known as a **quatrain.** The rhyme scheme might be such that all the lines rhyme (*aaaa*):

> *The woods are lovely, dark and deep,*
> *But I have promises to keep,*
> *And miles to go before I sleep,*
> *And miles to go before I sleep.*
>
> —Robert Frost

Or every other line may rhyme (*abab*):

> *"Farewell!" she sang to her friends one night*
> *She was mighty sad to leave 'em*
> *But she ran away that dark hot night*
> *Ran looking for her freedom.*
>
> —Eloise Greenfield

Or the first and fourth lines may rhyme while the second and third lines also rhyme (*abba*):

> *Over back where they speak of life as staying*
> *("You couldn't call it a living, for it ain't"),*
> *There was an old, old house renewed with paint,*
> *And in it a piano loudly playing.*
>
> —Robert Frost

Or the first, second, and fourth lines may rhyme (*aaba*):

My little horse must think it queer
To stop without a farmhouse near
Between the woods and frozen lake
The darkest evening of the year.

—Robert Frost

Or just the second and fourth lines may rhyme (*abcb*):

After all, my erstwhile dear,
My no longer cherished,
Need we say it was not love,
Just because it perished?

—Edna St. Vincent Millay

You may notice that a remarkable number of poems employ stanzas that are four lines long. Four is a symmetrical number. We have four limbs. There are four main directions. Many locales have four seasons. Traditionally, there are four basic elements: earth, water, fire, and air. The number four connotes wholeness and completion. Perhaps that's why four is such a proper and becoming number of lines for a stanza of poetry.

SONNET

The **sonnet**, a fourteen-line rhyming poem in iambic pentameter, may be the most popular poetic structure (for a complete poem). It is quick and easy to read, its rhymes and rhythms are engaging, and its symmetry is very satisfying. The word *sonnet* comes from the Italian *sonetto*, which means "little song."

There are two primary traditional sonnet forms. The **Italian,** or **Petrarchan, sonnet** has a rhyme scheme of either *abba / abba / cdc / cdc* or *abba / abba / cde / cde*. The **English,** or **Shakespearean, sonnet,** on the other hand, has a rhyme scheme of *abab / cdcd / efef / gg*.

The Sonnet-Ballad

by Gwendolyn Brooks

Oh mother, mother, where is happiness?
They took my lover's tallness off to war.
Left me lamenting. Now I cannot guess
What I can use an empty heart-cup for.
He won't be coming back here any more.   5
Some day the war will end, but, oh, I knew
When he went walking grandly out that door
That my sweet love would have to be untrue.
Would have to be untrue. Would have to court
Coquettish death, whose impudent and strange   10
Possessive arms and beauty (of a sort)
Can make a hard man hesitate—and change.
And he will be the one to stammer, "Yes."
Oh mother, mother, where is happiness? |—

HAIKU

The **haiku** is a venerable poetic form, originating in Japan. Traditionally, the haiku has three lines and a total of seventeen syllables. There are five syllables in the first line, seven in the second, and five again in the third line.

The special charm of the haiku resides in its simplicity, directness, and luminous clarity.

by Matsuo Basho

The lightning flashes
And slashing through the darkness,
A night-heron's screech. |—

translated by Earl Miner

When Japanese haiku is translated into English, it often loses its 5–7–5 syllabic structure, yet retains its beguiling charm and surprising force.

by Issa

In the cherry blossom's shade
there's no such thing
as a stranger.

translated by Robert Haas

SESTINA

The **sestina** is a highly stylized and artistic form. It is a poem of thirty-nine lines in which six six-line stanzas repeat, in a systematic order, the words that conclude each of the lines of the first stanza. Then, a final three-line stanza uses the six repeating words two to a line. In the first six stanzas, the six repeated words come at the ends of lines, but they appear at the ends of *different* lines in different stanzas. That is, each repeated word appears once at the end of a first line, once at the end of a second line, once at the end of a third line, and so on. In this way, these repeated words become *themes* that dance around each other. In the following sestina by Elizabeth Bishop, the six repeated words are *house, grandmother, child, stove, almanac,* and *tears.*

Sestina

by Elizabeth Bishop

September rain falls on the house.
In the failing light, the old grandmother
sits in the kitchen with the child
beside the Little Marvel Stove,
reading the jokes from the almanac,   5
laughing and talking to hide her tears.

| continued on page 134 |

She thinks that her equinoctial tears
and the rain that beats on the roof of the house
were both foretold by the almanac,
but only known to a grandmother.   10
The iron kettle sings on the stove.
She cuts some bread and says to the child,

It's time for tea now; but the child
is watching the teakettle's small hard tears
dance like mad on the hot black stove,   15
the way the rain must dance on the house.
Tidying up, the old grandmother
hangs up the clever almanac

on its string. Birdlike, the almanac
hovers half open above the child,   20
hovers above the old grandmother
and her teacup full of dark brown tears.
She shivers and says she thinks the house
feels chilly and puts more wood on the stove.

It was to be, says the Marvel Stove.   25
I know what I know, says the almanac.
With crayons the child draws a rigid house
and a winding pathway. Then the child
puts in a man with buttons like tears
and shows it proudly to the grandmother.   30

But secretly, while the grandmother
busies herself about the stove,
the little moons fall down like tears
from between the pages of the almanac
into the flower bed the child   35
has carefully placed in front of the house.

| *continued on page 135* |

Time to plant tears, says the almanac.
The grandmother sings to the marvelous stove
and the child draws another inscrutable house. ├─

Listening to Shakespeare

Interestingly enough, save for a single phrase ("swallowed bait") the following sonnet by Shakespeare contains not one concrete noun. Read it two or three times. It is a description of lust, "the expense of spirit in a waste of shame," and its consequences.

Sonnet 129

by William Shakespeare

The expense of spirit in a waste of shame
Is lust in action; and, till action, lust
Is perjured, murderous, bloody, full of blame,
Savage, extreme, rude, cruel, not to trust;
Enjoyed no sooner but despised straight;   5
Past reason hunted, and, no sooner had,
Past reason hated as a swallowed bait
On purpose laid to make the taker mad;
Mad in pursuit, and in possession so;
Had, having, and in quest to have, extreme;   10
A bliss in proof, and proved, a very woe,
Before, a joy proposed; behind, a dream.
   All this the world well knows, yet none knows well
   To shun the heaven that leads men to hell. ├─

We stated in a previous chapter that it is very difficult for a poem to have much power if it relies entirely upon abstractions, without concrete images to anchor and embody the ideas. But does the force and momentum of Shakespeare's language stir you nonetheless?

In a journal entry, characterize the *rhythm* of his words. Where and how do repetition, alliteration, and assonance contribute to this poem's tone and rhythm? When you read this poem carefully, do the sounds and rhythms help bring his abstractions alive?

Rhythm, Content, and Tone

Finally, let us consider a poem by e. e. cummings that has a distinct music and an identifiable—if not altogether consistent—meter. Allow the sing-song rhythm to play gently on your inner ear as you read.

anyone lived in a pretty how town

by e. e. cummings

anyone lived in a pretty how town
(with up so floating many bells down)
spring summer autumn winter
he sang his didn't he danced his did

Women and men (both little and small)   5
cared for anyone not at all
they sowed their isn't they reaped their same
sun moon stars rain

children guessed (but only a few
and down they forgot as up they grew   10
autumn winter spring summer)
that noone loved him more by more

| *continued on page 137* |

when by now and tree by leaf
she laughed his joy she cried his grief
bird by snow and stir by still   15
anyone's any was all to her

someones married their everyones
laughed their cryings and did their dance
(sleep wake hope and then) they
said their nevers they slept their dream   20

stars rain sun moon
(and only the snow can begin to explain
how children are apt to forget to remember
with up so floating many bells down)

one day anyone died i guess   25
(and noone stooped to kiss his face)
busy folk buried them side by side
little by little and was by was

all by all and deep by deep
and more by more they dream their sleep   30
noone and anyone earth by april
wish by spirit and if by yes

Women and men (both dong and ding)
summer autumn winter spring
reaped their sowing and went their came   35
sun moon stars rain ⊢

The meter in this poem differs somewhat from line to line
and stanza to stanza:

ANy / one LIVED / in a PRET / ty how TOWN
with UP so / FLOAting / MANy bells / DOWN
SPRING / SUMMER / AUTUMN / WINTER
he SANG / his DIDn't / he DANCED / his DID

Although no particular meter rules the poem in a uniform fashion, its rhythms are, nonetheless, considerably more regular and identifiable than the rhythms of speech-like or free verse poems.

Like many of cummings's poems, the subject matter, or theme, is mildly ambiguous. We can, at the very least, gather that this poem concerns cycles of lives, loves, nature, seasons, and years. The words themselves must be considered, by most accounts, to be a little bit nonsensical, irrational, and dreamlike.

So this is not a poem that we can paraphrase or unravel into a coherent sentence or two. We might assume, then, that a great deal of the meaning lies in the *sounds* of the words and in the rhythms, which function, in a sense, as commentators on the theme.

In ascribing a childlike, sing-song rhythm to its subject, and in using very simple words in a distinctly nonchalant, playful manner, what kind of *perspective* does this poem take? How does this affect our perceptions and emotions? Can you imagine this poem written in a more "serious" fashion? Could it be?

Compare the cummings poem to these two choruses from the popular musical play *Fiddler on the Roof:*

Sunrise, sunset
Sunrise, sunset
Swiftly fly the years
One season following another
Laden with happiness and tears.

Sunrise, sunset
Sunrise, sunset
Swiftly flow the days
Seedlings turn overnight to sunflow'rs
Blossoming even as we gaze.

You will note that these choruses share some thematic common ground with cummings's poem. But the words selected, the images chosen, and the *sounds* of the words and rhythms all convey an entirely different set of connotations, an entirely different feeling-tone.

If you know the melody of the song, consider that as well. How does the tune and its rhythm affect the way you understand the words and the way you perceive the singer's attitude?

What is the singer's attitude? What is the narrator's attitude in cummings's poem? How would the singer of "Sunrise, Sunset" feel about the poem "anyone lived in a pretty how town"? How would the speaker in the poem feel about the song?

WRITING WORKSHOP

Listening for Rhythm

Listening closely, read the following poem by Langston Hughes.

| *Dream Variations*

by Langston Hughes

To fling my arms wide
In some place of the sun,
To whirl and to dance
Till the white day is done.
Then rest at cool evening   5
Beneath a tall tree
While night comes on gently
    Dark like me—
That is my dream!

| *continued on page 140* |

To fling my arms wide   10
In the face of the sun,
Dance! Whirl! Whirl!
Till the quick day is done.
Rest at pale evening . . .
A tall, slim tree . . .   15
Night coming tenderly
    Black like me. ⊢

Listening for rhythm is a good tool for bringing a poem alive in your mind and heart. Do you hear a rhythm in this poem? If so, how does the rhythm contribute to, or reinforce, the life of the poem? How does the rhythm complement the words? Write down your reactions.

DISCUSSION WORKSHOP

Repetition and Rhythm

Read the following poem by Margaret Atwood slowly, two or three times.

Variation on the Word Sleep

by Margaret Atwood

I would like to watch you sleeping,
which may not happen.
I would like to watch you,
sleeping. I would like to sleep
with you, to enter   5
your sleep as its smooth dark wave
slides over my head

| *continued on page 141*|

and walk with you through that lucent
wavering forest of bluegreen leaves
with its watery sun & three moons   10
towards the cave where you must descend,
towards your worst fear

I would like to give you the silver
branch, the small white flower, the one
word that will protect you   15
from the grief at the center
of your dream, from the grief
at the center. I would like to follow
you up the long stairway
again & become   20
the boat that would row you back
carefully, a flame
in two cupped hands
to where your body lies
beside me, and you enter   25
it as easily as breathing in

I would like to be the air
that inhabits you for a moment
only. I would like to be that unnoticed
& that necessary. |—   30

Is there a rhythm in this poem? How would you characterize it? How does Atwood's use of *repetition* create
rhythms that define the mood and tone of her poem? Compare your impressions to those of others in a small group
discussion.

Unearth a Poem

Find a poem in which sounds or rhythms contribute significantly. Bring it to a small group discussion and talk about how the elements of sound work within this poem. How do the sounds and rhythms affect you—your perceptions, your emotions—as you read? How do they bear on your attitude towards the poem's subject matter? How do they reveal the narrator's attitude?

What's in a Name?

Perhaps you are familiar with the term **onomatopoeia.** An onomatopoeia is a word that actually *sounds* like what it *means.* Examples include *buzz, crash, thump,* and *pop.*

Now and again, certain words strike us as being odd in that they seem to sound *unlike* what they mean. This is usually difficult to explain, but, nonetheless, we have this strange feeling about certain words. Can you think of any such words?

More commonly, we may say that people "look like" their names, or "don't look like" their names. "She looks like an Elizabeth." "He really doesn't strike me as someone who should be named Anthony. I just can't get used to it." "She looks like someone who should be named Isabelle, do you know what I mean?" What on earth do we mean by this? What is a *Lester,* or a *Graziella,* or a *Manuel,* or an *Ian* supposed to look like, and why?

If the sounds of names have certain connotative resonance and rhythms, can the character of these sounds be identified or articulated in some fashion? Can they be correlated to any associative, or even logical, thought process? Or to a feeling process? Presuming you are rash enough to try, how might you explain the character of sounds in a name?

Think about someone you know, or have known (it could even be yourself!), who either does or does not "look like" his or her name. Why would you say that this person does or does not look like that name? What is there about the sounds of the syllable(s), the number of syllable(s), or the ways in which your mouth forms the shapes of the syllable(s) that does or does not correspond to the character/ambience/appearance of the person bearing the name?

METAPHORS, SIMILES, AND SYMBOLS

6

The Power of Comparison

My People

by Langston Hughes

The night is beautiful,
So the faces of my people.

The stars are beautiful,
So the eyes of my people.

Beautiful, also, is the sun.   5
Beautiful, also, are the souls of my people.

In this direct and deceptively simple little poem, Langston Hughes makes three implicit comparisons. He compares the faces of his people, African Americans, to the night; he compares their eyes to the stars; and he compares their souls to the sun.

Sometimes, when we make comparisons, we are only comparing *one particular quality* that is similar in two different things. For example, if I say that my bag of books is as "heavy as a rock," I probably just mean that the bag is very heavy. I don't necessarily mean that the bag of books is like a rock in any other way.

But if I say that my father was as tall as a tree, there are *connotations* implicit within this comparison that go beyond height. A tree also has attributes of strength and endurance and even spiritual grandeur. So when I say my father was as tall as a tree, I might be implying that he shared some of these other treelike qualities as well.

When Langston Hughes states that African-American people have faces beautiful like the night, eyes beautiful like the stars, and souls beautiful like the sun, he is most definitely talking about beauty, but perhaps he isn't *just* talking about beauty.

Of course, there are different kinds of beauty. The beauty of an attractive face is different from the beauty of a lush spring day, which is also different from the beauty of a brand new, shiny sports car, or the beauty of a painting in a museum. To say that just as the night, the sun, or the stars are beautiful, so are my people, is very much different from saying that my people are beautiful just as sports cars, spring days, or a highly skilled painter's work is beautiful. The night, the stars, the sun . . . these are all beautiful in a very exalted way. Their beauty is of a divine, not earthly, variety.

Also, as the night is dark and rich, so are the faces of African Americans. As the stars shine (beaming inspiration and comfort across light-years of space), so do eyes. As the sun blazes with a brilliant, nurturing fire which makes all life possible, so do souls. As the night, the stars, and the sun seem eternal—or are as close to the eternal as almost anything we can imagine—so too, a race of people and its spirit.

Nor do the comparisons end here. When we think of things *in terms of other things,* more comparisons, more connections, and more perceptions keep coming. Understanding compounds and perspective expands in all directions.

Similes and Metaphors

According to some learning theorists, all new knowledge is formed on the basis of old knowledge. In other words, to assimilate new information or new ways of thinking, there must be some conceptual link to what is already known or understood. You can't learn multiplication or addition until you have a solid idea of what a number is. You won't understand the concept of *entropy* before you grasp the concepts *order* and *disorder.*

Whether it is true that all new thoughts are built on old ones, it is clear that we constantly think of things in terms of other things and we constantly compare. When we see a movie, we compare it to other movies we've seen (or even to real life). When we meet people, we compare them to other people we know or have known. We often compare sunsets to ones we've seen before. In this way, we make *links* in our imaginations. Poetry, of course, also employs comparisons.

All comparisons between things dissimilar in kind (that is to say, *not* two of the *same* thing, such as two cars, two sandwiches, or two people) are either *similes* or *metaphors.* A **simile** is a comparison between two things using the words *like* or *as,* and a **metaphor** is a comparison between two things that does not use the words *like* or *as.* So, to say that someone is "steady as a rock," "built like a fire truck" (use your imagination), or "saintlike" is to use similes. To say that someone "is a rock of dependability," "is a fire truck," or "is an angel" is to speak in metaphors.

Clearly, we make many comparisons with *like* and *as,* but we also use metaphors regularly in common speech: "She's a fish out of water." "They're peas in a pod." "It left a bad taste in my mouth." Certain metaphors, like the *leg* of a table or the *mouth* of a river, which implicitly compare inanimate objects to human beings (or to animals in general), are conventional and ordinary. Unusual metaphors crop up all the time, too. If you pay attention, you'll notice that we use metaphors every day.

We use metaphors because they are vivid, powerful communication tools. They *capture the imagination*. They invoke images. Former U.S. presidential candidate Ross Perot proclaimed that it was time to "put our financial house in order" and to "put a box around undisciplined spending." Referring to the issues at hand, he said that "asking the Democrats and the Republicans to solve these problems is like going to a heart surgeon that just lost his last thirty-two patients and suggest that he do heart surgery on you." Perot uses metaphors (and similes) constantly. This probably accounts for some of his popularity.

Sometimes metaphors come in the form of double meanings, as in the "smooth character" billboard advertisements for cigarettes. These implicitly liken the character of the cigarette (and by association the character of would-be smokers of the cigarette) to a "smooth character" who plays pool, races cars, plays jazz, and attracts beautiful women.

Metaphors are often used propagandistically, in advertising and political speech. It is good to be aware of the use of metaphors because they direct the imagination. It serves us to know when and how we are being directed by them.

In contrast, poetry uses metaphors in a frank, ambitious, exploratory manner. Poetry uses metaphors to challenge and stretch and stimulate the imagination, rather than to manipulate or co-opt it. Whereas the metaphors of advertising and politics try to slip by us so that we are scarcely aware that we've seen or heard a figure of speech, the metaphors of poetry draw attention to themselves by compelling us to wrestle with and question them.

Sounds like Pearls

by Maya Angelou

Sounds
    Like pearls
Roll off your tongue
    To grace this eager ebon ear.

Doubt and fear,   5
    Ungainly things,
With blushings
    Disappear.

"Sounds like Pearls" by Maya Angelou employs a simile in the first stanza and a metaphor in the second. In the first stanza, sounds—nonphysical phenomena—are compared to pearls—physical objects—which we can then visualize rolling off of someone's tongue. In the second stanza, the emotions doubt and fear are implicitly likened to people, as they are "ungainly," or clumsy, and they blush.

We have already seen a great many similes and metaphors in poems from previous chapters. From Pablo Neruda's "Ode to Tomatoes" (Chapter 2) comes the simile "light is halved like a tomato." The first stanza of Laureen Mar's "The Window Frames the Moon" (also Chapter 2) gives two metaphors for the moon: "the curve of a comb" and "a plate broken perfectly in half." And in Margaret Atwood's "Variation on the Word *Sleep*" (Chapter 5), sleep is metaphorically cast as a "smooth dark wave." You can find many more examples throughout this book.

WRITING WORKSHOP

Noticing Similes and Metaphors

Noticing similes and metaphors is a useful tool for uncovering layers of depth in a poem. Here is another poem by former poet laureate Rita Dove of Ohio.

November for Beginners

by Rita Dove

Snow would be the easy
way out—that softening
sky like a sigh of relief
at finally being allowed
to yield. No dice.   5
We stack twigs for burning
in glistening patches
but the rain won't give.

So we wait, breeding
mood, making music   10
of decline. We sit down
in the smell of the past
and rise in a light
that is already leaving.
We ache in secret,   15
memorizing

a gloomy line
or two of German.
When spring comes we promise to act
the fool. Pour,   20
rain! Sail, wind,
with your cargo of zithers! ├─

This is a poem about waiting for weather to change and
how the seasons of the spirit may reflect and correspond to
the external seasons. There is a simile and at least one metaphor in this poem. Can you find them? What are they?

Metaphors That Link Ideas

Examine the following lyric by Canadian singer-songwriter Bruce
Cockburn:

Distant times and distant lands
Worthless money changing hands
Changing them to what? I wonder . . .

Cockburn's words plainly express an attitude about money when he calls it "worthless." But, more than this, he takes the common colloquial expression "changing hands" and gives it a double meaning, which in turn translates to a metaphor. When we say money "changes hands," we mean that money moves from one person, or one set of hands, to another. We do not mean that money actually *changes hands*, as in causing the hands themselves to change and be different than they were before they came into contact with money. Cockburn knows this, of course, but what his sly metaphorical question asks is: How does money, and the commerce by which it arrives, change *us*?

Apparently hands stand for the whole person here. When Cockburn says "changing them to what, I wonder" he is considering how *people* change, not just their hands. But hands also represent our *agency* in the world: what we do, how we behave, what we make. Hands are a *symbol* for how we engage the world, how we hold things, what we take from the world, and what we give in turn.

Note that "Changing them to what?" implies more than "changing them *how?*" Asking *what* something changes *to* implies that something can turn into something else—like magic—becoming something altogether different. Can money change people so drastically? We, along with Cockburn, may well wonder.

Note also that, while a *comparison* is not implicit in Cockburn's words, he is nonetheless framing certain phenomena—the human spirit and its movements—in terms of other phenomena—money and its movements. He uses the double meaning of the word "changing" and the symbolic meaning of "hands" as devices to link, or leap from, one kind of idea to another.

In Section 6 of his epic poem, "Song of Myself," the great American poet Walt Whitman employs both metaphors and idea linking/leaping to speculate in wondrous fashion about the nature of life and death.

Song of Myself (Section 6)

by Walt Whitman

A child said, What is the grass? fetching it to me with full hands;
How could I answer the child? . . . I do not know what it is
   any more than he.

I guess it must be the flag of my disposition, out of hopeful
   green stuff woven.

Or I guess it is the handkerchief of the Lord,
A scented gift and remembrancer designedly dropped,   5
Bearing the owner's name someway in the corners, that we
   may see and remark, and say Whose?

Or I guess the grass is itself a child . . . he produced babe of
   the vegetation.
Or I guess it is a uniform hieroglyphic,
And it means, Sprouting alike in broad zones and narrow zones,
Growing among black folks as among white,   10
Kanuck, Tuckahoe, Congressman, Cuff, I give them the same, I
   receive them the same.
And now it seems to me the beautiful uncut hair of graves.

Tenderly will I use you curling grass,
It may be you transpire from the breasts of young men,
It may be if I had known them I would have loved them;   15
It may be you are from old people and from women, and from
   offspring taken soon out of their mothers' laps,
And here you are the mothers' laps.

The grass is very dark to be from the white heads of old mothers,
Darker than the colorless beards of old men,
Dark to come from under the faint red roofs of mouths.   20

| *continued on page 153* |

O I perceive after all so many uttering tongues!
And I perceive they do not come from the roofs of mouths
   for nothing.

I wish I could translate the hints about the dead young men
   and women,
And the hints about old men and mothers, and the offspring
   taken soon out of their laps.

What do you think has become of the young and old men?   25
And what do you think has become of the women and children?

They are alive and well somewhere;
Their smallest sprout shows there is really no death,
And if ever there was it led forward life, and does not wait at the
   end to arrest it,
And ceased the moment life appeared.   30

All goes onward and onward . . . and nothing collapses,
And to die is different from what anyone supposed, and luckier. $\vdash$

In the first stanza, Whitman tells a little story in which a child
poses a simple question: What is grass? The next three or four
stanzas offer tentative metaphorical answers to this query.

"I guess it must be the flag of my disposition, out of hopeful green stuff woven." This compact sentence contains a remarkable combination of metaphors and conceptual links.

First, it suggests that the grass could be a kind of flag. We
normally think of flags as representing nations, states, or cities—
corporate political and cultural entities. A club or a school or any
official organization may also have a flag. But when Whitman says
"flag of my disposition," we are also given to imagine that one
person's mood, one person's peculiar constellation of thought,
feeling, and outlook, could be strong and significant enough to
merit a flag. Then "out of hopeful green stuff woven" implicitly
likens individual blades of grass to the cloth fibers from which

flags are woven. These grass fibers are also afforded the quality of *hopefulness,* which underscores that they are alive, conscious, and feeling, just like our narrator, who sees some essential dimension of himself reflected in the grass.

The next metaphor is "handkerchief of the Lord." The grass is indeed "scented" like some handkerchiefs but in what sense does it "bear the owner's name someway in the corners"? Perhaps the answer lies in the qualification "someway," which indicates that the name may take some effort to locate or read. Perhaps this effort of looking and reading is the very point, the reason that the "handkerchief" was "designedly dropped" in the first place: "that we may see and remark, / and say Whose?" That we may, essentially, be moved to search after a Creator. And this search could occupy one for an entire lifetime. After all, if all the grass covering the earth was one large handkerchief, how would we even begin to find the "corners"?

Three metaphors follow in the next stanza, two very quickly and one at the end. The grass is the child or "babe" of vegetation. The grass is a "uniform hieroglyphic" or a single symbolic message, which Whitman interprets: "Sprouting alike in broad zones and narrow zones, / Growing among black folks as among white, / Kanuck, Tuckahoe, Congressman, Cuff, I give them the same, I receive them the same." In addition to bespeaking the essential equality of human beings, this message is a reminder that we all arise from the stuff of earth and ultimately return to it. The grass, or earth, "gives" us our life and "receives" us all back. In this way, we are all related.

"And now it seems to me the beautiful uncut hair of graves." Although there are one or two more metaphors yet to come, it is from this metaphor that the rest of the poem proceeds.

In the next stanza, Whitman speculates about whose particular "hair" it is that he currently contemplates in the form of grass. Reflecting that it could be the "hair" of "offspring taken too soon out of their mothers' laps"—infants or children, perhaps, who died young—he redeems the tragedy, as such, by metaphorically concluding, "And here you are the mothers' laps." Our ultimate mother, the body from which all of us spring, is the earth, and the grass is her lap. And so the babies, along with the rest of us, are returned to her primordial embrace and nothing is lost, nothing is wasted; everything is reclaimed in a rightful place.

As Whitman continues to speak of grass as "transpiring" from graves and their contents, he implies one more metaphor two stanzas later—the blades of grass as "so many uttering tongues!" He perceives that they "do not come . . . for nothing" and he proceeds to tentatively "translate" what these tongues/voices "hint" at concerning what has become of those who have passed away.

In the last two stanzas, he is forthright and positive about what it all means, what the grass attests to: "They are alive and well somewhere; / The smallest sprout shows there is really no death / . . . nothing collapses, / And to die is different from what anyone supposed, and luckier." Combining metaphorical thinking with spiritual intuition, Whitman has triumphed over fear of death. And, insofar as we have followed the movements of his mind, we have triumphed with him.

WRITING WORKSHOP

Noticing Metaphors and Similes in Conversation

Metaphors and similes crop up frequently in conversation. Some are common expressions that we would never think twice about, like a "*train* of thought" or the "*branch* of a bank." Some come along as dramatic and delightful surprises. A few weeks ago I was having a particularly cheerful and energetic day and my friend Gwen commented, "You look like you're a bumblebee and it's the first day of spring." Most conversational metaphors and similes, however, fall somewhere in between these two extremes. You might miss them if you're not listening, but as soon as you're paying attention, there they are.

Listen a little bit more closely than usual to your conversations for the next few days. Try and catch at least seven metaphors or similes as they appear. Write them down.

Personification

Personification is the technique of ascribing human qualities, traits, or capabilities to nonhuman animals or objects; or ascribing *living* qualities to abstractions or inanimate things. Any personification is a metaphor: Nonhuman things are implicitly likened to human beings, or nonliving things are likened to living things.

Earlier in this chapter, Maya Angelou personified doubt and fear by suggesting that they *blush*. In "The Window Frames the Moon" (from Chapter 2), Laureen Mar personifies the moon when she states that it "refuses" to fit in her window and that it "pushes back" when she pushes it. In "Sorrow" (Chapter 1), Joules Graves describes sorrow itself as a sad, lonely woman. Personification is a very popular device; you may find more instances of it in this book. Here is a poem in which *rain* is personified.

| *Enjoying the Rain*

by Ts'ai Chih

Heaven's covering, how complete and broad!
It lavishly nourishes the host of men.
If it spurns them there is inevitable suffering;
If it cherishes them there is exciting prosperity.
Propitious clouds come from the north,   5
And dense-darkly move to the southwest.
Timely rain falls in the middle of the night;
A long peal of thunder envelops my garden.
Good seedlings fill the rich earth;
The autumn harvest will be full. |—   10

translated by George W. Kent

The personification in this poem occurs in the third and fourth lines, wherein rain "spurns" and "cherishes." Arguably, "lavishly nourishes" from the second line might be considered a personification too.

Death is something that has been personified in many legends and cultures. It has been cast as the "Grim Reaper," the "Angel of Death," and so on. Here are two poems that personify death in very different ways.

Death, All Riddled with Holes

by Miguel Hernandez

Death, all riddled with holes
And gorings from your very self,
In the hide of a bull you walk and graze
On a bullfighter's shining meadow.

He gives volcanic roars in sudden flashes,   5
And then steams with the fierce smoke
Of a love for everything that is born
As he kills the quiet rancheros.

Wild, hungry, loving beast, you can
Feed on my heart, on tragic grass,   10
If you like its bitter flavor.

A love for everything torments me now
As it does you, and towards it all
My heart spills out dressed in its burial clothes.

translated by John Crow

Poem #712

by Emily Dickinson

Because I could not stop for Death—
He kindly stopped for me—
The Carriage held but just Ourselves—
And Immortality.

| continued on page 158 |

We slowly drove—He knew no haste   5
And I had put away
My labor and my leisure too,
For His Civility—

We passed the School, where Children strove
At Recess—in the Ring—   10
We passed the Fields of Gazing Grain—
We passed the Setting Sun—

Or rather—He passed Us—
The Dews drew quivering and chill—
For only Gossamer, my Gown—   15
My Tippet—only Tulle—

We paused before a House that seemed
A Swelling of the Ground—
The Roof was scarcely visible—
The Cornice—in the Ground—   20

Since then—'tis Centuries—and yet
Feels shorter than the Day
I first surmised the Horses' Heads
Were toward Eternity— ⊢

In Miguel Hernandez's poem, Death is seen as a bull, "wild, hungry, loving," giving "volcanic roars in sudden flashes." By contrast, Emily Dickinson's Death is a dapper coachman, whose manner is "kindly," unhurried, and relaxed, possessed of marked "Civility."

Spotting Personification

Here's a short one:

| *Flock*

by Lance Henson

across the road
ice huddles against the trees

there is only a whisper of
leaves among the cottonwoods

and over the joyless valley   5

snow moves
like an ancient herd ⊢

Where does personification appear in this poem? Discuss
this with a friend.

Symbols

Up until now, we have discussed metaphors and similes as ways
of understanding things in terms of other things, and we have
referred to *symbols* as items that *stand for* other things. But we
have not yet looked closely at what symbols are and what they
do.

What is a symbol? Let's begin by defining what a symbol is
not. A symbol is not a *sign* that stands for a particular thing. A
stoplight, which has green, yellow, and red lights that stand for
go, slow down, and stop, respectively, is a sign, not a symbol. A
circle with a cigarette in the middle and a diagonal slash through
it is a "No Smoking" sign, not a symbol.

While a symbol may indeed stand for something, a symbol never stands for *just one* simple thing. The meanings of a symbol are always *bottomless*. Rather than signifying one thing, a symbol generates a *complex of associations* that only grows larger the closer we look. A **symbol** is an object, word, or action representing an ambiguous number of items and ideas beyond itself.

The fruit in Gary Soto's poem "Oranges" (from Chapter 3) are symbolic: They certainly signify more than just oranges. Among other things, they stand out for their bright, vibrant color on a gray, colorless day—a day when the narrator's feelings are running high and fiery in counterpoint to the weather. (Walt Whitman might say that the oranges are "the flag of the boy's disposition.")

The moon in Laureen Mar's "The Window Frames the Moon" is also loaded with symbolic value. Here the moon reflects and represents (among other things) the narrator's alternating sense of order and chaos about her world.

In the following poem, Linda Hogan invests *red, flower,* and *fire* with strong symbolism.

Geraniums

by Linda Hogan

Life is burning
in everything, in red flowers
abandoned in an empty house,
the leaves nearly gone,
curtains and tenants gone,   5
but the flowers red and fiery
are there and singing,
let us out.

| continued on page 161 |

Even dying they have fire.

Imprisoned, they open,   10

so like our own lives blooming,

exploding, wanting out,

wanting love,

water,

wanting.   15

And you, with your weapons and badges

and your fear about what neighbors think

and working overtime

as if the boss will reward you,

you can't bloom that way   20

so open the door,

break the glass. There's fire

in those flowers. Set off the alarm.

What's a simple crime of property

when life, breath, and all   25

is at stake? ├─

In this poem, the abandoned geraniums, valiantly blooming despite their imprisonment and lack of nurture, exemplify the life force that animates all living beings. "Life is burning"—red and fiery—because life is fierce, insistent, voracious as fire. This is the force that impels us to fulfill our basic needs and to *burst free* of suffocating circumstances, be they physical or spiritual. Just as a room with little air and no water will starve and suffocate the flowers, so too a life with no vibrancy or authentic meaning will suffocate a human soul. It seems, in the final stanza, that the poem's speaker is exhorting someone to recognize this life force, to reconnect with its furious energy, and to "break the glass" (like a fire explodes a window) before it is too late.

Keep these brave geraniums in mind when you remake the acquaintance of Sylvia Plath's tulips later in this chapter.

For the moment, let's revisit "The Wood-Pile" by Robert Frost.

The Wood-Pile

by Robert Frost

Out walking in the frozen swamp one gray day,
I paused and said, "I will turn back from here.
No, I will go farther—and we shall see."
The hard snow held me, save where now and then
One foot went through. The view was all in lines   5
Straight up and down of tall slim trees
Too much alike to mark or name a place by
So as to say for certain I was here
Or somewhere else: I was just far from home.
A small bird flew before me. He was careful   10
To put a tree between us when he lighted,
And say no word to tell me who he was
Who was so foolish as to think what *he* thought.

He thought that I was after him for a feather—
The white one in his tail; like one who takes   15
Everything said as personal to himself.
One flight out sideways would have undeceived him.
And then there was a pile of wood for which
I forgot him and let his little fear
Carry him off the way I might have gone,   20
Without so much as wishing him goodnight.
He went behind it to make his last stand.
It was a cord of maple, cut and split
And piled—and measured, four by four by eight.
And not another like it could I see.   25
No runner tracks in this year's snow looped near it.
And it was older than this year's cutting,
Or even last year's or the year's before.
The wood was gray the bark warping off it
And the pile somewhat sunken. Clematis   30
Had wound strings round and round it like a bundle.
What held it though on one side was a tree
Still growing, and on one a stake and prop,

| *continued on page 163* |

. These latter about to fall. I thought that only
Someone who lived in turning to fresh tasks   35
Could so forget his handiwork on which
He spent himself, the labor of his ax,
And leave it there far from a useful fireplace
To warm the frozen swamp as best it could
With the slow smokeless burning of decay. ⊦—   40

Earlier we noted that this poem describes a man walking in a swamp and his fascination in the end with a pile of wood which someone apparently cut, stacked, and forgetfully left behind.

If we look closer we see that there are symbols in this poem. In particular, in the final image of the woodpile which is apart from any "useful fireplace" and "warming" the swamp with "the slow smokeless burning of decay," we can almost picture something emanating from the pile of wood. It is not smoke exactly, but smokelike, some ethereal substance, some "warmth" that is not really warm somehow. This is the activity or "burning of decay," that goes on after the life of something is finished. There is a macabre sensibility to this, a certain darkness, particularly in contrast to the forgetful woodcutter who "lived in turning to fresh tasks" and so left the woodpile there to rot quietly.

If we linger on this image, we may begin to perceive some essential dichotomy between looking into the light and looking into darkness—turning to the "fresh tasks" of life, keeping busy with daily distractions and activities, or turning one's gaze to death, contemplating the "smokeless burning of decay." When we do the latter, along with the narrator in the poem, we see that death goes on and on; it doesn't stop; it is not a simple end, but rather it keeps "burning" without smoke. The darkness grows deeper as we look.

Possibly, we may also be moved to reflect on *abandonment* in general. Abandoned people and things are often subsequently forgotten, but they do not forget in turn. The woodcutter may have forgotten the woodpile when he turned to his fresh tasks, but perhaps the woodpile did not forget the woodcutter. There is something haunting in this.

The longer we "stay with it," the more symbols and symbolic resonances we will perceive. The bird in the poem is, perhaps, not merely a bird. Note the bird's skittishness and "little fear" in contrast to the solemn stolidity of the woodpile. What does the bird represent? What does a bird call to mind?

What does the "useful fireplace" stand for? In what sense does the woodpile "warm" the frozen swamp? What are the symbolic connotations of the swamp being "frozen"?

At this point, you might be saying, "Oh come on. If you want to think that way, then *anything* can be a symbol." You're absolutely right. Anything *can* be a symbol. More than that, everything *is* a symbol. Everything you can think of is symbolic, because everything exists in relationship to other things and thus, to some extent, *points* to an infinite range of other things.

"Well," you say, "that's one way of looking at life. But you don't *have* to take things symbolically. You can just take things for what they are and be done with it." Wrong! Make no mistake about it: We live by symbols. Every minute of every day, something is happening that affects you *symbolically*.

Even babies recognize and respond to symbols, such as facial expressions and tones of voice which signify love and approval and a gamut of other emotions. These facial expressions and tones of voice are not *the thing itself*, but rather are vivid *representations* of the thing itself, which the baby responds to.

Symbols convey meaning, and humans respond to meaning just as they do to substance. Consider: Are words substantive or symbolic? How often do words affect your feelings, your mood, your sense of well-being?

Perhaps I'm making a false distinction here. There is nothing insubstantial about symbols. Everything translates to something else, including the food we eat. An apple is not merely an apple, but also a set of potentialities: sweetness in the mouth, nourishment to the stomach, sugars in the blood. When we talk about *symbols,* we are merely referring to a *level* of symbols that is more abstract than the common symbolic activity we engage in all the time.

Even children understand and manipulate this more symbolic level of things. My friend's four-year-old nephew, Chance, told people, "My Uncle Darryl is going to beat you up!" whenever he got mad, so his mother called Darryl and asked him to set her son straight. "Chance?" Darryl said into the phone. "Hi buddy, this is Uncle Darryl. Listen, I hear you've been telling people that I'm going to beat them up. I want you to stop doing that, okay? I don't like to hurt people and I'm not going to beat anybody up. Okay?" There was no response from Chance. He had dropped the phone's receiver into the garbage.

Adults, of course, are also reflexively symbolic. A woman I know once told her new boyfriend, "I want to give you a key to my house, but I'm not sure I trust you enough yet." This was not because she imagined that this man might possibly use the key to rob her, or even to visit when he wasn't welcome. But the key held symbolic value for her; giving the man a key symbolized (among other things) a depth of emotional intimacy and trust she had not conceived for him yet. The issue really had nothing to do with how he might use the key. Nor did the boyfriend fail to understand. We all know that a key carries tremendous symbolic import. In fact, the boyfriend agreed he "wasn't ready" for a key just yet.

DISCUSSION WORKSHOP

Caged Bird Symbols

The following poem by Maya Angelou is filled with symbolism. Nearly *every word* brims with symbolic connotations.

Caged Bird

by Maya Angelou

A free bird leaps
on the back of the wind
and floats downstream
till the current ends
and dips his wing   5
in the orange sun rays
and dares to claim the sky.

But a bird that stalks
down his narrow cage
can seldom see through   10
his bars of rage
his wings are clipped and
his feet are tied
so he opens his throat to sing.

The caged bird sings   15
with a fearful trill
of things unknown
but longed for still
and his tune is heard
on the distant hill   20
for the caged bird
sings of freedom.

Becoming aware of symbols is a potent tool for unpeeling layers and seeing beneath the surface of a poem. In a small group, discuss how you see symbols working in "Caged Bird." What symbols are you aware of? What do they signify? What symbolic statement(s) or message(s) do you perceive?

Metaphors Are Symbols

We have, in a sense, distinguished symbols from metaphors. We have noted that while a metaphor is a way of speaking about something in terms of something else, a symbol stands for many things and indicates a host of associative meanings.

But we have also observed that a metaphor is usually an *open-ended* comparison that can imply many different meanings and call forth a host of associations. When we speak of the *arm* of a chair, this is not a symbolic metaphor because it only means one thing: the part of the chair where the sitter rests an arm. But when we speak of the *head* of a company, this metaphor has more than one meaning: the head directs the rest of the body, the head is at the top of the body, the head often surfaces when the rest of the body is submerged, and the head is the most visible part of the body.

With poetry, the distinction between a mere metaphor and a symbol is even less clear. When Whitman calls grass the *flag* of his disposition, we are inspired to think of pageantry and celebration and artistic design, as well as the literal resemblance of blades of grass to fibers or strands of thread. When Langston Hughes says that "The stars are beautiful, / So the eyes of my people," we are moved to reflect on vast distances and profound mysteries as well as on tiny spots of whiteness against a midnight background.

So it might be safe to say that whereas a symbol is not necessarily a metaphor (because it does not necessarily compare *one particular thing* with something else), we rarely find metaphors that do not also function as symbols, that possess no symbolic content, that do not suggest a plethora of associative meanings.

Consider again the following poem by Sylvia Plath, which is full of metaphors and similes which carry a multitude of symbolic connotations.

Tulips

by Sylvia Plath

The tulips are too excitable, it is winter here.
Look how white everything is, how quiet, how snowed-in.
I am learning peacefulness, lying by myself quietly
As the light lies on these white walls, this bed, these hands.
I am nobody; I have nothing to do with explosions.   5
I have given my name and my day-clothes up to the nurses
And my history to the anaesthetist and my body to surgeons.

They have propped my head between the pillow and the sheet-cuff
Like an eye between two white lids that will not shut.
Stupid pupil, it has to take everything in.   10
The nurses pass and pass, they are no trouble,
They pass the way gulls pass inland in their white caps,
Doing things with their hands, one just the same as another,
So it is impossible to tell how many there are.

My body is a pebble to them, they tend it as water   15
Tends to the pebbles it must run over, smoothing them gently.
They bring me numbness in their bright needles, they bring me
    sleep.
Now I have lost myself I am sick of baggage—
My patent leather overnight case like a black pillbox,
My husband and child smiling out of the family photo;   20
Their smiles catch onto my skin, little smiling hooks.

I have let things slip, a thirty-year-old cargo boat
Stubbornly hanging on to my name and address.
They have swabbed me clear of my loving associations.
Scared and bare on the green plastic-pillowed trolley   25
I watched my tea-set, my bureaus of linen, my books
Sink out of sight, and the water went over my head.
I am a nun now, I have never been so pure.

| *continued on page 169* |

I didn't want any flowers, I only wanted
To lie with my hands turned up and be utterly empty.   30
How free it is, you have no idea how free—
The peacefulness is so big it dazes you,
And it asks nothing, a name tag, a few trinkets.
It is what the dead close on, finally; I imagine them
Shutting their mouths on it, like a Communion tablet.   35

The tulips are too red in the first place, they hurt me.
Even through the gift paper I could hear them breathe
Lightly, through their white swaddlings, like an awful baby.
Their redness talks to my wound, it corresponds.
They are subtle: they seem to float, though they weigh me down, 40
Upsetting me with their sudden tongues and their color,
A dozen red lead sinkers around my neck.

Nobody watched me before, now I am watched.
The tulips turn to me, and the window behind me
Where once a day the light slowly widens and slowly thins,   45
And I see myself, flat, ridiculous, a cut-paper shadow
Between the eye of the sun and the eyes of the tulips,
And I have no face, I have wanted to efface myself.
The vivid tulips eat my oxygen.

Before they came the air was calm enough,   50
Coming and going, breath by breath, without any fuss.
Then the tulips filled it up like a loud noise.
Now the air snags and eddies round them the way a river
Snags and eddies round a sunken rust-red engine.
They concentrate my attention, that was happy   55
Playing and resting without committing itself.

They are opening like the mouth of some great African cat,
And I am aware of my heart: it opens and closes
Its bowl of red blooms out of sheer love for me.
The water I taste is warm and salt, like the sea,   60
And comes from a country as far away as health. ⊢

By calling tulips "excitable" in the first line, Plath employs the metaphorical technique of personification. As we shall see, she further personifies the tulips later in the poem.

In the second stanza, Plath compares her head between the pillow and sheet to an eye that will not shut, and she compares the nurses to seagulls. On the surface, these are strictly visual imagistic comparisons, but we may also infer other meanings.

For example, given statements regarding the speaker's past and family, we might assume that she is in the hospital because of a failed suicide attempt. If so, perhaps the eye that will not shut is analogous to the tormented life of her mind, which similarly refuses to shut down, or end. She has tried, but failed, to "put out the light" in her head. The eye stays ruthlessly, implacably, open.

The nurses look like gulls because of their white caps, and, like gulls, they all do the same things (to the patient). But could the speaker also be insinuating that these nurses appear as simple and stupid and untroubled as seagulls? Could she be envious of their freedom to "fly inland" and leave again?

In the next stanza she says her body is a "pebble to them" and she helpfully elaborates on her analogy: Just as water smoothes pebbles, so the nurses smooth her with narcotics and fresh sheets and so forth. But again, a pebble is a dense, inanimate, very small piece of matter. Perhaps the patient half-consciously assumes these attributes as well?

More metaphors follow: the "little smiling hooks" in her family photos. She views herself as a "thirty-year-old cargo boat." She states, "I am a nun now, I have never been so pure." There is surely irony, even sarcasm, in these expressions, as well as symbolism.

"Little smiling hooks." Though a smiling mouth may in fact be vaguely hook-shaped, one rarely associates smiles with hooks. Hooks hurt and ensnare, while smiles normally express and inspire pleasure. But the faces in the photo "hook" the patient, against her will, to a history she has presumably "given up." In doing so they invoke (we may imagine) an array of painful and confused emotions.

As a self-described "cargo boat," has she spent thirty years accumulating her "load"? What does this load consist of and how heavy must it be?

"I have never been so pure." To be wiped clean of identity, "swabbed . . . clear of . . . loving associations," is a kind of purity. It is a purity of emptiness, a dark purity of nonbeing and death, not precisely the brand of purity one generally ascribes to nuns. See how, even in irony, the symbolism is active.

In the fifth stanza, she speaks of being "utterly empty." What does she mean? In what sense is she empty? She likens this emptiness, this "free" state, this "peacefulness," to a Communion tablet that the dead shut their mouths on. Again, we hear her voice as cynical, ironic, and resentful—and still her words and her analogy reverberate hauntingly, for she raises troubling questions about death, religion, faith, and life's presumed value.

In her last four stanzas, the focus is on the tulips which someone apparently brought for her. She describes an antagonistic relationship with them; she says they hurt her. She personifies them by saying that she hears them breathe; they have "sudden tongues" and "their redness talks"; they watch her; they "eat" her oxygen; they have "eyes." The tulips, to her, are monsters. They fill the air like a loud noise. "The air snags and eddies round them." The flowers open like "the mouth of some great African cat." They are invasive and terrifying.

But why? What makes flowers seem so monstrous to this hospital patient? What about them alarms and repels her (even if she is, perhaps, being somewhat ironic)? If we assume that these tulips are really just flowers, not strange, scary life forms from another planet, then we might also assume that it is not the flowers themselves, but rather what they *represent* that is so disturbing to the speaker in this poem.

She refers to their "redness" and she calls them "vivid." Everything else in the room is white, muted, "empty." The tulips then, with their vivid red presence, shout of life, vitality, activity, all the things the speaker wishes to escape from. Furthermore, when they open, she becomes aware of the opening and closing of her own heart and its "bowl of red blooms." Is it then, in some sense, that the tulips are her heart, and her heart the tulips—neither of which she would have open again if she could prevent it?

This activity of opening and closing, "out of sheer love" of her, brings to her a reluctant awareness and a taste in her mouth of warm water that comes from "a country as far away as health." In this final metaphor, she likens health, well-being, and the attendant qualities joy and optimism, to a faraway country. Perhaps then her dread of the tulips is that they represent, among other things (there are *always* other things), all the merciless, insistent, witless forces that drive her—despite her exhaustion and unwillingness—to undertake an arduous metaphorical *journey* she had thought she need never attempt again.

The Symbolic Dimension of Simple Things

We stated earlier that all things are symbolic. It may be more accurate to say that all things have a symbolic dimension as well as a limited and literal dimension. Sometimes we feel things to be more symbolic than we do at other times. This is particularly true of simple things, like the weather. We've all experienced rainstorms, for example, that felt symbolic as well as ones that were merely very inconvenient. It depends largely on our point of view. Driving home on the freeway from a distant city, a thunderstorm may feel less symbolic than when you're lying in bed in the wee hours of the night.

Consider the point of view in the following poem, which concerns weather, winter weather in particular. (We have seen this poem once before in Chapter 2.) Read the poem very carefully. Read it more than twice.

The Snow Man

by Wallace Stevens

One must have a mind of winter
To regard the frost and the boughs
Of the pine-trees crusted with snow;

| continued on page 173 |

And have been cold a long time
To behold the junipers shagged with ice,   5
The spruces rough in the distant glitter

Of the January sun; and not to think
Of any misery in the sound of the wind,
In the sound of a few leaves,

Which is the sound of the land   10
Full of the same wind
That is blowing in the same bare place

For the listener, who listens in the snow,
And, nothing himself, beholds
Nothing that is not there and the nothing that is. ├—   15

We are presented with images of "frost," "pine-trees crusted with snow," "junipers shagged with ice," and "the distant glitter / Of the January sun." There is a suggestion of "misery in the sound of the wind, / In the sound of a few leaves." The wind blows in a "bare place."

By placing the word *the* in front of the word *nothing*, the final line suggests that "nothing" can actually be a kind of "something," with a nature of its own, a nature of *nothingness*. The word "nothing" comes to signify not an absence, but a *presence* of some faintly imaginable state or feeling.

All in all, this wintry scene might be described as "the soul of desolation." It is not merely a portrait of winter weather. There are intimations of mood and portent and feeling. The poem is loaded with symbolism.

Looking closely, we see that, syntactically, the poem is actually one long sentence, which reads:

One must have a mind of winter to regard the frost and the boughs of the pine-trees crusted with snow; and have been cold a long time to behold the junipers shagged with ice, the spruces rough in the distant glitter of the January sun; and not to think of any misery in the sound of the wind, in the sound of a few leaves, which is the sound of the land full of the same wind that is blowing in the same bare place for the listener, who listens in the snow, and, nothing himself, beholds nothing that is not there and the nothing that is.

When we look at this poem as one (relatively) straightforward sentence, we may notice two or three provocative and peculiar things. In the middle of the sentence/poem, where the focus is drawn to the "sound" that is present, we have ". . . any misery in the sound of the wind, in the sound of a few leaves, which is the sound of the land full of the same wind that is blowing in the same bare place for the listener, who listens in the snow. . . ."

The word "sound" is used three times as the poem cites the sound of the wind, the sound of the "few leaves," and the sound of the land. And it is all *just one sound*, the same sound, as the poem states "Which is the sound of the land / Full of the same wind." The sound then, as well as the wind, is both within and above the land. What *characterizes* this wind, this sound, which blows through everything, around and about and within and without? Certainly we could assume that it is a very *cold* wind. Aside from that, we can refer to our symbolic/connotative associations with wind, in particular a winter wind, a howling wind that fills all things. And we also have, from the poem itself, the word "misery."

We may also note that the wind blows "For the listener, who listens in the snow." This is peculiar too, isn't it? Does the wind really blow for anyone in particular? And who is this listener anyway?

This listener is the subject of the sentence that *is* the poem. This listener's point of view is what gives the poem its character and depth. The poem starts off: "One must have . . ." This "One" is our listener, our subject, our point of view. What do we know about this listener? And what, if anything, does this listener do, besides listen?

This listener *regards* the frost and boughs. He *beholds* the junipers shagged with ice. He *does not think* of any misery in the sound of the wind. (Why not? We do.) He *listens* in the snow and *beholds,* "Nothing that is not there and the nothing that is."

So this listener regards, beholds, and listens, but does not think. He also has "a mind of winter" and is "nothing himself." What kind of a listener is this? Why, a snowman, of course, as the title indicates.

And so we have a barren wintry landscape, desolate and dreary in itself, but even more so from the point of view of a cold, frozen, insensate being dwelling within it. A being *made* of its very essence, the frozen snow. This being, the snowman, has literally "a mind of winter," and, for all intents and purposes, is "nothing himself."

Yet, even though he is "nothing," we still perceive him as "something." This is a paradox we cannot avoid. We have been tricked into imagining his point of view, although, by definition, he has no point of view. This is strange and haunting, even as we attempt to dismiss it as nonsense and wordplay. It is mere wordplay only if it fails to capture your imagination; once your imagination has been enticed, it transcends wordplay and becomes mind-play.

But play is not a pointless or frivolous thing. This particular kind of play stimulates realms of our imaginations that we may not have even known existed before. This poem is very much a "machine made of words," an imagination machine, a machine that engenders new forms in our imaginations which do not fall into accustomed categories. This is the power of combined poetic and symbolic thinking.

WRITING WORKSHOP

Taking the Symbolic Measure of Simple Things

Consider the following poem by Gary Soto.

Old House in My Fortieth Year

by Gary Soto

The clod's stubbornness gives in to my fist.
The snail groans a single bubble under my shoe
The roots of every chinaberry I've swung from
Needle even further into the moist earth.
I'm home in these weeds. I'm home in these bones,   5
This flesh with its laughter and fatherly scent,
Flesh held up by a frayed belt on its last hole.
I don't have to walk far to hear the jay
Or a vicious dog, a coal breathing in each eye.

The old house has been smoothed by sand   10
And the rake of years. I don't know this place,
Really, or the boy buried in this flesh of mine.
One error, and I'm the man pushing a cart.
Another error, and I march a long row of cotton
Or beets. The stars wheeled around an icy comet,   15
And by fortune, I'm now at home in this body—
The heart down to business
And slapping blood through its swinging door. ⊢

    This poem contains a metaphor at the end of each stanza. In stanza one, the pupils in a vicious dog's eyes are likened to breathing coals, and in stanza two, the valves of the speaker's heart are likened to a "swinging door." There is other figurative language as well, such as the phrase "the rake of years," which could be a metaphor for the eroding influences of time.

    Yet the heart and soul of this poem lie in its nonfigurative concrete details: the snail under the shoe, the chinaberry roots, the speaker's flesh "with its laughter and fatherly scent," the song of the jaybird, and, of course, the old house itself. If you consider these images for a little while, do they take on any symbolic—or at least connotative—character?

How about the images in the second stanza: the man with the cart, the cotton fields, the stars wheeling around a comet? What is their purpose? Why are they here? Do they have any symbolic value? Ponder this in a journal entry.

The Mercurial Nature of Symbols: A Note about Warmth and Cold, Darkness and Light

I warned you previously, but it bears repeating: Don't take my word for granted. Never let me *dictate* your experience of a poem. *A dictated experience is a bankrupt experience.*

This is especially apparent with a poem like "The Snow Man." I stated that this poem strikes a chord of desolation and dreariness. Indeed, for me it does, but for you it may not. Many people feel a pristine serenity, simplicity, and even spiritual joy emanating from this poem.

In George Orwell's novel *1984,* the protagonist, Winston Smith, has a dream about a character named O'Brien who tells him, "We shall meet in the place where there is no darkness." Though Winston does not really know this man, he trusts him and feels overwhelmingly optimistic about these words.

O'Brien turns out to be a profoundly evil and sadistic man. The "place where there is no darkness" is a torture cell, wherein the light is glaringly bright all the time, twenty-four hours a day, and Winston Smith can never find refuge in darkness or sleep.

Just as we need light in our lives, so we require respite from light occasionally. Metaphorically and literally, light *reveals* things. We often speak of the "light of knowledge" or the "light of understanding." What remains in darkness is obscure and unknown. We are naturally afraid of the unknown, which is why children are often afraid to go to sleep in a dark room by themselves.

But darkness is also the place of rest, and, incidentally, the source of all that we perceive in light. The womb is darkness. The creative process takes place within a dark mystery. Bruce

Cockburn sings: "May your life be filled with light / except for when you're trying to sleep."

When we speak of the "forces of darkness," we usually mean evil. And it would *be* evil to turn all light into darkness, obscuring everything, and throwing all things into chaos, confusion, blindness, and lack of understanding. Bigotry, prejudice, and ignorance are all forms of darkness. Fear exists in darkness, but also in certain kinds of light.

It is said: "Ye shall know the truth, and the truth shall make you free." Knowledge is a form of light. Perhaps the ultimate light, which is knowledge of Truth with a capital *T,* knowledge borne of an absolute understanding of all things (presuming this is possible), is entirely kind and good. But there are, as poor Winston Smith discovered, other, less benign varieties of light. Remember, it is also said that "a little knowledge is a dangerous thing."

The point is that symbols can work in contradictory ways, depending on context and perception. The archetype symbols light and dark are obvious examples of this. Warmth and cold, spring and winter are further examples.

At a glance, warmth may symbolize life, vitality, exuberance, comfort, and happiness, whereas cold may connote death, sterility, pain, and joylessness. But cold and frozen things are also beautiful, stark, and clear, and what is frozen is preserved. There is a certain purity, even holiness, about the cold and about a bare winter landscape.

On the other hand, the sun rots things. Things become lax and wilted under too much heat. Warmth dries out organic matter, drains it of moisture and "juice." The light of summer glares and burns, gives us headaches, and makes concentration difficult. I do my best work and feel my mind to be sharpest on cold, rainy days.

If you read the poem "The Snow Man" and it made you feel sweet and high and clear (before you read my commentary), then consider your first impression correct because *that* was your *authentic* experience and a thoroughly legitimate reading of the poem. Nobody can dictate what a poem means for you, and no one can ultimately interpret a symbol for you either.

Mind-Healing Metaphors

When his best friend died, my brother-in-law was heartsick and disconsolate. In an attempt to ameliorate his grief, I gave him the following verse from Kahlil Gibran's *The Prophet:*

On Death

by Kahlil Gibran

Then Almitra spoke, saying, We would ask now of death.
And he said:
You would know the secret of death.
But how shall you find it unless you seek it in the heart of life?
The owl whose night-bound eyes are blind unto the day
    cannot unveil the mystery of light.   5
If you would indeed behold the spirit of death, open your heart
    wide unto the body of life.
For life and death are one, even as the river and the sea are one.

In the depth of your hopes and desires lies your silent
    knowledge of the beyond;
And like seeds dreaming beneath the snow your heart dreams
    of spring.
Trust the dreams, for in them is hidden the gate to eternity.   10
Your fear of death is but the trembling of the shepherd when
    he stands before the king whose hand is to be laid upon him
    in honor.
Is the shepherd not joyful beneath his trembling, that he shall
    wear the mark of the king?
Yet is he not more mindful of his trembling?

| *continued on page 180* |

For what is it to die but to stand naked in the wind and to melt
    into the sun?
And what is it to cease breathing, but to free the breath from
    its restless tides, that it may rise and expand and seek God
    unencumbered?   15

Only when you drink from the river of silence shall you indeed sing.
And when you have reached the mountaintop, then you shall
    begin to climb.
And when the earth shall claim your bones, then shall you
    truly dance. |—

My brother-in-law taped this poem to his mirror and reread it often. He said it gave him comfort.

Gibran employs a host of similes and metaphors in his exposition on the nature of death. In a small group, identify some of these metaphors and similes and discuss their symbolic ramifications. How might they affect the way one conceives of death? Is Gibran's symbolic/metaphorical thinking convincing and compelling? Is he saying or suggesting anything specific about what may be in store for us after we die?

Would Walt Whitman have appreciated this passage? In what ways does this passage resonate with the section of "Song of Myself" that we examined earlier? How are Gibran's words different in character from Whitman's? How do their respective views of death differ? How are they similar?

Why do you suppose this passage comforted and consoled my grief-stricken brother-in-law?

DISCUSSION WORKSHOP

Visions in the Darkness

Reflectively absorb the following Robert Frost poem.

Acquainted with the Night

by Robert Frost

I have been one acquainted with the night.
I have walked out in rain—and back in rain.
I have outwalked the farthest city light.

I have looked down the saddest city lane.
I have passed by the watchman on his beat   5
And dropped my eyes, unwilling to explain.

I have stood still and stopped the sound of feet
When far away an interrupted cry
Came over houses from another street,

But not to call me back or say good-by;   10
And further still at an unearthly height,
One luminary clock against the sky

Proclaimed the time was neither wrong nor right.
I have been one acquainted with the night. ├─

In a small group, discuss possible symbolic or metaphorical meanings attendant to any of the following words or phrases:

- night —
- rain —
- farthest city light —
- saddest city lane
- watchman
- interrupted cry —
- luminary clock
- time was neither wrong nor right —
- acquainted with the night

time —
shame —

A Radiant Poem

The following poem by eighteenth-century mystic poet William Blake is entirely symbolic and should be read as such. Everything in this poem stands for more than itself. This luminous poem *radiates* with symbolism. It *explodes* with meaning—wave upon wave and layer upon layer of meaning.

The Sick Rose

by William Blake

O Rose, thou art sick.
The invisible worm
That flies in the night,
In the howling storm,

Has found out thy bed   5
Of crimson joy,
And his dark secret love
Does thy life destroy.

Consider the following questions in a journal entry. As you allow the images of the sick rose, the invisible worm, the howling storm, and so forth to form in your mind, note the shapes they assume. Does the phrase "dark secret love" evoke anything? What about "bed of crimson joy"? Feel your way into this poem. Leave aside rational evaluation. What is it about?

You might brainstorm the connotations of individual phrases in this poem as a tool for forging your way in. You may, if you like, offer possible interpretations of what this poem is saying and what kind of situation it is depicting. But consider also the *relationships* between various elements in the poem—between, say, the worm and the rose, "love" and life, the "howling storm" and the "bed of crimson joy."

───────────────────────────────── WRITING WORKSHOP

Unearth a Poem

Find a poem that employs symbols, metaphors, or similes (or some combination of these devices), and discuss *one or two specific ones* in two to three paragraphs. Describe how they *work* in the poem. What do they imply? How do they affect your perception or understanding of what you read?

───────────────────────────────── WRITING WORKSHOP

A Symbolic Object

In one to three paragraphs, discuss an *object* that has symbolic value for you. It may be a book, a car, a photograph . . . you name it. What does this object represent to you, and why?

A Grab Bag of Devices

7

A poetic device is any element in a poem that engages the imagination in a special way, thereby enabling the poem to perform a certain magic. We have already examined many poetic devices, including imagery, metaphor, symbol, and sound play. While we do not need to have a technical definition for every poetic device, it is worth briefly discussing some of the main ones that we have neglected thus far.

Line Breaks

Perhaps the most important poetic device we have yet to examine closely is the strategic use of line breaks in poems. We have discussed the images that the words create on a page; line breaks, of course, are an integral part of this. We have also discussed rhythms in lines of poetry. Line breaks, since they create automatic pauses, play a large part in determining rhythm.

But line breaks are also much more than this. The primary function of a line break is in the way that it *points our attention* as we read. Following are some dramatic examples of this from poems we have looked at in other contexts.

From Elizabeth Bishop's "In the Waiting Room," final stanza:

> *Then I was back in it.*
> *The War was on. Outside,*
> *in Worcester, Massachusetts, . . .*

The first line of this stanza is a complete, simple sentence. But the second line contains a sentence and also an extra word. This extra word could, syntactically and sensibly, have been part of the sentence in this line. Instead, the word "Outside" introduces the next sentence, which continues on the following line. We automatically do a double-take here because for a moment we see it as part of the previous sentence, as in: "The war was on outside." The result is that we linger for an extra moment or two on the word "Outside," and its connotations are amplified accordingly.

From e. e. cummings's "i carry your heart":

> *i carry your heart with me(i carry it in*
> *my heart)i am never without it(anywhere*
> *i go you go,my dear;and whatever is done*
> *by only me is your doing,my darling)*
>   *i fear*
> *no fate(for you are my fate,my sweet)i want*
> *no world(for beautiful you are my world,my true) . . .*

The first line break sets up a dramatic surprise. What can a heart be carried in? What might we be half-imagining before our eyes skip down and over to the answer?

In the second line break, the word "anywhere" compels a semantic double-take, much like the word "Outside" in Bishop's poem. We read the line at first as "i am never without it anywhere," but then find that the word is really part of "anywhere i go you go."

The next line break also sets up a surprise. "Whatever is done" is a large and grand phrase, something on the order of "anything that happens." But then we discover, as we read on, that the phrase is actually meant in a far more limited sense ("by only me"). Or is it?

Then, of course, "i fear" and "i want," both of which could stand as complete thoughts and sentences unto themselves, turn out to be *beginnings* of sentences that express the opposite of what we anticipate. The effect, again, is one of surprise, possible double meanings, and magnified connotations.

From Robert Frost's "The Wood-Pile":

A small bird flew before me. He was careful
To put a tree between us when he lighted, . . .

Here again, we have a word, "careful," that does a kind of double duty. The bird was, on the one hand, careful to put a tree between himself and the narrator, and, on the other hand, the bird was simply *careful*.

Many of the poems we have read have employed provocative line breaks. Take a look again at Rita Dove's "November for Beginners."

November for Beginners

by Rita Dove

Snow would be the easy
way out—that softening
sky like a sigh of relief
at finally being allowed
to yield. No dice.   5
We stack twigs for burning
in glistening patches
but the rain won't give.

| continued on page 188 |

So we wait, breeding
mood, making music   10
of decline. We sit down
in the smell of the past
and rise in a light
that is already leaving.
We ache in secret,   15
memorizing

a gloomy line
or two of German.
When spring comes we promise to act
the fool. Pour,   20
rain! Sail, wind,
with your cargo of zithers! ⊢—

Many, perhaps even most, of Dove's lines in this poem deliberately break at ambiguous points in her sentences. In the second
line, for example, "softening" could be seen as a gerund-noun
(*softening* as a thing in itself), until we jump to the next line and
realize it is an adjective for "sky."

In the second stanza, first line, "So we wait, breeding" could
be a complete thought. *Breeding* normally refers to making babies.
But here it turns out to mean something else, something
metaphorical: breeding "mood."

A few lines down we have "and rise in a light/that is already
leaving." "Rise in a light" has connotations of meeting a brand
new day. Thus "already leaving" comes as a small shock, almost
a contradiction.

A couple of lines farther down, the stanza ends with the one-
word line "memorizing." This word hangs between the stanzas,
suggesting that "memorizing" here denotes a general activity, a
general exercise of memory—until, at the beginning of the last
stanza, it is further defined as "memorizing / a gloomy line / or
two of German." Note the funnel effect achieved by these line
breaks: from "memorizing" (very general), to "line" (more spe-

cific, but still ambiguous), to "or two of German" (very specific—and a little surprising).

Another funnel-like surprise occurs two lines later: "we promise to act / the fool." Here again, "we promise to act" might be the complete thought, as in "we promise to do something." "Act the fool," however, is more specific—and it means something altogether different. "We promise to act," by itself, may connote acting productively or responsibly, but "the fool" contradicts this.

DISCUSSION WORKSHOP

Connecting with Line Breaks

Most of the line breaks in the following story-poem by William Carlos Williams occur where you might expect them, at the ends of discrete phrases and sentences. But some of them are slyly strategic, creating surprises or multiple meanings or ambiguous connotations. Which ones are they, and what is their effect? With a friend, talk about your reactions to these breaks.

The Last Words of
My English Grandmother

by William Carlos Williams

There were some dirty plates
and a glass of milk
beside her on a small table
near the rank, disheveled bed—

Wrinkled and nearly blind   5
she lay and snored
rousing with anger in her tones
to cry for food,

| continued on page 190 |

Gimme something to eat—
They're starving me—
I'm all right I won't go
to the hospital. No, no, no

Give me something to eat
Let me take you
to the hospital, I said
and after you are well

you can do as you please.
She smiled, Yes
you do what you please first
then I can do what I please—

Oh, oh, oh! she cried
as the ambulance men lifted
her to the stretcher—
Is this what you call

making me comfortable?
By now her mind was clear—
Oh you think you're smart
you young people,

she said, but I'll tell you
you don't know anything.
Then we started.
On the way

we passed a long row
of elms. She looked at them
awhile out of
the ambulance window and said,

10

15

20

25

30

35

| continued on page 191 |

What are all those
fuzzy-looking things out there?
Trees? Well, I'm tired
of them and rolled her head away. ├─ 40

Note, in particular, line 16 at the end of the fourth stanza. In a poem such as this, wherein a single sentence might run through multiple stanzas, the word or words that *end a stanza* linger for a moment before the sentence resumes at the beginning of the following stanza.

Allusion

An **allusion** is a reference, overt or subtle, to something outside the poem, something that is presumably within the reader's, as well as the writer's, frame of reference. It may be an historical event or, even more commonly, another work of literature.

There is a baseball poem by Robert Fitzgerald entitled "Cobb Would Have Caught It." This is an allusion to baseball great Ty Cobb. Perhaps the author assumes that anyone interested in reading a poem about baseball would also have heard of Ty Cobb, though the poem itself has nothing to do with the man.

The following humorous poem by Anthony Hecht alludes to the line, "A rose by any other name would smell as sweet," from Shakespeare's play *Romeo and Juliet*. The meaning of the line, in this poem, gets turned on its head. The Capulets and the Montagues were the feuding families in the play.

| *Nominalism*

by Anthony Hecht

Higgledy-piggledy
Juliet Capulet
Cherished the tenderest
Thoughts of a rose:

| *continued on page 192* |

"What's in a name?" said she,   5
Etymologically,
"Save that all Montagues
Stink in God's nose." ├─

In the following lines from her poem "The Sandpiper," Elizabeth Bishop alludes to the poet William Blake. Keep in mind that she is describing a bird on the beach.

He runs, he runs to the south, finical, awkward,
in a state of controlled panic, a student of Blake.

This would necessarily fall into the category of subtle, rather than overt, allusion. In assuming that the reader will understand her, Bishop must also assume a number of other things. First, she must assume not only that her reader has heard of the poet William Blake, but also that the reader knows Blake's poetry well enough to be familiar with his line about perceiving "a world in a grain of sand." The line is from the following poem.

─┴─

by William Blake

To See a World in a Grain of Sand
And a Heaven in a Wild Flower,
Hold Infinity in the palm of your hand
And Eternity in an hour. ├─

Bishop must assume that when the reader reads her lines, she will think of no other Blake but William, and she will specifically recall the first line of this poem. Blake meant to describe a visionary, wondrous, expansive perception. Bishop's sandpiper, by contrast, is locked into a most limited and tiny perspective in that its world is *reduced* to the size of a grain of sand. So this is a cleverly humorous, ironic allusion, but it requires a certain degree of poetic education to be understood.

The following poem by Oregon poet Karynn Fish is based on a far less obscure allusion: the story of Job from the Bible. (The Bible is probably the most common object of poetic allusion in the English language.) Fish assumes that even if her readers haven't read the Bible cover to cover, most of them will at least be familiar with the broad outline of the Job story: how he lost his first family and all he had, and was then rewarded for his faith with a second "set."

| Coda for Job

by Karynn Fish

I might as easily have been his second wife as his first.
I might have sprung up beside the wheat
In his vast, untended fields, one day
Black and seeded with salt, the next an Eden
Shot to heaven with green   5
In time for harvest. It is just
That simple.

Sometimes I want to ask him, can't you taste
The bones of your children in the flour
That made this bread? But I know   10
He'd be only too happy to find his mouth
Full of dust.

I've caught him bathing alone at the river, seen him
Fingering his many faint scars with reverence
As though his body were a tablet spelling out   15
A new law, the letters etched with his own blood.
And maybe it is.

It is a strange life, this coda to his strange song.
I walk at sunrise to the well with my daughters
And the village wives scatter, but leave behind   20
Tiny packets of spice so I won't know they're afraid.

| *continued on page 194* |

And he never asks about our other
Firstborn son, though this child wears
The same clothes, with the same
Simple prayers woven into the hem.   25

Job comes at evening from his vineyards, pockets stuffed
With grapes too sweet for such an early vintage.
We taste them in the darkness. He wonders
If I am happy: I say
I wish for nothing. ├─   30

Fish takes the voice of Job's wife (though she is ambiguous as to which one, the first or second). In doing so, she conveys an obliquely ironic commentary on the famous story (note the double meaning of "just" where the poem's fifth line breaks), and also teases out other themes for our consideration, such as compassion, grief, tenderness, and spiritual resurrection.

Thematic Recurrence, or Motif

A **motif** is a subject or image that recurs within a work of art, music, or literature. In a poem then, a motif is any word, set of words, or image that repeats. These recurring words or images take on the quality of a *theme* in that they come to represent ideas.

In e. e. cummings's poem "anyone lived in a pretty how town," the names of the seasons are a motif representing, perhaps, the idea of cyclical time. Bells are a motif in Poe's "The Bells." Their chiming, swelling, groaning, and jingling symbolize a veritable host of ideas in the poem. In "Geraniums" by Linda Hogan, fire is a motif which embodies the raging power of the survival instinct.

In the following verse, Jimmy Santiago Baca employs wind as a motif, wind as a kind of all-knowing, all-pervasive presence that "stirs up" events in the barrio.

from *Meditations
on the South Valley*

by Jimmy Santiago Baca

XVII
I love the wind
when it blows through my barrio.
It hisses its snake love
down calles de polvo,
and cracks egg-shell skins   5
of abandoned homes.
Stray dogs find shelter
along the river,
where great cottonwoods rattle
like old covered wagons,   10
stuck in stagnant waterholes.
Days when the wind blows
full of sand and grit,
men and women make decisions
that change their whole lives.   15
Windy days in the barrio
give birth to divorce papers
and squalling separation. The wind tells us
what others refuse to tell us,
informing men and women of a secret,   20
that they move away to hide from. ⊢

Sometimes motifs are less obvious than in the preceding
examples. For example, an idea or image may reoccur only once
or twice, perhaps spread widely apart, which makes the resonance
more subtle. But a diluted dose of resonance can still be quite
effective.

Consider these uses of the words "eye" and "eyes" in Sylvia
Plath's "Tulips."

*They have propped my head between the pillow and the
    sheet-cuff*
Like an eye between two white lids that will not shut.

Five stanzas later:

And I see myself flat, ridiculous, a cut-paper shadow
Between the eye of the sun and the eyes of the tulip, . . .

All of these "eyes" are metaphorical: her head, the sun, and
the tulips, respectively. And all of these "eyes" remain unrelent-
ingly open. Thus the quality of an eye, in this poem, becomes
uniformly horrific—whether or not we consciously notice it. By
virtue of their reappearance in the poem, eyes come to symbolize the notion of a menacing, intractable witness to shame or
frailty or grief.

A more quiet and unobtrusive thematic recurrence takes place
in Elizabeth Bishop's "In the Waiting Room." In the first line of
this lengthy poem, she employs the words "Worcester, Massachusetts," and then she does so once more at the poem's conclu-
sion. Thus she effectively *frames* this poem—wherein a young girl
traverses vast distances in her thoughts—inside the idea of a very
pointed and specific locality, a small town.

WRITING WORKSHOP

Extracting the Motif

The image of snow in the following poem by Kenneth
Patchen is a very pronounced motif. What does it represent?
What does it call to mind? How is Patchen using snow to
express an emotion or idea which runs like a thread through
this poem? Write a paragraph answering these questions.

The Snow Is Deep on the Ground
by Kenneth Patchen

The snow is deep on the ground.
Always the light falls
Softly down on the hair of my beloved.

This is a good world . . .
And war shall fail.   5
God shall not forget us.
Who made the snow waits where love is.

The sky moves in its whiteness
Like the withered hand of an old king.
God shall not forget us.   10
Who made the sky knows of our love.

The snow is beautiful on the ground.
And always the lights of heaven glow
Softly down on the hair of my beloved. ⊢

Understatement, or Withheld Image/Emotion

At times in conversation, we deliberately understate a fact or an emotion to convey ironic emphasis or humor. For example, on a day when everything goes wrong, one might say, "I've had better days." Or, for another example: "Say, how do you feel about that huge raise and promotion you just got?" "I am not displeased."

An understatement indicates something *withheld* or *unsaid*. Think about it. In the first example above, what is unsaid, though implied, is not only that the speaker has seen better days, but also that this particular day was quite dreadful. In the second example, the speaker isn't merely "not displeased," she is also probably thrilled.

One reason that things are left unsaid is for ironic effect, and another reason is that some things, particularly very strong feelings, are often difficult to give words to. It may be easier to only *imply* whatever the unsaid thing is. It's a lot simpler to state "I've had better days" than to try and describe just how unpleasant this particular day has been. Also, at times the implication may be just as descriptive, or even more so, than a straightforward explanation.

Poetry, too, uses understatement in the same ways we use it in conversation, and perhaps in one or two more ways. The following two miniature poems illustrate this.

Upon the Death of Sir Albert Morton's Wife

by Sir Henry Wotton

He first deceased; she for a little tried
To live without him, liked it not, and died. ├

On the Spartan Dead at Thermopylae

by Simonides

Go tell at Sparta, thou who passest by,
That here obedient to her laws we lie. ├

Both of these poems understate the emotional import of what they describe, and both imply more than they say.

In the case of the Spartan dead, what is withheld is the images of bodies ravaged by spears and swords in battle. These soldiers were not merely "obedient to her laws"; they gave their very lives for those laws and for the state. There may even be an implied criticism of Sparta here, for what she asked and received from her obedient young men.

In the case of Sir Albert Morton's wife, we know that "liked it not" is a vast understatement, that she must have died of sorrow or, in some way, been dependent on her husband and unable to live without him. To describe her feelings in such an offhand manner is to chuckle at matters of some gravity: death and grief. But the tone of this epigram is considerably less grim than that of "Spartan Dead," so we may receive it in a lighter spirit as well.

The following remarkable poem by e. e. cummings (which we've seen in the first chapter) employs a number of provocative devices to good effect, including strategic line breaks, unorthodox indentation, and parentheses. All of these bear examination and comment. But for the moment, we will only consider how cummings uses unsaid words.

if there are any heavens

by e. e. cummings

if there are any heavens my mother will (all by herself) have
one. It will not be a pansy heaven nor
a fragile heaven of lilies-of-the-valley but
it will be a heaven of blackred roses

my father will be (deep like a rose   5
tall like a rose)

standing near my

(swaying over her
silent)
with eyes which are really petals and see   10
nothing with the face of a poet really which
is a flower and not a face with
hands
which whisper
This is my beloved my   15

            (suddenly in sunlight
he will bow,

& the whole garden will bow) ├─

Clearly, this poem is about cummings's mother and it describes his reverential and loving feelings for her, illustrated by the singular heaven in which he places her.

There are two instances in this poem in which the possessive pronoun "my" is not followed by a noun-object. In the first instance, the word which is implied, and which we might naturally fill in, is *mother*. In the second instance, the word might be *wife*. And yet, these are not the *only* words which could conceivably fit into these places, and herein lies the point.

Why does cummings withhold the words that should follow "my"? Perhaps because *mother* and *wife* won't do. Perhaps they don't even come close to describing his subject. Perhaps there are no words that can serve as accurate and fully descriptive designations for a person so splendid and ineffable. And in the case of cummings's father, perhaps there are no words, besides "beloved," which can even begin to express the devotion and love that so thoroughly possesses him as he beholds her.

Perhaps, in both cases, awe has taken breath away and speakers are left speechless. So rather than pick words which fall short of doing his mother justice, cummings deems it more accurate to say nothing at all and to leave *implied* that which cannot be said.

Overstatement, or Hyperbole

We are all familiar with hyperbole: "If I told you once, I've told you a million times." "That's got to be the worst movie ever made." "This job is torture." **Hyperbole** is an obvious and extravagant exaggeration or overstatement. When we use hyperbole, we don't expect people to take us literally, but we want them to know how strongly we feel. Poetry uses hyperbole to the same end.

| *Spoils*

by Robert Graves

When all is over and you march for home,
The spoils of war are easily disposed of:
Standards, weapons of combat, helmets, drums
May decorate a staircase or a study,
While lesser gleanings of the battlefield—   5
Coins, watches, wedding-rings, gold teeth and such—
Are sold anonymously for solid cash.

The spoils of love present a different case,
When all is over and you march for home:
That lock of hair, these letters and the portrait   10
May not be publicly displayed; nor sold;
Nor burned; nor returned (the heart being obstinate)—
Yet never dare entrust them to a safe
For fear they burn a hole through two-foot steel. ┝

Graves has found a hyberbolic way of saying that the "spoils" or mementos of lost love retain more emotional significance and power than do the spoils of military war. (He is also insinuating that love itself can be a kind of battleground.) You can lock away those old love letters in a safe or in some metal box, but you will know they are there and they will continue to "burn" you even when you don't look at them. Perhaps Graves is also indicating that the invisible injuries inflicted upon a disappointed lover's heart are as deep and as lingering, or even more so, than any physical injury.

DISCUSSION WORKSHOP

Hyperbole, Homelessness, and You

The following poem is by street poet Julia Vinograd, who spends a great deal of time on Telegraph Avenue where the homeless of Berkeley, California, gravitate, sitting or lying on sidewalks, soliciting passersby for change. This poem employs overstatement in an extraordinarily dramatic and unrelenting fashion. Her hyperboles echo and compound each other.

Sparechangers

by Julia Vinograd

20 on a block and by the time
you get to the end of the block
your innocence is gone.
You're a horrible miser
who lets people starve in front of you;   5
you're guilty of the hawking cough
and the plastic bag raincoat
and the broken shopping cart
packed with all that's left.
It isn't much and it's getting wet   10
and it's your fault it's raining too.
If you looked in a mirror
it would break with disgust,
you couldn't spare a quarter?
You were just walking down the street   15
minding your own business,
maybe thinking about someone you just met
and the light on their hair
and wondering if they liked you as much
when all of a sudden there's this empty hand   20
in your path
and you're a mass murderer and there's no excuse.

You can buy spare parts of your self-respect
back from the sparechangers
but the motor's broken for good.   25
You can call the garage and get them
to tow your conscience away, it doesn't work anymore.
Nothing works anymore.

| *continued on page 203* |

And you want your innocence back.
You have a right to the self you were   30
before you walked down the block,
you spent a whole life working at it,
it's yours.
And the homeless want their homes back,
they have a right to the selves they were before,   35
it's theirs.
> Whole lives broken.
> Whole lives blaming.
> One block. ├─

There are many hyperboles in this poem, including:

"your innocence is gone"

"You're a horrible miser / who lets people starve in front of you."

"you're guilty of the hawking cough"

"it's your fault it's raining too"

"If you looked in a mirror / it would break with disgust"

"you're a mass murderer and there's no excuse."

"You can call the garage and get them / to tow your conscience away, it doesn't work anymore."

"Nothing works anymore."

Does Vinograd have a political purpose in this poem? Is she sincerely and angrily accusing the passerby/reader of inhuman negligence, callousness, and gross irresponsibility? Or is she merely describing how a passerby might be induced to feel about herself as she walks by rows of forlorn, woeful homeless people? Or is she doing a little of both? Or neither? What does she mean when she states "Nothing works anymore"? Who is she blaming? *Is* she blaming someone?

What feeling is she trying to convey? What *do* we feel about it as we read?

Could she have accomplished her task without overstatement? Is overstatement, in this context, a misrepresentation? Or does overstatement (even as we know it to be such) make for a more *accurate* depiction of something?

Synesthesia

Synesthesia is the term for when one kind of sensory data is perceived or interpreted in terms of a different sense. For example, when we say someone *dresses quietly,* we are describing *visual* phenomena—the appearance of a person's clothes—in terms of the *hearing* sense ("quietly"). When we see a *sweet* smile, we are ascribing a *taste*-related sensation to a *sight*. When musicians speak of the *texture* of a piece of music, they are describing sound in terms of touch. And so on. We use synesthesia a great deal in day-to-day speech.

Poetry also uses this "overlapping" of the senses for expressive purposes.

WRITING WORKSHOP

Synesthetic Synergy

| *The Blindman*

by May Swenson

The blindman placed
a tulip on his tongue for purple's taste.
Cheek to grass, his green

was rough excitement's sheen
of little whips.   5
In water to his lips

| *continued on page 205* |

he named the sea blue and white,
the basin of his tears and fallen beads of sight.
He said: this scarf is red;

I feel the vectors to its thread   10
that dance down from the sun I know
the seven fragrances of the rainbow.

I have caressed
the orange hair of flames. Pressed
to my ear,   15

a pomegranate lets me hear
crimson's flute.
Trumpets tell me yellow. Only ebony is mute. ⊢

How many instances of synesthesia occur in this poem? How does synesthesia work with metaphor and symbol in this poem, and to what effect? Write a paragraph responding to these questions.

Synecdoche and Metonymy

A **synecdoche** (pronounced "si-NEK-du-kee") refers to a thing or a person in terms of *one part* of that thing or person. We do this often in common speech. For example, sometimes we might refer to a car as "a set of wheels."

Michael Heron, of the former group the Incredible String Band, used synecdoche in his song "Puppies":

*Fiddlehead ferns and daffodils made me want to play
to the puppies having a little breakfast.
So I took out six fine strings and I began to play
what I thought that new-born fur would like best.*

One synecdoche is the word "fur" in the fourth line, which is only one part, one feature of puppies. Another synecdoche is "six fine strings" in the third line, signifying an entire guitar.

There is also a different kind of synecdoche, which is the exact opposite of the first type. This is when a more *inclusive* or *general* term is used to refer to a *part* or a *specific expression* of the larger item. For example, after the Apollo astronauts made the first lunar landing, it was said that *humankind* had reached the moon and that *America* had gotten there first.

Metonymy is similar to synecdoche but slightly different. Metonymy uses something *associated* with a person or a thing for a designation. For example, a group of businessmen might be referred to as *suits*. In the Old West, "a famous gun" might have meant "a well-known outlaw."

In her song "In the Garden," Kristin Deelane of the folk duo Adam and Kris sings:

> *In the mirror I'm growing older*
> *The years sinking into my skin.*

Of course it is not "the years" themselves that sink into the skin, but rather those lines, impressions, and sets of facial expressions that come with the passing of the years.

In the poem "Tulips," Sylvia Plath speaks of the nurses bringing her "numbness in their bright needles." What the nurses actually bring is anesthetic medication in needles. *Numbness* tells us this—in a more tangible, less clinical fashion—through metonymy.

A Word about Poetic Devices

Any of these devices may or may not appear in a particular poem. Poetic devices comprise a menu of colorful ways to convey thoughts, ideas, and feelings. This doesn't mean that a poet will sit down and think, "Hmm . . . I bet a good synecdoche would work well there, and maybe I could add a little allusion over here, and perhaps I could introduce some thematic recurrence a little later on, and maybe an unconventional line break or two would spice things up nicely." In fact, it's unlikely that poets consciously think in terms of devices at all as they compose, any more than we consciously think of understatement, synesthesia, or allusion as we speak.

For our purposes as readers, we may observe poetic devices as a means of becoming increasingly aware of how we are affected by the uses of language and the play of words, and as a way of boring our way deeper into the life of a poem.

WRITING WORKSHOP

Unearth a Poem

Find a poem that employs strategic line breaks. Discuss the dramatic effect of these line breaks. How do the line breaks direct your attention? What do they emphasize? Do they suggest any ambiguous or double meanings?

WRITING WORKSHOP

Unearth Another Poem

Find a poem that employs allusion, motif, understatement, overstatement, synesthesia, synecdoche, or metonymy. Discuss the impact of this device in the poem.

DISCUSSION WORKSHOP

Creating a Quilt

In a small group, make up a short story together. Patch the story together in sentences that pack in as much allusion, motif, understatement, overstatement, synesthesia, synecdoche, and metonymy as possible. Don't worry about using every one of these devices, but do incorporate at least a few of them. Designate one person to transcribe the story onto paper.

IRRATIONALITY, DREAMS,
AND PARADOX

8

Calculated Nonsense

Most of the time, we prefer things to make sense. When things make sense to us, they fit into our understanding of the world and allow us to feel more or less in control of things. That's one of the reasons why we sometimes find poetry confounding—sometimes it doesn't make sense at first. So we attempt to make sense of it by looking at it systematically, analyzing it piece by piece, until we can say with some measure of assuredness, "Ah, now I *see what it means.* Now I *get it.* Now I *understand!*"

We've already seen, of course, that this analytical approach is not necessarily the right one or the best one to take with poetry. Many good poems contain multiple ambiguities and are best apprehended through feeling before reason. Nonetheless, we might assume that every poem has a rational meaning, or a set of rational meanings, even if it is impossible to put all or most of them into words.

The error we could be making in assuming this lies in thinking that all meaning is rational—or that only "meaning," as we understand it, has a point, and that nonsense is a waste of time and has no point whatsoever. There are those who hold that the opposite is true: Human rationality is an extremely narrow and limiting system that *locks out* more meaning than it preserves. They feel that the only cure for too much rationality is a dose of calculated nonsense, or irrationality.

Avante-garde thinkers and artists of the early twentieth century felt that if common sense had led the human race into World War I, then perhaps "craziness" could have no worse results, and they wrote poems such as this one:

What the Violins
Sing in Their Baconfat Bed

by Jean Arp

the elephant is in love with the millimeter

the snail dreams of lunar defeat
its slippers are pallid and drained
like a gun made of Jell-O that's held by a neodraftee

the eagle has the gestures of an alleged vacuum   5
his breast is swollen with lightning

the lion sports a mustache that is pure gothic of the flamboyant
    type
his skin is calm
he laughs like a blot from a bottle of oink

| continued on page 211 |

the lobster goes *grr* like a gooseberry   10
he is wise with the savvy of apples
has the bleeding-heart ways of a plum
he is fiendish in sex like a pumpkin

the cow takes a path that's pathetic
it peters out in a pond of flesh   15
every hair of this volume weighs volumes

the snake hops with prickety prickling
around about washbowls of love
full of hearts with an arrow in each

the butterfly stuffed is a popover made of papaya   20
papaya popovers grow into papapaya papapovers
papapaya papapovers grow into grandpapapaya grandpapapovers

the nightingale sprinkles on stomachs on hearts on brains on guts
what I mean is on lilies on roses on lilacs on pinks
the flea puts his right leg behind his left ear   25
his left hand in his right hand
and on his left foot jumps over his right ear ├──

translated by John Frederick Nims

A poem like this can surprise, tickle, and amuse us, and perhaps, at moments, even jolt us into odd new ways of seeing things. Stepping back a bit we might note that the poet uses a great deal of alliteration and that most of the lines are or could be syntactically complete sentences. The momentum and rough regularity of the poem's rhythms lend this fanciful wordplay a quality of self-assurance, or even, conceivably, a force of credibility.

This phenomenon of the sheer phonetic and syntactic *feeling* and *force* of words, affording them a kind of semantic feasibility, is most famously illustrated in the Lewis Carroll poem "Jabberwocky" from *Through the Looking Glass,* the sequel to *Alice in Wonderland.*

Jabberwocky

by Lewis Carroll

'Twas brillig, and the slithy toves
    Did gyre and gimble in the wabe;
All mimsy were the borogoves,
    And the mome raths out gabe.

"Beware the Jabberwock, my son!   5
    The jaws that bite, the claws that catch!
Beware the Jubjub bird and shun
    The frumious Bandersnatch!"

He took his vorpal sword in hand;
    Long time the manxome foe he sought—   10
So rested he by the Tumtum tree,
    And stood awhile in thought.

And, as in uffish thought he stood,
    The Jabberwock, with eyes of flame,
Came whiffling through the tulgey wood,   15
    And burbled as it came!

One, two! One, two! And through and through
    The vorpal blade went snicker-snack!
He left it dead, and with its head
    He went galumphing back.   20

"And hast thou slain the Jabberwock?
    Come to my arms, my beamish boy!
O frabjous day! Callooh! Callay!"
    He chortled in his joy.

'Twas brillig, and the slithy toves   25
    Did gyre and gimble in the wabe;
All mimsy were the borogoves,
    And the mome raths outgabe.

As Alice herself put it, "Somehow it seems to fill my head with ideas—only I don't exactly know what they are!"

Despite the percentage of nonsense words in the poem, we not only understand the story (more or less), but we can also guess the meanings of some of the made-up words. "Slithy," for example, which sounds a good deal like *slimy*, is clearly an adjective, as is "frumious," which calls to mind words like *furious* and *fumes*. "Gyre" and "gimble" must be verbs; "wabe" must be a noun, and so on.

Other adjectives include "mimsy," "vorpal," "manxome," "tulgey," and others. Verbs include "whiffling," "burbled," and "galumphing." Nouns include "borogoves," "Bandersnatch," and "Jabberwock." These fantasy words give this poem its flavor. We may not understand their meanings exactly, but their sounds tip us off and our imaginations fill in bits and pieces of vaguely rational sense.

We can similarly detect bits of sense, if we try, in the following excerpts from Roger McGough's fanciful and irreverent poem, "What You Are."

| from *What You Are*

by Roger McGough

you are the moment
before the noose clenched its fist
and the innocent man cried: treason

you are the moment
before the warbooks in the public library   5
turned into frogs and croaked khaki obscenities

you are the moment
before the buildings turned into flesh
and windows closed their eyes

| continued on page 214 |

you are the moment   10
before the railwaystations burst into tears
and the bookstalls picked their noses

you are the moment
before the buspeople turned into teeth
and chewed the inspector   15
for no other reason than he was doing his duty

you are the moment
before the flowers turned into plastic and melted
in the heat of the burning cities

you are the moment   20
before the blindman put on his dark glasses

you are the moment
before the subconscious begged to be left in peace

you are the moment
before the world was made flesh   25

you are the moment
before the clouds became locomotives
and hurtled headlong into the sun ⊢

There is certainly tremendous energy, drama, color, and rhythmic momentum in these lines. But do they have a point?

DISCUSSION WORKSHOP

Anything There?

Are there any hints of sense or symbolism in the preceding McGough stanzas? What germs of meaning or significance, if any, do they contain? Compare your impressions with those of others in a small group.

Enlightenment and Irrationality

There is a serious side to all this nonsense. As was mentioned a little earlier, there are those who feel irrationality is a necessary tonic for the tunnel vision of logic and reason. They feel that without irrationality we are doomed to the tiny prisons of our conditioned conventional thoughts, instead of enjoying the boundless, infinite universe of perception.

Zen Buddhism is a centuries-old spiritual tradition in which methods are employed to focus the student/seeker's conscious attention on the present moment and to shock him out of the confinement of his conceptual understanding of reality. The most well-known device for doing this is the Zen *koan,* a riddle posed by a Zen master, such as "What is the sound of one hand clapping?" or "What was your original face, before your parents were born?" The idea is that such riddles are patently impossible to answer rationally, and so, in the attempt, the student's rational thought processes will ultimately wear out and break down. In the Zen philosophy, this is the beginning of enlightenment, the opportunity for the light of true awareness to shine into a mind previously obstructed by walls of rational thought.

In a related vein, there is much poetry which expresses the Buddhist idea that there is no true *self* as we conceive it, that our individual identity, as such, is an illusion known as *ego*. Each of us, at essence, is one with the all-encompassing divine spirit, and all the things we conceive of as facets of our individuality are like layers of an onion, the core of which is vacant. Rational thought then, is one of our primary structural reinforcements for this illusion of separateness.

by Angelus Silesius

God, whose love and joy
    are present everywhere,
can't come to visit you
    unless you aren't there

In Buddhism, the ultimate goal of meditation and contemplative practice is to dissolve the distinction between the perceiver and the perceived until there is no longer an *I* who has *an experience*. Rather, there is just the phenomenon of an experience happening, or "experience experiencing itself."

by Li Po

The birds have vanished into the sky,
and now the last cloud drains away.

We sit together, the mountains and me,
until only the mountain remains.

Note how a few simple images can bring the imagining mind to a place where the mind does not exist.

WRITING WORKSHOP

Grasping the Ungraspable

Consider the following poem.

by Antonio Machado

In our souls everything
moves guided by a mysterious hand.
We know nothing of our own souls
that are unundersrandable and say nothing.

The deepest words   5
of the wise man teach us
the same as the whistle of the wind when it blows
or the sound of the water when it is flowing.

Is there anything Zenlike about this poem? Are there any irrational statements? If so, what are they? Are there intimations of spiritual significance here? Ponder these questions in writing.

Can you paraphrase this poem?

Dream and Paradox

Between the extremes of wildly playful and irreverent irrationality on the one hand, and the calculated, purposeful irrationality of spiritual tradition on the other, lies a vast and fertile expanse of poetic prerogative, in which intimations of sense may be mixed with sheerest nonsense or vice versa. In this expanse, perspective may be jostled and bandied about to varying effect and the mind may be lifted briefly from accustomed norms of perception into intriguing new configurations.

One source of irrational imagery which we are all familiar with is dreams. Many poets, we can safely assume, draw much of their raw material from their dreams. The two poems which follow contain simple examples of dream images and events. The scenarios which they depict are not too far removed from reality; in fact they both make sense. But there is something a little askew in each poem.

My Dream

by Lew Blockcolski

"I had this dream.
I was on the old town square,
holding a white man down.
My brother was nearby shouting.
Anyway, I was going to scalp this man.   5
Then I remembered I didn't know how to scalp.
I asked my brother. He didn't know either.
The man started to laugh and laugh and laugh.
I woke up." ⊢—

Galloping in the South

by Pablo Neruda

Forty leagues on horseback,
the ranges of Malleco;
the fields are newly washed,
the air electric and green.
Regions of rocks and wheat,   5
a sudden bird breaks out,
the water slithers and scrawls
lost letters in the earth.

It rains, rains a slow rain,
it rains perpetual needles   10
and the horse which was galloping
dissolved into rain:
later, it took shape
with the grave-digging drops,
and I gallop on in the wind   15
astride the horse of the rain.

| *continued on page 219* |

Astride the horse of the rain
I leave behind these regions,
the vast, damp solitude,
the ranges of Malleco. |—   20

translated by Alastair Reid

In the first poem, Cherokee/Choctaw poet Lew Blockcolski dreams he is about to scalp someone, but then realizes he doesn't know how to. There are at least two irrational things going on here: If he does not know how to scalp, then, certainly, in real life he would have realized this before getting ready to try. And, as for the "white man" who is being forcefully held down, chances are he would have little to "laugh and laugh and laugh" about, even if a scalping was not in store.

In the Neruda poem, of course, what is dreamlike is the image of the horse dissolving into rain and then re-forming as a horse made of rain.

Perhaps you can discern symbolic or connotative implications in one or both of these poems. All the same, neither poem offers us a sense of any clear, rational explanation for the fantastical events that occur.

Paradox refers to things that are apparently self-contradictory. Our dreams often contain paradoxical elements. The following short poem is both dreamlike and paradoxical.

| *The Mask*   *by Ya-Ka-Nes (Patty L. Harjo)*

While upon the journey of life
I found a mask lying beside
The winding road
I bent down

| *continued on page 220* |

In jest placed it on my brow   5
Then, I saw the world
In all its ugliness
And I cried ⊢—

The episode itself, of course, is quite dreamlike. One does not typically find a mask lying by the side of the road, let alone one which, upon wearing it, will alter one's perceptions. This episode also contains some apparent contradictions, some effects which are the very opposite of what we might logically expect.

When someone puts on a mask, it is normally the *wearer's* appearance that is changed, not the appearance of *what the wearer sees* through the mask. Also, a mask is usually something that creates a *disguise,* but here a mask enables someone to see the world more clearly, albeit less pleasantly. Finally, masks are generally associated with celebration and laughter, as opposed to tears. (Then again, in shamanistic traditions, masks are an important element of many rituals and sacred ceremonies which facilitate sight and deeper understanding, even at the cost of some pain or fear.)

This curious poem by Gary Snyder also features dreamlike images and paradoxes.

| *As for Poets*

by Gary Snyder

As for poets
The Earth Poets
who write small poems
Need help from no man.

The Air Poets   5
Play out the swiftest gales
And sometimes loll in the eddies.
Poem after poem,
Curling back on the same thrust.

| *continued on page 221* |

At fifty below

Fuel oil won't flow

And propane stays in the tank.

Fire Poets

Burn at absolute zero

Fossil love pumped back up.

The first

Water Poet

Stayed down six years.

He was covered with seaweed.

The life in his poem

Left millions of tiny

Different tracks

Criss-crossing through the mud.

With the Sun and Moon

In his belly,

The Space Poet

Sleeps.

No end to the sky—

But his poems,

Like wild geese,

Fly off the edge.

A Mind Poet

Stays in the house.

The house is empty

And it has no walls.

The poem

Is seen from all sides,

Everywhere,

At once. ⊢

There are at least three blatant paradoxes in this poem. "Burn at absolute zero" in the third section is a paradox. In the second-to-last section, the notion of poems and geese that "fly off the edge" of an *endless* sky is clearly paradoxical. Finally, in the last section, how can a house that is empty and has no walls *be a house?* Are not walls the very *definition* of a house?

WRITING WORKSHOP

Plumbing the Paradox

Of course, there are explanations for Snyder's paradoxes if we regard them symbolically. How might you explain them? Look at his paradoxes *in context*. One applies to "Fire Poets," the next to "The Space Poet," and a final one applies to "A Mind Poet." Do these designations fit in some fashion with their respective paradoxes? Write a paragraph or two explaining your answer.

Another Dreamy Paradox

The following poem by Karynn Fish contains the word "mystery" in its title for good reason: The poem's subject, "the turtle-woman," is shrouded in mystery and we are only given very obscure and vaguely contradictory clues as to her nature and character.

The Turtlewoman Mystery

by Karynn Fish

You never asked me about the turtlewoman.
You look for her in graveyards, in phone books,
You look for her at the missions where old men sleep,
But she is younger than you think, hatched in the corpseglow

| *continued on page 223* |

Of Neil Armstrong's 15 minutes on interspace t.v.,   5
She learned early to orbit your life in pennyspun ellipses
When you thought you were immune to gravity. Once,
When you touched my shoulders, you thought of her,
I could tell your fingers were searching
For the hard edge of her back. But you never asked me.   10
I would have told you if you had.
I have a picture of the turtlewoman
From high school, she's staring right at the camera
From the concessions line at a varsity football game, her
Birdnosed face and those scuffed-leather eyes   15
Staring right at you because you were the one
Who took that picture, though you only saw the coach's wife
Kissing the ice cream boy.
I know the turtlewoman kept your number
Years ago, tucked safe in the secret wrinkles   20
Inside her green glazed shell. I know because once
I lost it and she was there, and she shrank inside herself
And echoed the single digits out to me
While I dialed them, one by one. I used to think
She knew you better than I did.   25
Now you go looking for her like she's some wisewoman
Who can tell you why you've wasted so much time
With ribs, and thumbs, and wombs
Who can take you to a more primitive water
Where you can gasp at the slowness of your everevolving soul,   30
Limpid illusion of age. You think
She's something ancient, new-to-you
But I've heard her singing in the drains
For the past six years. I even knew you would leave
When finally she snapped and split out of herself   35
And squirmed through your dreams
To get your attention.
Don't look for her at the missions.
She's younger than you think, and richer, too.
I would have told you before if you had asked me. ├─   40

An intuitive, almost meta-rational, logic weaves tightly through and unifies this poem. We can infer a relationship of some kind exists, or has existed, between the speaker, the one spoken to, and the mysterious turtlewoman.

We will assume, strictly for the sake of convenience, that the speaker is a woman. The speaker intimates that she knows or understands this turtlewoman better than does the person to whom she is speaking, the one who now seeks the turtlewoman for ambiguous reasons. There is a discernible tinge of jealousy in the speaker's tone; is the person whom she addresses a past or present lover? This too is ambiguous. The line "When you touched my shoulders, you thought of her" could be alluding to an intimate moment, but quite possibly not.

In any case, if there is jealousy here, it may be of a more spiritual than sexual nature. The turtlewoman's "bird-nosed face and those scuffed-leather eyes" and her "secret wrinkles / Inside her glazed shell" do not signify physical attractiveness, at least not by any conventional standard. The attraction, such as it is, seems more to do with what the addressee in this poem imagines the turtlewoman can show or tell or teach: "Now you go looking for her like she's some wisewoman / Who can tell you why you've wasted so much time / With ribs, and thumbs, and wombs / Who can take you to a more primitive water."

The speaker asserts that the turtlewoman is younger and richer than thought and is not to be found in graveyards or missions. "Younger" and "richer" are adjectives intended to disillusion the addressee about the turtlewoman, to disqualify the turtlewoman somehow, perhaps by revealing her to be less profound and tragic than thought, more simple perhaps, more callow.

But all this is conjecture, of course. After a point, this poem defies logical speculation. If the turtlewoman is *not* down and out, what is she doing "singing in the drains" for six years? For that matter, if she's "in the drains," what could move her to sing? What does she sing *about*?

And what is the turtlewoman's relationship to outer space, to Neil Armstrong (a poetic *allusion* to the first man ever to walk on the moon), to ellipses, to orbits? All this seems in thematic counterpoint to the "primitive water" that the addressee presumes her to abide in, and which we too might associate more readily with turtles and turtle-type creatures.

Further questions remain as well, of course. What is the relationship of the poem's speaker to the turtlewoman, such that she would go to the turtlewoman for the phone number of the poem's addressee (how literally should we take this?), and such that she professes to understand the turtlewoman so well? What was the turtlewoman doing at a varsity football game? What pressures were brought to bear on the turtlewoman such that she "snapped and split out of herself," and why did she have to "squirm through dreams" to get the addressee's attention? Why did she (presumably) need or desire that attention, and, now that she compels that attention so thoroughly, why is she so elusive? Is the turtlewoman an actual or a symbolic personage to the speaker and the addressee?

It might be fun and interesting to come up with answers to these and other questions. Still, the poem essentially retains more of a dream-sense than a rational one. Like a dream, it ties together by its own self-referential logic; like a dream, it yields more puzzles the more you scratch the surface. Like a dream, it brims with energy and significance, and like a dream, it stands as one piece, ultimately irreducible to analysis.

DISCUSSION WORKSHOP

Who Might She Be?

Who, or what, is the turtlewoman? Explain her, to your own way of thinking, in a small group discussion.

Dreamy, Paradoxical, and Irrational

The following poem by Wallace Stevens is similarly dreamlike, elusive, and laden with innuendo. But the form is quite different. In a sense, it is a "package" of thirteen small poems in one.

It is advisable to gently reflect on each in turn before forging ahead to the next.

Thirteen Ways of Looking at a Blackbird

by Wallace Stevens

I

Among twenty snowy mountains,
The only moving thing
Was the eye of the blackbird.

II

I was of three minds,
Like a tree
In which there are three blackbirds.

III

The blackbird whirled in the autumn winds.
It was a small part of the pantomime.

IV

A man and a woman
Are one.
A man and a woman and a blackbird
Are one.

V

I do not know which to prefer,
The beauty of inflections
Or the beauty of innuendoes,
The blackbird whistling
Or just after.

5

10

15

| continued on page 227 |

VI
Icicles filled the long window
With barbaric glass.
The shadow of the blackbird   20
Crossed it, to and fro.
The mood
Traced in the shadow
An indecipherable cause.

VII
O thin men of Haddam   25
Why do you imagine golden birds?
Do you not see how the blackbird
Walks around the feet
Of the women about you?

VIII
I know noble accents   30
And lucid, inescapable rhythms;
But I know, too,
That the blackbird is involved
In what I know.

IX
When the blackbird flew out of sight,   35
It marked the edge
Of one of many circles.

X
At the sight of blackbirds
Flying in a green light,
Even the bawds of euphony   40
Would cry out sharply.

| *continued on page 228* |

XI

He rode over Connecticut
In a glass coach.
Once, a fear pierced him,
In that he mistook   45
The shadow of his equipage
For blackbirds.

XII

The river is moving.
The blackbird must be flying.

XIII

It was evening all afternoon.   50
It was snowing
And it was going to snow.
The blackbird sat
In the cedar-limbs. ├─

For Wallace Stevens, perception and imagination were insep-
arable. In the act of perceiving, one automatically—and cre-
atively—imposes order and meaning on that which is perceived.
Stevens held this to be an exalted function of the human mind,
one which affords us an almost god-like status as determiners of
our own reality.

Therefore, much of his poetry "teases out" this reality-
ordering function. In "Thirteen Ways of Looking at a Blackbird,"
Stevens offers ambiguous hints, images, and some blatantly
incredible, even paradoxical statements such as "It was evening
all afternoon." No explanation is given; he leaves it to the inherent, automatic, reality-ordering capacity of our imaginations to
"fill in the blanks," to afford some sense to his peculiar statements
and juxtapositions.

But the statements and images are not *random*. Quite the con-
trary, they are veritably pregnant with suggested significance, and
therein lies the art. *Randomness* is a category that our minds

understand; when we see something we judge to be random, we simply leave it as such and move on. But Stevens's words cannot be so casually dismissed; they are too deliberate, too precise; they compel more careful appraisal.

The engine of this poem is its use of juxtaposition—the way images and ideas are placed next to one another. Each of these juxtapositions beg intriguing questions. In stanza XII, for example: "The river is moving. / The blackbird must be flying." What, we wonder, could be the correlation between blackbirds and rivers? How are they related such that one might indicate something about the other?

Or stanza IV: "A man and a woman / Are one. / A man and a woman and a blackbird / are one." We are all familiar with the idea of a man and woman being metaphorically "one" in love, or in marriage, or in complementarity, or what-have-you. But where does the blackbird fit into this equation? How does the blackbird alter the equation? What does it mean to be "one" with a blackbird?

Or stanza XIII: "It was evening all afternoon. / It was snowing / And it was going to snow. / The blackbird sat / In the cedar-limbs." As we noted before, the first line seems completely illogical at first glance. But when it is followed by the second and third lines, we see that there is a common theme here of things that are *impending* and yet are somehow already present. As afternoon must eventually turn to evening, so "going to snow" always leads to "snowing." In this context then, it seems the thing that is about to happen is already *contained* in that which precedes it. And the blackbird on the cedar limbs? What does *it* indicate is impending? What does *it* already contain?

Or stanza II: How is a blackbird analogous to a mind, and in particular, to a divided one? Or stanza IX: What sort of "circles" are perceived, and what do these circles demarcate? Or stanza I: Why is the eye of the blackbird the only moving thing and what does this portend? And so on.

Chances are, you can conceive answers to these questions (and others). In fact, with little or no effort, your subconscious, prerational imagination automatically supplies answers—though these answers may be difficult or even impossible to articulate. Even as you sit perplexed, saying to yourself, "Well, this doesn't make sense," there is a deep and basic impulse that urges you to impose a sense on it—even if you don't altogether *understand* the very sense that you yourself create. And that's the point.

Irrationality, at its best, supersedes and transcends understanding.

WRITING WORKSHOP

Articulating the Sense That You Impose

While it is true that much of what we "make out of" non-rational data, such as Stevens's "Thirteen Ways of Looking at a Blackbird," cannot be articulated, much of it can be. For example, I could say that the reason the eye of the blackbird is the only moving thing among twenty snowy mountains is that something cataclysmic is about to happen, an act of God perhaps, and the knowledge of this imminent event renders all things extraordinarily still. The eye of the blackbird, however, keeps moving, because it is the symbolic eye of all vigilant beings, the sharp, alert eye of poised readiness, the focal point of all awareness, the conscious sight-organ of the mountains themselves.

Pick any one, or two, or three of Stevens's stanzas and make an assertion as to what is implied by the juxtaposition of images and statements contained therein.

WRITING WORKSHOP

Your Own Dreamy Nonsense

The dream realm is an extraordinary resource for all kinds of ideas, rational and irrational. Have you had any interesting dreams lately? Write one down. Then see if you can turn it into a poem. You are free to embellish it; you don't have to adhere faithfully to what happened in the dream. If you like, you might combine scenes and events from two or more dreams. Be sure to spend time fleshing out distinct images.

WRITING WORKSHOP

Unearth a Poem

Find another poem that strikes you as largely irrational, dreamlike, or paradoxical. Identify irrational elements in the poem. What *questions* do they call to mind? Which questions feel intuitively answerable and which ones do not? In your journal, speculate as to what the "irrational sense" is, or describe your own "dream-sense" of it, as the case may be.

WELDING IT TOGETHER 9

Meaning and Being

Archibald MacLeish concludes his poem "Ars Poetica" with the famous lines:

A poem should not mean
But be.

By this proclamation then, a poem should not contain a message about something else, but rather should speak for itself, a kind of luminous object.

With this in mind, let's read two poems (one of which you've seen in Chapter 5).

Eternity

by William Blake

He who binds himself to a joy
Does the winged life destroy.
But he who kisses the joy as it flies
Lives in eternity's sun rise. ├─

Sestina

by Elizabeth Bishop

September rain falls on the house.
In the failing light, the old grandmother
sits in the kitchen with the child
beside the Little Marvel Stove,
reading the jokes from the almanac,   5
laughing and talking to hide her tears.

She thinks that her equinoctial tears
and the rain that beats on the roof of the house
were both foretold by the almanac,
but only known to a grandmother.   10
The iron kettle sings on the stove.
She cuts some bread and says to the child,

It's time for tea now; but the child
is watching the teakettle's small hard tears
dance like mad on the hot black stove,   15
the way the rain must dance on the house.
Tidying up, the old grandmother
hangs up the clever almanac

| *continued on page 235* |

on its string. Birdlike, the almanac
hovers half open above the child,   20
hovers above the old grandmother
and her teacup full of dark brown tears.
She shivers and says she thinks the house
feels chilly and puts more wood on the stove.

It was to be, says the Marvel Stove.   25
I know what I know, says the almanac.
With crayons the child draws a rigid house
and a winding pathway. Then the child
puts in a man with buttons like tears
and shows it proudly to the grandmother.   30

But secretly, while the grandmother
busies herself about the stove,
the little moons fall down like tears
from between the pages of the almanac
into the flower bed the child   35
has carefully placed in front of the house.

Time to plant tears, says the almanac.
The grandmother sings to the marvelous stove
and the child draws another inscrutable house. ⊢

There's no escaping it—the first of these two poems *means*
something. But William Blake is widely regarded as one of the
most brilliant poets ever to have written in the English language.
So, notwithstanding Mr. MacLeish's admonishments, Blake's cre-
dentials are impeccable and we may safely reckon his poem a
poem. The meaning, as such, is fairly straightforward and involves
a bit of advice about how to live and how best to receive life's
joys.

By contrast, Bishop's "Sestina" apparently *is* much more than
it *means.* It is elegant and balanced in form; being a sestina, here
is beauty and symmetry in the *body* of the poem itself. There is

also a gentle and pleasing succession of images in this poem, like tiny pictures from a fairy tale. Magical events occur: The stove talks, the almanac talks, and the almanac weeps moons that fall like tears into the child's drawing. Rain is falling outside; water is boiling and tears are streaming inside. We don't need to analyze to be captivated and absorbed into the world of this poem. There need be no message.

So which do you prefer, meaning or being? Is the distinction clear and absolute?

Blake's poem, while purposeful, is certainly not devoid of *being*. His metaphors, images, and symbols—joy as a "winged" thing, "eternity's sun rise," joy as something that can be "kissed"—are quite sensual and aesthetic onto themselves. Furthermore, although his words *could* be paraphrased into common speech along the lines of "Trying to hang on to pleasure only squeezes the joy out of it; it is best to take life's joys as they come and then let them go," his words are a good deal more graceful and pleasing to the eye and ear. The symbols he employs are *vibrant* with significance. They do not *end* with the message contained in the paraphrase; they *radiate* with *life*.

If we look closely, we may detect some ripples of significance (or meaning) in Bishop's "Sestina." There are *themes* within this poem, including the theme of concealed or suppressed grief, which is illustrated by the grandmother holding back her tears and the almanac's tears buried in the garden of the child's drawing.

There is also the theme of hidden, mysterious knowledge and secrets. Something that has been foretold is "only known to a grandmother." But, quietly: "*It was to be,* says the Marvel Stove," and "*I know what I know,* says the almanac." The little moons fall "secretly" from the almanac's pages. The house in the child's drawing is "inscrutable." Everything is imbued with some invisible presence or spirit or destiny.

Can something really *be* without *meaning,* or *mean* without *being?*

Let's look at two more poems and see if they shed any further light on this question.

I Know I'm Not Sufficiently Obscure
by Roy Durem

I know I'm not sufficiently obscure
to please the critics—nor devious enough.
Imagery escapes me.
I cannot find those mild and gracious words
to clothe the carnage.   5
Blood is blood and murder's murder.
What's a lavender word for lynch?
Come, you pale poets, wan, refined, and dreamy:
here is a black woman working out her guts
in a white man's kitchen   10
for little money and no glory.
How should I tell that story?
There is a black boy, blacker still from death,
face down in the Korean mud.
Come on with your effervescent jive   15
explain to him why he ain't alive.
Reword our specific discontent
into some plaintive melody,
a little whine, a little whimper,
not too much—and no rebellion!   20
God, no! Rebellion's much too corny.
You deal with finer feelings,
very subtle—an autumn leaf
hanging from a tree—I see a body! ⊢

Anonymous

Spun in high, dark clouds,
Snow forms vast webs of white flakes
And drifts lightly down. ⊢

Now, these two poems, if any, represent the poles of meaning and being (if, in fact, they are poles). In "I Know I'm Not Sufficiently Obscure," Roy Durem makes a clear, direct statement in which, among other things, he flatly disdains the "pure being" dimension of poetry. Yet, for all his straight-from-the-hip shooting, he also employs a fair amount of technique. Even as he declares, "Imagery escapes me," he uses imagery effectively, particularly at the end, where he contrasts the image of an autumn leaf with that of a body—both of which can be seen hanging from a tree. He even rhymes once or twice, and the phrase "a lavender word for lynch" contains both alliteration and synesthesia. Finally, his choice to cast his statement *as a poem* indicates that he is concerned, to some degree, with the *form* as well as the content of his message—even if we assume he only wrote it this way to get our attention.

The haiku is brisk and simple, like most haiku, and its imagery is not spectacular. You might say that it simply *is*, and that it does not seek to mean anything. And yet this little poem rests on metaphors, the metaphor (implicit) of silk for snow and web (explicit) for snowflakes. Any metaphor, of course, is a comparison, and any comparison is a kind of commentary or interpretation. So this poem, too, makes a *statement* of sorts in how it interprets the snow.

It seems there is no escaping it: Meaning and being are inextricably intertwined. As in the Oriental yin/yang symbol, which shows that darkness and light must each contain a bit of the other—and that, symbolically, all things must contain some part of their opposite—so it is that being and meaning cannot exist entirely apart.

DISCUSSION WORKSHOP

How about Us?

Which do we do more of—mean or be? Which is more important to us? To you personally? Do some people *mean* more than they *are,* and vice versa? How do these terms apply to our lives? Do our lives have to "mean something"? What does it mean to "be somebody"? Are there times when we *are* more than we *mean,* and other times when we *mean* more than we *are?* Can you give examples?

Discuss these questions in a small group and see what you come up with.

Where Poetry Lives

Do we know what poetry is at this point? Do we have a working definition?

Poetry is a machine made out of words, said William Carlos Williams. But even the best machines wear down, and so a favorite poem read hundreds of times will, eventually, fail to fire the imagination as it once did. We mature and change as well; what captured us today may leave us unmoved tomorrow. So we continually need new machines, new poems.

A metaphor is a kind of a machine too, and this particular one—the metaphor of a poem as an imagination machine—is starting to wear thin around the edges. You may have already noted ways in which the comparison breaks down. For one thing, a machine, unlike a poem, performs precisely the same function for anyone who uses it. There can be little argument as to what a machine is for, whereas a poem is generally open to interpretation. More importantly, there will always be room in the world for more poetry, but, arguably, there may not always be room for more machines.

So what is poetry? When we see uneven lines of words on a page, with a title at the top, perhaps a few rhymes, and the author's name somewhere, we recognize this as a poem. But other things may also qualify as poetry by a broader definition.

We can probably agree that poetry, whatever form it takes, will be made of words. Poetry is an art of words. Words fill our lives. It's not *all* poetry, is it? Or does that depend on how we *hear* the words? Is it possible to find poetry everywhere, in everything?

Does finding the poetry in life simply require a perceptual shift? By reading and immersing ourselves in poetry, might we become more aware of connotations in speech, metaphors and symbols in language, levels of ambiguity in various words, and the play of sound? Could life become more rich, textured, vibrant, colorful, and full of meaning?

The answers must come from your own experience. Essentially, your own experience—your unique, uncensored, unqualified, unabridged, immediate sensory, emotional, and cognitive experience—is what poetry addresses, what poetry is about, and where poetry lives.

Keeping Poetry with Us

Now that you are almost done reading this text, how are you going to keep poetry in your life?

For approaching new poems, you are now equipped with a fairly complete set of tools. With patience, you can gauge the emotional connotations latent in words. You can envision images, listen for the sounds and rhythms, spot similes and metaphors, and plumb the depths of symbols. You can detect and reflect on motifs and strategic line breaks, and you can navigate your rational mind through dream and paradox.

One way to enlarge the presence of poetry in your life is to share poems you love, when you find them, with friends and associates. Comparing perceptions and responses will enrich your understanding and experience. You might also want to keep a journal of the poems you love the most, describing why they're important to you.

Another pleasant way to keep poetry with you is to discover a poet. Go to a bookstore or a library and look in the poetry section. Peruse the books until you find a poet whom you've never read before and whose work strikes you and moves you. Check out or buy the book.

You might also want to write poems for yourself or others. There are many books and articles that give guidance and instruction on how to write poetry. Strictly speaking, this is not one of them. But if you want to write, you have a lot of options. You can pick up a pen or pencil (or crayon) and simply begin writing. You can find a teacher, a class, or books about how to write poetry, or you can join or start a writers' group. You can show your work to other people, or you can keep a private journal. You may even want to publish some of your poetry, and there are many places to do this as well.

One caution: Although writing can be fun and exciting, poems seldom flow spontaneously from writers' pens. Some poems take a very short time to read, but those same poems may take ten times as long or more to write. Most poets revise their poems several times before the poems "feel right" to them. Poets craft their work very carefully; they choose words very deliberately. They may add words, they may subtract words, they may change words, and sometimes they may even throw the whole thing away in despair. So take your time. It's just as well; the things we work hardest to accomplish are usually those that afford us the most lasting satisfaction and value.

If there are poetry readings in your area, this is another wonderful way to absorb more poetry. You will experience it directly from the source, in an entirely different manner from reading. The oral interpretation given by a poet to her poem can be unlike what you might expect simply from having read the words on the page.

In short, if you want to keep poetry in your life, keep reading, keep thinking, keep listening, and keep watching. But *do* you want to keep poetry in your life? If so, why?

The Original Question

This book began with the question of whether poetry really matters. Does it? No one but you can say. We have looked at many poems together. Do any of them matter to you?

When we say that something *matters*, we usually mean that it somehow *makes a difference*. So let's ask: Does poetry make a difference to your life? Would your life be any better or worse without poetry? Has poetry ever changed or affected how you think or feel, or even what you do?

We noted, in the section about poetry and sound, that words fill our minds all the time, if not our ears at every second. I have noticed, in particular, that the lyrics to songs course through my mind almost constantly, as a kind of subliminal running commentary on whatever I'm thinking or doing. One July morning I looked out my window and in my mind I heard "Summer deep is in the hills again," which is a line from an old T. Rex song entitled "Summer Deep." Another time, I was ascribing unworthy motives to a friend who had disappointed me and I distinctly heard—from the song "God Is a Real Estate Developer" by Michelle Shocked—the line "I say it's all speculation."

It seems odd how I do not consciously control what words I hear in my head most of the time. I have noticed that if I hear news reports on the radio or TV, or even if I just glance through a newspaper, my mind picks up the nonstop verbiage about whatever the latest headlines are, be they elections, murders, or football games. Exposure to mass media creates, for me, a kind of "internal chatterbox" which goes on incessantly about the issues of the day in clipped jargonistic phrases and hackneyed, unimaginative—yet emotionally charged—language.

This points to one reason why poetry may be important for some of us. Whatever poetry is, it is not chatter, nor does it induce chatter in the mind. Poetry, to a certain extent, stills and focuses the mind; it lets in air. It opens the windows. It flushes out the chatter. It is a fresh breeze, a new light. Poetry introduces unique, often exotic textures into our lives.

At its best, poetry can open our minds, our senses, our imaginations, and even our hearts. What could be more important than this?

One More Poem

It is only fitting to end with one last poem. But what should it be?

Sometimes it's nice to come home to a nice, grounded poem. While the following poem by Gary Snyder leaves us, at the end, looking out from a high tower, it nonetheless speaks matter-of-factly of sunlight in the voices of nature.

And if we are metaphorically inclined, we might also consider the light of wisdom, or the light of imagination, or even the light of poetry itself, to be as particles of that larger light. That would be up to us.

The Uses of Light

by Gary Snyder

It warms my bones
      say the stones

I take it into me and grow
Say the trees
Leaves above   5
Roots below

A vast vague white
Draws me out of the night
Says the moth in his flight—

Some things I smell   10
Some things I hear
And I see things move
Says the deer—

A high tower
on a wide plain.   15
If you climb up
One floor
You'll see a thousand miles more.

Glossary

Abstract | Denoting ideas or things that cannot be seen, touched, or perceived by any of the five senses.

Alliteration | The repetition of a consonant sound in a line or verse of poetry.

Allusion | A reference, within a poem, to something that exists outside the poem, such as a famous person, an historical event, or another work of literature.

Anapest | A metrical foot of three syllables, stressing the final syllable only.

Approximate rhyme | *See* **Slant rhyme.**

Archetype | An image or idea that has been imprinted in the human race's unconsciousness, which carries profound emotional charges and associations.

Assonance | The repetition of a vowel sound within a line or verse of poetry.

Ballad | A poem that tells a story of events, usually historical events, that are not personal to the narrator of the poem.

Blank verse | Poetic verse in unrhymed iambic pentameter.

Concrete | Denoting beings or things that can be seen, touched, or otherwise apprehended by one of the senses.

Connotation | The *associative* meanings that a word *points to* beyond its simple dictionary definition.

Dactyl | A metrical foot of three syllables, stressing the first syllable only.

Denotation | The dictionary definition of a word.

Enjambment | When a sentence within a poem runs from line to line.

Foot | A discrete metrical unit of syllables within a line of poetry.

Free verse | Poetry which disregards fixed conventions of rhyme or meter, but usually approximates rhythms of natural speech.

Haiku | A three-line poem of seventeen syllables, with five syllables in the first line, seven in the second line, and five in the third line. Haiku originated in Japan. Not all haiku translated into English retains its strict syllabic structure.

Hyperbole | An extravagant overstatement.

Iambic meter | A meter in which one stressed syllable follows each unstressed syllable.

Iambic pentameter | Verse constructed in iambic meter, with five metrical feet per line.

Image | A descriptive representation of a sensory impression, such as a sight, sound, smell, taste, or touch.

Internal rhyme | Rhyming within a single line of poetry.

Medicine Wheel | A Native American term that conceives of the world, and all that the world contains, as a great mirror.

Metaphor | A comparison between two dissimilar things that does not employ the words *like* or *as*.

Meter | The formal structure of a line of poetry, in terms of stressed and unstressed syllables.

Metonymy | The technique of referring to a person or thing in terms of something associated with that person or thing.

Motif | A repeating image, word, or phrase within a poem, which comes to represent a *theme* or idea.

Narrator | The speaker, or voice, in a poem.

Onomatopoeia | A word, such as *pop* or *thump*, that sounds like what it means.

Paradox | Something that is apparently self-contradictory, yet possesses some quality of sense or truth.

Parallel structure | A technique of casting similar grammatical units in a series, such that they appear all together or at regular intervals.

Personification | The technique of ascribing human qualities, traits, or capabilities to a nonhuman animal or object; or ascribing *living* qualities to abstractions or inanimate things.

Quatrain | A rhyming four-line stanza.

Rhyme | A succession of words that end in identical or highly similar vowel-consonant combinations/sounds.

Rhyme scheme | The pattern of rhyming lines in a poem, as represented by a series of letters.

Rhythm | The musical mood or beat in a line of poetry, as defined by the meter, speed, and sound of the syllables.

Sestina | A poem of thirty-nine lines in which six six-line stanzas repeat, in a systematic order, the words concluding each of the lines in the first stanza. The final three-line stanza uses the six repeating words two to a line.

Simile | A comparison between two dissimilar things using the word *like* or the word *as*.

Slant rhyme | A rhyme that is inexact; the rhyming syllables are similar but not identical.

Sonnet | A rhyming poem of fourteen lines, in iambic pentameter. The **Italian,** or **Petrarchan,** sonnet has a rhyme scheme of *abba / abba / cdc / cdc* or *abba / abba / cde / cde.* The **English,** or **Shakespearean,** sonnet has a rhyme scheme of *abab / cdcd / efef / gg.*

Spondee | A metrical foot of two stressed syllables.

Symbol | An object, word, image, or action that represents an ambiguous number of ideas and items beyond itself.

Synecdoche | The technique of referring to a thing or person in terms of one part of that thing or person. Or, conversely, referring to a thing or person in terms of something more inclusive of which the thing or person is a part or a member.

Synesthesia | The technique of interpreting one kind of sense data in terms of a different sense. For example, "a loud smell."

Theme | A unifying idea or concept.

Tone | The attitude conveyed by the voice of the narrator in a poem.

Trochee | A metrical foot of two syllables in which a stressed syllable is followed by an unstressed syllable; the reverse of iambic meter.

Zen | A centuries-old spiritual tradition that employs irrationality as a means of breaking down conceptual barriers to enlightenment.

ACKNOWLEDGMENTS

The author says "Thank you" to the following people for inspiration, encouragement, and advice:

Judy Brock, Darryl Purpose, Erica Wolfsong & Barry Green, Cynthia Walker, Gwen Gilliland, Ellen Hertzmann, Sandra Niemann, Kathleen Hallam, Jennifer Lowood, Vista College PACE students, Karynn Fish, Brenda & Dan Cohen-Peltier, David Baumgarten, Ira and Ronnie Polonsky, Kim Voigt, Patrick Miller & Laurie Fox, Paul Otteson and Mary Hageman, the GPMFGND family, Marisa L. L'Heureux, and, last but not least, my astute and supportive editor Lisa A. De Mol.

Literary Credits

Angelou, Maya. "Caged Bird" from *Shaker, Why Don't You Sing?* by Maya Angelou. Copyright © 1983 by Maya Angelou. Reprinted by permission of Random House, Inc. "Sounds Like Pearls" and "When I Think About Myself" from *Just Give Me A Cool Drink Of Water 'Fore I Die* by Maya Angelou. Copyright

© 1971 by Maya Angelou. Reprinted by permission of Random House, Inc.

Arp, Jean. "The Violins Sing in Their Baconfat Bed" by Jean Arp, from *Arp on Arp: Poems, Essays, Memories* by Marcel Jean (editor), translated by Joachim Neugroschell, translation copyright © 1969, 1972 by The Viking Press, Inc. Used by permission of Viking Penguin, a division of Penguin Books USA Inc.

Atwood, Margaret. "Variation On the Word 'Sleep' " from *Selected Poems II: Poems Selected and New 1976–1986* by Margaret Atwood. Copyright © 1987 by Margaret Atwood. Reprinted by permission of Houghton Mifflin Company. All rights reserved. Also from *Selected Poems 1966–1984.* Copyright © Margaret Atwood 1990. Reprinted by permission of Oxford University Press Canada.

Baca, Jimmy Santiago. Section XVII from "Meditations on the South Valley" by Jimmy Santiago Baca, from *Martin and Meditations on the South Valley.* Copyright © 1987 by Jimmy Santiago Baca. Reprinted by permission of New Directions Publishing Corp.

Baraka, Imamu Amiri. "Ka'Ba" by Amiri Baraka from *Black Magic Poetry.* Reprinted by permission of Sterling Lord Literistic, Inc. Copyright © 1969 by Amiri Baraka.

Bishop, Elizabeth. "In The Waiting Room," "Sestina," "The Fish," and excerpt from "Sandpiper" from *The Collected Poems 1927–1979* by Elizabeth Bishop. Copyright © 1979, 1983 by Alice Helen Methfessel. Reprinted by permission of Farrar, Straus & Giroux, Inc.

Blockcolski, Lewis. "My Dream" by Lewis Blockcolski. Reprinted by permission of the author.

Bock, Jerry and Sheldon Harnick. Lyric excerpts of "Sunrise, Sunset" by Sheldon Harnick and Jerry Bock. Copyright © 1964 Alley Music Corp. and Trio Music Co., Inc. Copyright renewed and assigned to Mayerling Productions Ltd. and Jerry Bock Enterprises for the United States and to Alley Music Corp., Trio Music Co., Inc. and Jerry Bock Enterprises for the world outside the United States. International Copyright Secured. Used by permission. All rights reserved.

Brooks, Gwendolyn. "The Bean Eaters" and "The Sonnet-Ballad" by Gwendolyn Brooks. Published in *Blacks* by Gwendolyn Brooks. © 1991 by Gwendolyn Brooks. Publisher, Third World Press, Chicago. Reprinted by permission of the author.

Chih, Ts'ai. Trans. by George W. Kent. "Enjoying the Rain" by Ts'ai Chih from *Worlds of Dust and Jade: 47 Poems and Ballads of the Third Century Chinese Poet Ts'ai Chih,* translated by George W. Kent, 1969. Reprinted by permission of the Philosophical Library, New York.

Cockburn, Bruce. "The Gift" words and music by Bruce Cockburn. © 1988 Golden Mountain Music Corp. Taken from the True North album *Big Circumstance.* Used by permission. "January In The Halifax Airport Lounge" words and music by Bruce Cockburn. © 1977 Golden Mountain Music Corp. Taken from the True North album *Joy Will Find a Way.* Used by permission.

cummings, e. e. "anyone lived in a pretty how town," "i carry your heart with me (i carry it in," "if there are any heavens my mother will (all by herself) have," "nor women/(just as it be," and excerpt from "O sweet spontaneous" from *Complete Poems: 1904–1962* by e. e. cummings, edited by George J. Firmage. Copyright 1923,1925, 1926, 1931, 1935, 1938, 1939, 1940, 1944, 1945, 1946, 1947, 1948, 1949, 1950, 1951, 1952, 1953, 1954, © 1955, 1956, 1957, 1958, 1959, 1960, 1961, 1962, 1963, 1966, 1967, 1968, 1972, 1973, 1974, 1975, 1976, 1977, 1978, 1979, 1980, 1981, 1982, 1983, 1984, 1985, 1986, 1987, 1988, 1989, 1990, 1991 by the Trustees for the E. E. Cummings Trust. Copyright © 1973, 1976, 1978, 1979, 1981, 1983, 1985, 1991 by George James Firmage. Reprinted by permission of Liveright Publishing Corporation.

Deelane, Kristin. From *In The Garden* by Adam and Kris. Copyright © 1993 by Kristin Deelane, If You Want It Done Right Records. Reprinted by permission.

Dove, Rita. "November for Beginners" from Rita Dove, *Museum,* Carnegie-Mellon University Press. Copyright © 1983 by Rita Dove. Used by permission of the author. "The Wake" and "Your

Death" from *Grace Notes* by Rita Dove. Copyright © 1989 by Rita Dove. Reprinted by permission of the author and W.W. Norton & Company, Inc.

Durem, Roy. "I Know I'm Not Sufficiently Obscure" by Roy Durem.

Fearing, Kenneth. "Any Man's Advice to His Son" from *Complete Poems of Kenneth Fearing* by Kenneth Fearing. © 1994 The National Poetry Foundation, University of Maine, Orono, Maine 04469. Reprinted by permission.

Fish, Karynn. "Coda for Job" and "The Turtlewoman Mystery" by Karynn Fish. Reprinted by permission of the author.

Frost, Robert. "Acquainted with the Night" and "Stopping by Woods on a Snowy Evening" from *The Poetry of Robert Frost,* edited by Edward Connery Lathem. Copyright 1936, 1942, 1951, © 1956 by Robert Frost. © 1964, 1970 by Leslie Frost Ballantine. Copyright 1923, 1928, © 1969 by Henry Holt & Co., Inc. Reprinted by permission of Henry Holt & Co., Inc. "The Investment" by Robert Frost from *The Poetry of Robert Frost,* edited by Edward Connery Lathem. Copyright 1956, 1951, 1958 by Robert Frost. © 1967 by Leslie Frost Ballantine, copyright 1923, 1928, 1930, 1939, © 1969 by Henry Holt & Co., Inc. Reprinted by permission of Henry Holt & Co., Inc.

Graves, Joules. "Sorrow" by Joules Graves. Reprinted by permission of the author.

Graves, Robert. "The Spoils" from *The Collected Poems of Robert Graves* by Robert Graves. Copyright © 1958 by Robert Graves. Used by permission of Oxford University Press, Inc.

Greenfield, Eloise. "Harriet Tubman" from *Honey, I Love* by Eloise Greenfield. Text copyright © 1978 by Eloise Greenfield. Used by permission of HarperCollins Publishers.

Harjo, Patty. "Wishes" and "The Mask" by Ya-Ka-Nes (Patty L. Harjo).

Hecht, Anthony and John Hollander. "Nominalism" by Anthony Hecht. Reprinted with the permission of Scribner, a divison of Simon & Schuster from *Jiggery-Pokery* by Anthony E. Hecht and

John Hollander. Copyright © 1966 by Anthony Hecht and John Hollander.

Henson, Lance. "Flock" by Lance Henson. Reprinted by permission of the author.

Hernandez, Miguel. Trans. by John A. Crow. "Death All Riddled with Holes" by Miguel Hernandez. From *An Anthology of Spanish Poetry: From the Beginnings to the Present Day, including both Spain and Spanish America,* compiled and edited by John A. Crow. Copyright © 1979 by Louisiana State University Press. Used with permission.

Heron, Michael. *Puppies* by Mike Heron © 1969 Warner-Tamerlane Publishing Corp. All Rights Reserved. Used by Permission. Warner Bros. Publications U.S. Inc., Miami, FL 33014.

Hogan, Linda. "Geraniums" is from *Savings* by Linda Hogan, Coffee House Press, 1988. Copyright © 1988 by Linda Hogan. Reprinted with permission of the publisher.

Hughes, Langston. "Dream Variations" and "My People" by Langston Hughes. From *Selected Poems* by Langston Hughes. Copyright 1926 by Alfred A. Knopf, Inc. and renewed 1954 by Langston Hughes. Reprinted by permission of the publisher.

Joseph, Jenny. "Warning" by Jenny Joseph from *Selected Poems* published by Bloodaxe Books Ltd. Copyright © Jenny Joseph, 1992. Reprinted by permission.

Lee, Li-Young. "Early in the Morning," "Eating Together," and "The Gift," copyright © 1986 by Li-Young Lee. Reprinted from *Rose,* by Li-Young Lee with the permission of BOA Editions Ltd.

Lim, Genny. "Departure" by Genny Lim. © Genny Lim. Reprinted by permission of the author.

Lorca, Frederico Garcia. Trans. by W. S. Merwin. "Song of the Barren Orange Tree" by Frederico Garcia Lorca, translated by W.S. Merwin, from *Selected Poems of Federico Garcia Lorca.* Copyright © 1955 by New Directions Publishing Corp. Reprinted by permission of New Directions Publishing Corp.

Lorde, Audre. "Black Mother Woman" from *From a Land Where Other People Live* by Audre Lorde. Reprinted by permission of Broadside Press.

Machado, Antonio. Trans. By Willis Barnstone. Reprinted with permission from *The Dream Below the Sun: Selected Poems of Antonio Machado,* "Summer Night," p. 55 translated by Willis Barnstone, © 1981. Published by The Crossing Press: Freedom, CA. Trans. by Robert Bly. "In Our Souls Everything" by Antonio Machado from *Times Alone: Selected Poems of Antonio Machado* translated by Robert Bly. © 1983 Wesleyan University Press with University Press of New England.

MacLeish, Archibald. Excerpt from "Ars Poetica," *Collected Poems 1917–1982* by Archibald MacLeish. Copyright © 1985 by The Estate of Archibald MacLeish. Reprinted by permission of Houghton Mifflin Company. All rights reserved.

Mar, Laureen. "The Window Frames the Moon" by Laureen Mar. Copyright © 1982 by Laureen Mar. Reprinted by permission of the author.

McDonald, Wm. G. "Zen and the Art of Peanut Butter" by Wm. G. McDonald originally appeared in *The Sun,* Issue 93, August, 1983. Reprinted by permission of the author.

McGough, Roger. From "What You Are" by Roger McGough, from *The Mersey Sound: Penguin Modern Poets 10* by Adrian Henri, Roger McGough and Brian Patten. Reprinted by permission of The Peters Fraser and Dunlop Group Limited on behalf of Roger McGough. Copyright © Penguin Books Ltd, 1967.

Millay, Edna St. Vincent. Excerpt from "Passer Mortuus Est" by Edna St. Vincent Millay. From *Collected Poems,* HarperCollins. Copyright 1921, 1948 by Edna St. Vincent Millay. Reprinted by permission.

Neruda, Pablo. Trans. by Allistair Reid. "Galloping in the South" from *Extravagaria* by Pablo Neruda, translated by Alastair Reid. Reprinted by permission of Farrar, Straus & Giroux, Inc. Trans. by Margaret S. Peden. "Ode to Tomatoes" from *Selected Odes of Pablo Neruda* by Pablo Neruda, translated by Margaret S.

Peden, 1990. Reprinted by permission of the University of California Press and the author.

Patchen, Kenneth. "The Snow Is Deep On the Ground" by Kenneth Patchen from *The Love Poems of Kenneth Patchen.*

Plath, Sylvia. "Tulips" and excerpt from "Daddy" from *Ariel* by Sylvia Plath. Copyright © 1962 by Ted Hughes. Copyright renewed. Reprinted by permission of HarperCollins Publishers, Inc. and Faber and Faber Ltd.

Po, Li. Trans. by Rewi Alley: "Looking for a Monk and Not Finding Him" by Li Po from *Li Pai: 200 Selected Poems* by Li Po translated by Rewi Alley, 1980. Trans. by Sam Hamill: "Zazen on the Mountain" by Li Po. From *Midnight Flute: Chinese Poems of Love And Longing* translated by Sam Hamill, © 1994. Reprinted by arrangement with Shambhala Publications, Inc. 300 Massachusetts Ave., Boston MA 02115.

Prevert, Jacques. "Autumn" by Jacques Prevert. Translation © copyright 1958 by Lawrence Ferlinghetti. Reprinted by permission of City Lights Books.

Reed, Ishmael. "Beware: Do Not Read This Poem" by Ishmael Reed. © 1988 by Ishmael Reed from *New and Collected Poems* (Atheneum) Reprinted by permission.

Roethke, Theodore. "The Premonition" copyright 1941 by Theodore Roethke. "The Waking" copyright 1953 by Theodore Roethke. From *The Collected Poems of Theodore Roethke* by Theodore Roethke. Used by permission of Doubleday, a division of Bantam Doubleday Dell Publishing Group, Inc.

Shocked, Michelle. "God Is a Real Estate Developer" by Michelle Schocked and Matthew Fox. © 1989 Cooking Vinyl Ltd. (PRS) all rights on behalf of Cooking Vinyl Ltd. administered by BMG Music Publishing Ltd. (PRS) all rights for the U.S. on behalf of BMG Music Publishing Ltd. Controlled by BMG Songs Inc. (ASCAP). Reprinted by permission.

Silko, Leslie Marmon. "Alaskan Mountain Poem #1" by Leslie Marmon Silko. "Where Mountain Lion Lay Down with Deer" by Leslie Marmon Silko.

Snyder, Gary. "As for Poets" and "The Uses of Light" from *Turtle Island* by Gary Snyder.

Soto, Gary. "Old House in my Fortieth Year" and "Oranges" by Gary Soto. © 1995 from *New and Selected Poems,* published by Chronicle Books, San Francisco. Reprinted by permission of the publisher.

Swenson, May. Reprinted with the permission of Simon & Schuster Books for Young Readers, an imprint of Simon & Schuster Children's Publishing Division from *The Complete Poems to Solve* by May Swenson. Copyright © 1993 The Literary Estate of May Swenson.

Vinograd, Julia. "Sparechangers" by Julia Vinograd from *Cannibal Carnival 1986–1996,* Zeitgeist Press, 1996. Reprinted by permission of the publisher.

Williams, William Carlos. "The Young Housewife" and "The Last Words of My English Grandmother" by William Carlos Williams, from *Collected Poems, 1909–1939, Volume I.* Copyright © 1938 by New Directions Publishing Corp. Reprinted by permission of New Directions Publishing Corp.

Williamson, Robin. From "Darling Belle" by Robin Williamson. Copyright © 1972 Warlock Music Ltd. (BMI) All rights for North & South America controlled and administered by Pubco. Lyrics used by permission of Rykomusic. All rights reserved.

The publisher has made every effort to contact copyright holders. Any omissions or errors will be corrected upon written notification.

INDEX

THE POETRY READER'S TOOLKIT

*A Guide to Reading
and Understanding Poetry*

MARC POLONSKY

NTC Publishing Group
a division of NTC/CONTEMPORARY PUBLISHING COMPANY
Lincolnwood, Illinois USA

Contents

FOREWORD

The Poetry Reader's Toolkit is designed to be used in a flexible, intuitive manner by teachers and students alike. The Writing Workshop and Discussion Workshop exercises should be considered menus of possible activities. It is up to your discretion to assign these or other exercises. One approach would be to tell students that they have a choice as to which exercises they will complete, so long as they do a given number.

Similarly, everything in this Instructor's Manual should be regarded as suggestion, never prescription. Consider this a resource book, a muse for teaching. It is expected that teachers will adapt *The Poetry Reader's Toolkit* to their own styles and priorities. With this in mind, what follows is a series of general recommendations.

It is a good idea to read the poems aloud, or to have students read them aloud, at least one time, if they are subject to class discussion.

Throughout the book, there are various assignments that involve students finding poems on their own. Sometimes, these poems will be shared in the context of class discussion. If your class is using a literature or poetry anthology in addition to the *Toolkit*, encourage students to draw their findings from that text (or from the *Toolkit* itself), so that the entire class can read along. But if the students find poems elsewhere, ask them to bring photocopies along to class if they would like to share what they've found. You may also want to photocopy one or two additional poems now and again, to illustrate a section's theme.

Do not allow a small clique of students to dominate class discussion week after week, no matter how intelligent these students are, or how reticent the rest of the class seems. If necessary, benignly force quiet students to participate by calling on them or asking them for their views, whether or not their hands are raised. The central point of *The Poetry Reader's Toolkit* is that poetry is essentially democratic; it does *not* take great sophistication or erudition to apprehend poems and to delight in them. All that is required is the ability to be patient and present with oneself and one's perceptions.

Many of the exercises in *The Poetry Reader's Toolkit* are geared to small-group discussion or dyads. You could ask students early on to choose discussion partners for the entire term, students with whom they might develop a "poetic rapport," or you might choose to let discussion groupings be different for each exercise.

Some of the written-work exercises in the text ask for "a journal entry." In a sense, a "journal" is more a frame of mind than a specific format. A journal is typically the place wherein thoughtful people record their reflections and musings, and so to call these exercises "journal entries," as opposed to, say, "homework," carries a different, hopefully more inviting, connotation. You may want to encourage or even require your students to keep an actual journal of their responses to poems. This may ultimately be of more value to them than a series of disconnected pieces of paper.

Emphasize every so often that it is not necessary for your students, as readers, to feel something special about every poem. The exercises in this book are calculated to make students give an appropriate measure of attention to poems, and to induce students to examine their perceptions. Students will often have surprising insights. This instructor's manual details some possible responses to the exercises, but by no means are these "answers" definitive or exhaustive.

Now and again, when students speak about poems, they will not answer the specific questions posed in the Writing or Discussion Workshop exercises, but instead will write or talk generally about why they like a poem or why they chose it. Sometimes, especially early in the curriculum, this is perfectly fine and acceptable. Generally speaking, however, over time, writing and conversation should become more focused, sharp, purposeful, and exciting.

At any given time, make sure that the class—and the speaker of the moment—is clear about what is being talked about. They shouldn't, for example, confuse a general assessment of a poem with the answer to a specific question such as, "How would you characterize the poem's speaker's voice?" It's acceptable to deviate from a stated purpose in these discussions, so long as that deviation is made explicit. As the teacher, this clarification will be your task.

Because so much about poetry will strike many students as *unclear,* at least initially, it is important that the discussions *about* poetry take place in an extremely well-defined context. If the students do not feel lost in the discussion, chances are that they will gain a sense of confidence that they need not feel lost within the poems either. Keep bearings clear. Make distinctions in subject matter obvious. If the subject has changed and people are no longer responding to the question at hand, it's fine to let conversation flow in a different direction for a little while, but make sure that everyone understands explicitly that the discussion has shifted course.

Most discussions can probably continue for as long as you see fit. There are always more images to examine, more symbols to analyze, and so forth. It is important not to let the class get bogged down in a mire of impressionistic exposition which will bore many students. If the discussion becomes too "far out," you may need to ground it, to reintroduce structure and coherence, perhaps by asking a well-calculated question at a strategic moment, or by summing up and synthesizing students' ideas.

Periodically, allow students to share poems that they find (per the assignments in the book) as well as their impressions and feelings about these poems. Allow some general class discussion about the poems unearthed by individual students.

Also, have a "report back" period after each small-group discussion, so that the groups may share their findings with the whole class.

You might ask, whenever it seems appropriate, What kinds of things can happen only in poems? Is there anything that poems can do that plays, stories, and songs cannot do?

The attitude to inculcate throughout the curriculum is that reading poetry is more a process of *discovery* than one of trying to understand.

WHY POETRY?

1

Suggestions for Teaching

The object of this chapter is to break the ice, to talk a little about poetry and what poetry means to students. Other objectives are to ease the fear of poetry and to set a comfortable class tone. Class discussion could be a good time to "air out" people's feelings and expectations on the subject. The best result would be an atmosphere of curiosity, a sense that the class is about to embark on an adventure of discovery.

Ask: Why is poetry important, or unimportant, in our lives? What constitutes *importance?* Why do people read poetry? How is it different from reading other kinds of literature, such as fiction or drama? What do people look for when they read a poem, as opposed to what they look for in a story? What expectations do people have of this class? What do they imagine they might gain from it? What are their concerns? Their fondest hopes? (You might express the conviction that their experience will largely depend on their attitudes and approaches, and that, therefore, their fondest hopes will probably come true.) Can anyone recall previous experiences with poetry, positive or negative, that made lasting impressions?

Discuss patience as a neglected virtue. What are the rewards of patience? Why do we get impatient? How do we become conditioned to expect instant gratification all the time? Do the best things always come right away?

Brainstorm reasons why we need to revisit poems, using this chapter's poems as examples. We come back to movies and novels to deepen our enjoyment and knowledge of these works; poems are comparatively easy to revisit, much like songs. Poems are often complex, multilayered, and rewarding to get to know. Our feeling about a poem deepens when we come back to it. Our perspective changes from reading to reading. Sometimes a poem, like a person, changes. Discuss how some of the poems they've already read, in this class or elsewhere, have changed.

Concerning the poems in this chapter, ask what people *noticed*. Did they notice an image, a rhythm, a rhyme? What kinds of *specific* things do they notice in these poems that are different from what they'd find in other forms of literature? Examples might include numbered stanzas, rhyme, unexpected line breaks, skewed syntax, lack of discursive explanation, and lack of narrative. Acknowledge these examples as they come: "Yes, that's there. No doubt about it." Then encourage some speculation as to what these odd features are *doing* there, what their effect is as we read, as well as how they direct our attention and alter our perception.

Allow some discussion of people's overall feelings about or "interpretations" of poems. These kinds of comments may be interspersed in the above discussion, but make sure that the class—including the speaker of the moment—is clearly aware that the subject is changed for the time being. This sort of gestalt apprehension/speculation is different from simply observing details and noticing one's reactions as one reads. Don't make this change of topic a "bad" thing; just point out that these are two distinctly different ways of coming to a poem, and that both are certainly quite useful and interesting.

Allow some time for students—in dyads or small groups—to compare responses to the Discussion Workshop exercises and to try to answer each other's outstanding questions. Then have a debriefing session wherein small groups report to the class about their discussions, their differing and similar perceptions about the poems, their tentative answers to each other's questions, and any as-yet unanswered questions. Let the entire class, as one large group, address any particularly provocative questions.

Perhaps not everyone will have a chance to give their report. This is acceptable because not everyone will necessarily want to share with the class.

Assume there will be some amorphous discussion of thoughts, feelings, and associations inspired by the poems. Allow it. At this point, it is fine not to focus too rigorously on the details of how poems work. Let the conversation stay relatively light, free-flowing, and impressionistic. Don't demand too much. This is just "first practice."

If class members have already had time to find other poems of interest, allow some of them to share the poems they have discovered, along with their impressions of and questions about these poems.

DISCUSSION WORKSHOP

Devising a Question (page 6)

In response to the poem "Wishes" by Ya-Ka-Nes, an observant student might question why the rainbow is blue, because by definition rainbows have more than one color. Perhaps this rainbow has different shades of blue, however, and a blue rainbow would, after all, stand out brilliantly and dramatically against an "ivory" sky. This poem is about a "Happiness bird." Is blue a happy color? Why or why not?

"What is a rainy day mountain?" someone might ask. A mountain is a mountain, rain or shine, is it not? You might point out that weather is a most ambiguous quantity in this poem, what with blue rainbows in a cloudless, yet white, sky. Perhaps the rainy day mountain signifies the mountain that the bird flies over on a rainy day. Or maybe it is a mountain on which life thrives most visibly in the rain. Or perhaps the writer is merely invoking an image here—an image of a mountain, seen from above, in the rain.

No doubt someone will ask what the "Happiness bird" is. It is possible that someone might equate the "Happiness bird" with the dove which flew forth from Noah's Ark in the Bible. "Happiness bird" can mean many things. It can be a literal bird, or perhaps it can represent the spirit or soul of the speaker or even a kind of deity. You might point out that the writer of this poem is a Laguna Pueblo Indian, and that Native Americans, in their legends and lore, ascribe profound and complex character qualities to many animals.

WRITING WORKSHOP

Developing Patience (page 9)

Students may be somewhat perplexed by "The Waking," which is not a simple poem to understand. Nonetheless, they may perceive the narrator as humble, perhaps religious ("God bless the Ground!"), uncertain but unafraid. They may question what is meant by "I hear my being dance from ear to ear." This could refer to the speaker's brain or to the voice he hears inside his mind when he talks to himself. Students may ask about "Light takes the Tree" and also about the relevance of "The lowly worm climbs up a winding stair." "Light takes the Tree" could be a comment about death and how little we understand the how and why of it. "Light" here might be short for lightning. As for the "lowly worm," this could be a metaphor for progress which is made slowly but steadily, with the end never in sight until it is reached. "This shaking keeps me steady" is a paradoxical statement that may intrigue some students and confuse others. One possible explanation is that, even while one is insecure and disoriented in life, the very response to that insecurity, the "shaking," the groping for direction and stability, is what ultimately keeps one on track.

Students may be puzzled by the refrain "I wake to sleep, and take my waking slow." One "interpretation" of this is that waking life, as we know it, is also a kind of sleep, a state of unknowing. Even when we wake up each day, there is a great deal that we are unaware of, that we do not understand, including the big questions: What are we doing here? Where did we come from? Where are we going? What is the meaning of life? Why are we here? So, in this sense, we wake up each day to merely a different kind of *sleep*.

Students will feel more confident in apprehending the voice and significance of "Ka 'Ba." Even if they have not heard of the author before, they should be able to gather that this is an African-American man addressing his people. Questions may revolve around the relative literal or nonliteral meanings of his words. What are the "grey chains"? Is he talking seriously about "magic," "spells," and "sacred words"? "Grey chains," of course, is almost undoubtedly figurative, representing poverty, oppression, and minority status in a racist society. It may also represent a "ghost" of the literal chains of slavery that continue to haunt African Americans in the United States. The "magic," "spells," and "sacred words" could be taken literally, or they could be figurative, or even both. Clearly this poet wants his people to collectively find will, strength, and self-knowledge. All of these are great inner resources that may require mysterious and unfathomable catalytic forces to be awakened.

Still More Patience (page 12)

There will undoubtedly be many questions regarding the curious structure of the cummings poem. In this discussion, it may be advisable to read the poem aloud as a series of complete, or nearly complete, sentences. There are two words missing in this poem, both after the word "my." In the first case the missing word might be *mother;* in the second it might be *wife.* Perhaps the students can speculate as to why the writer purposely omitted these words. (In Chapter 7, the section on understatement discusses the missing words in this poem.) Also, even if we set aside the words in parentheses, there is one particularly long and difficult sentence in this poem: "My father will be standing near my [mother] with eyes which are really petals and see nothing with the face of a poet really which is a flower and not a face with hands which whisper. . . ." Here cummings is casting his father as a flower, with petals for eyes, blind but still sensing the presence of his beloved as a flower senses the sun. He is playing with imagery here, superimposing human on flower on human on flower on human: "eyes," "petals," "face of a poet," "a flower and not a face," and "hands." The "hands" here may be seen as the small leaves that sometimes grow on the stems of roses, and which may wave in the wind expressively, like hands. Once this has been carefully examined, students might be asked how they feel about this blending of images.

Alert students should see immediately that the speaker in the García Lorca poem is in fact the orange tree, as the title indicates. The more alert students might realize that "Cut my shadow from me" is a request by the tree to be felled. Questions may revolve around the metaphorical statements in the second stanza. What "mirrors" are being referred to? What does it mean to say that the day "walks in circles" and that the night "copies" the tree in its stars? The mirrors, of course, are the day and the night themselves, against which the tree perceives the forlorn fact of its own existence. The "circles" are the cycles of ascending and descending sunlight from east to west. The "copies" in the stars indicate that, even at night (when the tree could be resting), the stars remind the tree that it too is a single point of light, or life. This sad and beautiful poem can be read literally or symbolically. The barren orange tree could stand for any life that is barren of the meaning and purpose it requires.

DISCUSSION WORKSHOP

Sharing Perceptions (page 15)

Discussions will vary.

WRITING WORKSHOP

Unearthing More Poems (page 16)

Responses will vary.

EMOTIONS

Suggestions for Teaching

The object of this chapter is to increase interest in poetry by demonstrating how various words trigger emotions. In general, people tend to take words for granted, forgetting how marvelous words are and how much power they contain. At this point in the curriculum, students should be aware that words and language *live*. Once they are interested in words, it should be a relatively easy step to get them interested in poetry, which is the art form that employs the power of words far more deliberately than any other.

Ask if anyone can think of or remember particular words in conversation which have affected them emotionally. Note that there are certain words which exist for the sole purpose of stimulating emotion, words such as *darling* and *sweetheart*, as well as, on the other hand, various denigrating terms. Be sure to call attention to the fact that emotional triggers are also often couched in more "ordinary" words, where we least expect them.

The Power of Words. Have the students close their eyes and simply note the feelings that arise as you say certain words. Perhaps start with the word *danger.* Say it clearly once, then wait a few moments and say it again. Let them sit with it for fifteen seconds or so. Then say a positive word such as *love* or *joy* or *friends.* Let them sit with that one for several seconds too. Have them open their eyes while you take brief comments from several class members as to how they responded inside, emotionally, to the words.

Then ask them to close their eyes again and repeat the process with more concrete or descriptive words, such as *crimson, detour, languish,* or *eucalyptus.* Then have them talk about their emotional responses, if any, to these words. Some students may say that, upon hearing any particular word, images come to mind. Point out that these images, in addition to any other feelings or associations that arise, constitute the word's *connotations* for them.

Explore the connotations of various synonyms. For example, what is the difference between a *smell,* an *odor,* a *scent,* or a *fragrance?* (You can subsequently apply this question to the poem "Departure" by Genny Lim, and the phrase "odor of stale incense.") Or "I want to convince you to . . ." as opposed to "I want to entice you to . . ." or "I want to persuade you to. . . ." Ask the class members for some synonyms and see if they can discern connotative differences between the synonyms that they come up with.

Allow a few individual class members, if they choose, to share one or two of their lists of connotations of particular words from the exercises in the book. Perhaps choose two or three words and let three to five people read aloud their connotations. You might remark on commonalities as well as differences and emphasize that we naturally share a pool of some common connotative associations, but that some connotations will be unique to us as individuals.

This is, in a sense, the last introductory session; up to this point, the curriculum focus has largely been on the students' internal universes, their worlds of inner feelings and imaginings and memories. Implicitly, poetry has been cast primarily as a vehicle for exploring the self. (In one sense, poetry *is* a vehicle for exploring the self, though, of course, that's not all.) This emphasis has been necessary to cultivate the ease and expansive mindset required to delve seriously and meticulously into poetry with patience and genuine interest. Beginning with the next chapter on images, the focus will shift to the poems themselves.

WRITING WORKSHOP

Examining Connotations (page 26)

Many lines in Genny Lim's poem "Departure" are pregnant with connotation. "The fog has lifted" connotes hope of fresh light and new life. "Yawn like a child" recalls the fact that the dying woman was once a child, and that her sister the narrator remembers this in an infinite number of ways. "Chinatown accent" suggests a host of ethnic associations. "Eyes staring out of their sockets like glass" calls to mind the hardness of glass, as well as its vulnerability to shattering. Finally, "3 cc's of morphine / shot through your brain" has horrific connotations of dehumanization, erosion of will and personality, the reduction of a human being to a mere organism that responds to drugs.

DISCUSSION WORKSHOP

Name That Tone (page 31)

The tone of Maya Angelou's "When I Think about Myself" is bitterly ironic, as is evidenced by lines such as "I almost laugh myself to death," "I laugh so hard I almost choke," and "I laugh until I start to crying."

The tone of Jenny Joseph's "Warning" is one of cheerful defiance. This is conveyed in all of her declarations. It is reinforced by the repetition of the affirmative "I shall" in the first stanza and illustrated particularly in phrases such as "gobble up samples," "learn to spit," and "make up for the sobriety of my youth."

WRITING WORKSHOP

The Textures of Emotion (page 33)

Responses will vary.

WRITING WORKSHOP

Connotation Dissection (page 36)

Here is a small example of the kind of list students may come up with:

Fate

- Destiny

- Death

- Chance meetings

- Meeting the love of your life

- Unavoidable

- Chance

- Mistakes

- No way out

- All things under control

- Everything predetermined

- The eyes of fate

- Free will

- No free will

- The nature you're born with

- The body you're born with

- The parents you're born to and your whole family

- Anything that happens

- Life as a series of coincidences

- No accidents

- The hand of God

- Unkind fate

- Merciless

- Useless struggle

- Everything turning out the way it's supposed to

- Master plan

(And so on. Some students' associations may seem much wider than this.)

WRITING WORKSHOP

Unearth a Poem (page 37)

Responses will vary.

WRITING WORKSHOP

Unearth Another Poem (page 37)

Responses will vary.

Share and Tell (page 38)

Responses will vary.

Strike Your Own Tone (page 38)

Responses will vary.

IMAGES

3

Suggestions for Teaching

The object of this chapter is to demonstrate the power of visual images as they are conjured onto the screen of the mind's eye by poems and poetic phrasing. Furthermore, we want to enable students to see how images can embody abstractions, how they inform the character of a poem, and how the content of imagery is at once tactile, emotional, and conceptual.

You might point out how our attention is constantly arrested by visual images on screens, on billboards, and in magazines. Mention that communication experts claim we gather most of our information through visual data, and we form our opinions of people and ideas based primarily on visual impressions.

In contrast to the visual images we see outside of ourselves, how vivid and distinct are the ones we see in our imaginations? How powerful are the ones that are conjured in our minds' eyes—by memories, suggestions, dreams, or poems—as compared to the ones which enter via our retinas? Are these internal images generally more powerful or less powerful than the external ones? Do they activate our emotions to greater or lesser effect?

When we see images in our minds' eyes, what sorts of images do we see? How *often* do we see internal images? All day long or on and off? Just during sleep? Only when reading? You might ask, "How many people have seen any internally-formed images since this discussion began?" You might also invite people to share what they've seen since the discussion began, and this could be interesting in a flashy sort of way, but don't let it go on more than a minute or two. People's fleeting mental imagery should not be confused with deliberately crafted poetic images, which are the ultimate subject of this discussion. The purpose of introducing the topic in this way is simply to illustrate how active and virtually tireless our internal "projectors" are, and how linked these images are to our emotions.

Now and again, direct the class's attention to the *ideas* that are *embodied,* or symbolically expressed, in images. Also, in examining imagery, ask what the *emotional effects* of the images are, what *connotations* the images carry. (This is different from looking for distinct conceptual *ideas* within images.)

WRITING WORKSHOP

A Quick Question (page 42)

With the poem "Autumn" centered and the lines becoming progressively smaller in length, a visual effect of *falling* or *thinning out* is created on the page. Students may have other ideas about this as well.

Prying Open the Images— Looking within and beyond (page 48)

The narrator of "The Window Frames the Moon" seems to feel that the moon is something she must tame and keep in its proper place, so that she may feel that she too has a rightful and unimpeachable place in the scheme of things, a secure home. This is evidenced in lines such as "I push the moon into place / as if it were a vase of flowers" and "when I push the moon, it pushes back / and fills my house, and I am forced to abandon. . . ." Objects in her room include the clock, the dresser, the chink in the wall, and the tablecloth; these objects are fixed and dependable, in contrast to the moon, which is not. These objects, in a sense, root and orient the narrator, providing a temporary sense of security that is upended when the moon grows too large and cannot be contained within the window frame. This poem, of course, can be viewed symbolically, in terms of the forces which subvert our sense of safety and certainty from time to time, and in terms of those objects or touchstones that we look to in our lives (superstitiously, as it were) for some reassurance that we will not be uprooted or disrupted.

It is also worth noting that the moon is an archetype. Among other connotations, the moon is unearthly, *lunatic,* and strange. In folktales, the full moon is a powerful harbinger of werewolves and other supernatural phenomena. You might point out that, in real life, the moon is too far away to *ever* actually *fill* the frame of any normal window. Therefore the moon described by this narrator is quite remarkably imposing—it even has the power, in the final stanza, to push her right out of the house!

Sense Data and Images (page 52)

In "Ode to Tomatoes," "the knife / sinks / into living flesh" is at once visual and tactile, as is the description of the meal itself. "Pepper / adds / its fragrance" and "the aroma / of the roast" are both olfactory images.

Unearth a Poem (page 60)

Responses will vary.

Images and Indentations (page 66)

The first long indentation in Leslie Marmon Silko's "Where Mountain Lion Lay Down with Deer" precedes the word *silently*. This indentation, or space, creates a small silence in the mind of the reader whose eyes are skimming along the lines. The next long indentation comes as a weighted pause, after the words "I descended" and before the words "a thousand years ago," a phrase we should be compelled to weigh the gravity of before moving on. The indentations after "It is better to stay up here" could be seen as illustrating the great distance between the narrator on the mountain above and the yellow flowers below. The final clause at the bottom, beginning with "How I swam away," concerns "tumbling down" and "spilling out," just as the words themselves do on the page.

Moods and Images (page 67)

In "Summer Night" by Anthony Machado, the "deserted square," "black shadows," and "clock's illuminated globe" all may be perceived to have ghostly connotations.

In Li Po's "Looking for a Monk and Not Finding Him," the images of an empty temple and the (ironically) dust-covered hair duster, as well as the sound of the narrator's "empty" sigh, connote gloom and colorlessness, while the image of "light rain" likened to "flowers falling from the sky, making a music of its own" certainly foreshadows the narrator's sense of being "filled with" the beauty of his surroundings in the end. Also, images of the moss-covered gate, the path in the valley, and the bird tracks may suggest a happy appreciation of the natural world. Then again, the moss-covered gate and bird tracks might also call to mind the lack of human presence, deserted places, and sadness.

Contrasting Images (page 69)

In "Eating Together" by Li-Young Lee, the first series of images are vibrant and tactile, occurring at lunchtime in his family home. Then there is, by contrast, the cold, barren, insensate image of an empty snow-covered road winding through old pines. (Some students may feel a deep peacefulness from this image, particularly through the phrases "lay down to sleep" and "lonely for no one.") What connects these two images is the thought of the narrator's father who, we might presume, has recently passed away, and therefore no longer sits at the table with his family, partaking of the life of this ritual-like meal and all its textures.

Constructing Vibrant Imagery (page 70)

Responses will vary.

Stories

4

Suggestions for Teaching

The objectives of this section are to examine how stories are cast in poems, how poetic narratives differ from prose narratives, and to reveal the purpose, the power, and the peculiar charm of stories that are rendered as poems.

One good way to open discussion might be to talk about the importance of stories in general. How important are stories really? Does the class agree that stories are what we are and that, as the *Toolkit* claims, we are constantly making up our own stories as we live? What about the idea that memory is something to be nurtured and maintained? Upon reflection, does this notion match their own experience?

What kinds of things do we remember from, say, early childhood, and what kinds of things do we forget? Why? Do we remember things that are apparently random, isolated incidences and sensations? Or do we remember specific things that fit into particular *stories* that happened to us? Or both?

Can *anything* be made into a "story"? What, if anything, cannot be? What are the criteria? How does something become a *story* as opposed to merely an event or a perception or, for that matter, a thought?

Sometimes a story, a life experience, or a poem contains more than one level of significance, more than one meaning. How do the poems in this section express this inherent ambiguity in the stories they tell? Another concept to emphasize is that of *timing* within the poems—how certain critical perceptions are "set up" by what has come before.

Consider presenting the two inaugural poems "The Gift Outright" by Robert Frost, which was read at President Kennedy's inauguration in 1961, and "On the Pulse of Morning" by Maya Angelou, which was read at President Clinton's inauguration in 1993. Both poems tell the story of the American nation in a particular way. Have the class carefully read and paraphrase these stories with your assistance. Then have them compare the two stories.

When evaluating a poem, or any life experience for that matter, we must work from what we *currently* know, our knowledge and experience to date. Discuss ways that our understanding of life—and our understanding of poems—is deepened and enriched over time by further life experiences. Offer and solicit examples of both kinds of enriched appreciation—appreciation of life events and of poems.

WRITING WORKSHOP

A First Date Story (page 76)

Nearly every line in Gary Soto's "Oranges" recalls some concrete detail about his experience on this day. Among the ones not cited in the text are the dog barking, the tiny bell that rang when they entered the drugstore, the frost cracking beneath his steps, and the rouge on the girl's face. In the store, Gary Soto's narrator realized that he did not have enough money to buy the girl the chocolate she wanted, so he placed a nickel and an orange on the counter. The saleslady understood that he was proffering the orange in lieu of the extra five cents he lacked and that he wanted to buy the chocolate to impress the girl. The saleslady played along with him and didn't comment on the unusual currency of this transaction.

The oranges stand imagistically in contrast to the grey of the day, and the "fire" an orange makes in the narrator's hands could be a reflection of the "fire" of excitement he feels inside, being out with this girl. Oranges also have a sharp tangy flavor, a burst of nourishing sweetness contained within their thick skin, just as this day contains a sharp sweet vitality for the narrator, beneath the surface of its foggy cold exterior.

DISCUSSION WORKSHOP

How the Story's Told (page 89)

In Rita Dove's "Your Death," the day should probably have belonged to the narrator herself and to the new baby inside her. She is angry in a reflexive, irrational way at the man whose passing has made a tragedy and a horror of what should have been a celebratory day. Her irrational resentment might be a temporary defense against an impending tidal wave of grief. Every movement she makes now, even the mundane activity of eating a sandwich, is imbued with incredible pain and thoughts of the one whom she has lost. There is no escaping him; he fills and "owns" everything. Nothing "tastes" or feels the same.

Referring to her menstrual cycle as "lunar clockwork" is a way of perceiving pregnancy as a matter of great fate, something cosmic and inexplicable, the genesis of new life. The image of her womb as an "urn, filling with wine" has connotations of sacred Communion as well as connotations of death. The stepson's headache may have been a premonition that something was wrong; apparently it went away once the news was known.

The tone in "The Wake" is more subdued, more grief-stricken, less angry. Some days have passed and the reality of death has set in. Images of ethereality and emptiness abound: "Your absence distributed itself," "the rooms still gaped," "the green hanger swang empty," "an empty plate," "your warm breath fell over my shoulder," and "trying to cover the silence." This is in marked contrast to the busyness and noise of Bloomingdale's and the "copper skillets," "collapsible baskets," "china," "subway," and "tuna fish sandwich" of "Your Death."

In the last stanza particularly, the narrator's feelings of mute helplessness are illustrated: "I lay down between the sheets / I lay down in the cool waters / of my own womb / and became the child / inside, innocuous. . . ." Here she only yearns to escape the pain of grief; she is no longer in rebellion.

In "The Gift," Li-Young Lee superimposes one incident over another. He recalls vividly how his father was able to soothe his fears and his terror by telling a story and speaking in a low, calm voice as he removed a shard of metal from his young son's palm. The two episodes are different in that the narrator is now an adult, and it is he who is removing the splinter from the thumb of another, his wife. But the episodes are similar in that, in each case, someone is administering a delicate, necessary, and painful operation on a loved one.

Literally speaking, the "gift" probably refers to the shard that the narrator's father removed and then gently placed back on the surface of the son's palm: "a silver tear, a tiny flame." Figuratively, perhaps the gift is that the narrator has learned from his father how to perform such an operation with consummate tenderness, so that it is not frightening or traumatic. Phrases such as "Metal that will bury me" represent what the seven-year-old boy's experience *might* have been like, had his father not been so extraordinarily gentle. Perhaps the gift of tenderness alluded to in this poem is a more general gift as well, one that has many applications in the narrator's life, beyond removing splinters.

WRITING WORKSHOP

What's the Difference? (page 97)

Ballads have in common a certain *distance* from their subject matter, whereas personal-story poems, with their singular detail and point of view, pull the reader into a more *immediate* experience of the story. Also, ballads tend to describe events that take place over a longer period of time, while personal-story poems are generally concentrated on *moments* rather than on months or years. Also, reading a ballad is usually somewhat less demanding than reading a personal-story poem because ballads are very straightforward, whereas personal-story poems tend to be idiosyncratic and even enigmatic in their structure and word choice.

WRITING WORKSHOP

Why This Story? (page 101)

Robert Frost's "The Wood-Pile" is analyzed in more depth and detail in Chapter 6, in the section on symbols. For the purposes of this discussion, it might be sufficient to note that this story does seem to be largely *about* the woodpile, as nearly half of the poem is devoted to a description of it, and the rest is preamble to the narrator's encounter with it. As to why the narrator wants to call our attention to this woodpile, for now you can let the students speculate as they will. Maybe it was simply an unusual thing, a striking image. If this story had been told in prose rather than poetry, details may have been articulated differently, and colorful phrases such as "his little fear," "useful fireplace," and "smokeless burning of decay" might have been absent.

A Mother-Daughter Story (page 103)

The daughter-narrator in "Black Mother Woman" seems to be appreciating her mother in a new light, cast by experience and the perspective of years. She seems grateful, both for her mother's apparent shortcomings and for her deep-seated strengths. In the first lines, she states "I cannot recall you gentle / yet through your heavy love / I have become. . . ." Here she acknowledges that while she may have missed a certain softness and tenderness in her childhood, her mother's love was nonetheless abiding and tangible. "When strangers come and compliment me / your aged spirit takes a bow . . ." indicates her mother's spirit lives inside her now and makes her the best of what she is. "I have peeled away your anger / down to the core of love / and look mother / I Am / a dark temple where your true spirit rises. . . ." These lines seem to indicate that the mother is no longer with the daughter in flesh and blood, but lives inside the daughter in spirit. These words also tell that, although on the surface the narrator's mother may have been beaten and in pain, at her core she was whole and pure and strong, and this is the ultimate legacy she has bequeathed to her daughter. "And if my eyes conceal / a squadron of conflicting rebellions / I learned from you / to define myself / through your denials." Like her mother before her, this daughter will go through the world cloaking her true strength in a posture of resentment and resistance.

Unraveling the Yarn (page 105)

There are a number of ways to read the e. e. cummings "nor woman" poem. Many people assume that the bundle in the poem must be a baby that has been left to die and hence cannot be hurt anymore. Perhaps this baby has been left because there is no one to properly care for it. Then again, the bundle might well be the "he" of the poem himself; it may be his own body he has gratefully left behind. Perhaps this is why the poem begins with "nor woman" and why "nor woman" stands prominently outside the parentheses; perhaps it was a woman who hurt him the most. The poem itself, on the page, vaguely resembles a pregnant belly, but if we turn it sideways it might also resemble a coffin.

Most of the lines, which are oddly broken up, end in vowel sounds (or in *w* or *h*), leaving the reader's mouth ajar, as if in wonderment. This reinforces the ethereal, ghostly mood of the poem. Word fragments such as "be," "o," and "elf" are also somewhat ethereal in connotation. "Hush" spread over four lines (including a blank one) is more ethereal yet, and calls to mind an extended, softly fading utterance of "Shhhhhh. . . ."

The fact that all but the first and final lines end in broken words may indicate that the protagonist's world is also broken and disintegrating into pieces. Also, the broken words "pro / pped" and "can / 't" are paradoxical in that they both carry *affirmative* connotations that are subsequently contradicted.

Unearth a Story (page 107)

Responses will vary.

What's Your Story? (page 108)

Responses will vary.

SOUND

5

Suggestions for Teaching

The purposes of this chapter are to cultivate an awareness of how the sounds of the words in a poem affect the reader's emotional experience; and to make students cognizant of such elements as alliteration, assonance, rhythm, and rhyme, and what these devices *accomplish* in a poem.

General discussion might begin with questions such as these: Is it true or is it not true that we hear sounds in our minds all the time? What is it that we hear when we pay attention to these sounds? How do these internal sounds reflect, or bear on, our moods? Do we hear words as we read them? Is the *voice* we hear speaking them always the same voice, or does it change?

Which sense is more important to us, sight or sound? Why?

In what ways are poems like songs? Possible responses: We can read (or listen to) them over and over. They are often composed of verses. They may linger with us, like a favorite tune.

We can share poems with friends and, like sharing songs, it only takes a matter of minutes. Like listening to music, reading poetry is not an entirely cerebral experience, but a sensual one as well.

In looking at poems, always direct the class's attention to the *connotations* of various sounds. What do they *do?* Don't let anyone simply point out that a slant rhyme, or a lilting rhythm, or a repeated consonant sound is *there*. Ask what it is *doing* there; how does it imbue, or provide subliminal commentary on, the semantic content of the poem? Do the sounds and rhythms reinforce the words? Do they contradict the words in some fashion?

Emphasize that all sound has a distinctive *character*. Identifying poetic sound patterns or devices should never degenerate into a mechanical exercise. You must ask students to use their imaginations and *feel* what the sounds *do* inside of them, what kinds of *atmosphere* the sounds bestow. This is very demanding, but it is good exercise for the imagination, and students should have no fear of being wrong, because no one else can speak for their inner experiences and responses.

WRITING WORKSHOP

The Sounds in Your Mind (page 111)

Responses will vary.

WRITING WORKSHOP

Unearth a Poem (page 115)

Responses will vary.

The Emotional Weight of Sounds (page 122)

There is an intricate, systematic rhyming structure in Theodore Roethke's "The Waking." The first and third lines of each stanza all end in either the *oh* or *oo* vowel sound, while the second lines end in either *eer* or *air*, thus creating continuous exact or slant rhymes throughout the poem. There is assonance in the refrain "I wake to sleep, and take my waking slow," and alliteration in "I feel my fate in what I cannot fear" as well as in "Light takes the Tree" and "worm climbs up a winding stair."

The Emotional Weight of Rhythms (page 126)

The entire poem is in iambic pentameter, which makes the rhythm uniform and steady. The poem's repetition and its measured rhythmic structure reinforce the theme of taking things slowly, easily, unhurriedly, carefully. The sounds of the words are also gentle and repetitive, soothing, lulling, like an incantation or a lullaby.

Listening to Shakespeare (page 135)

In Shakespeare's "Sonnet 129," there is an alliteration of s sounds in the first line, *l* sounds in the second line, *b* sounds in the third line, *s* sounds in the fourth and fifth lines, *p* sounds in the next four lines, and *h* sounds in the tenth line. The third line contains assonance with "perjured, murderous." In the seventh line, "Past reason hated" echoes "Past reason hunted" from the sixth line. "Hunted" and "hated" contain three identical consonant sounds in the space of a mere two syllables. The repetition of sounds throughout this poem creates a forceful and passionate rhythm. The parallel structure of the series of adjectives in the third and fourth lines is also powerful and emphatic.

WRITING WORKSHOP

Listening for Rhythm (page 139)

The rhythm of "Dream Variations" by Langston Hughes is fast and happy. This is largely accomplished by the preponderance of single-syllable words in this poem. The short words go quickly as we read; there is nothing to slow the reader down. The repetition of the words "whirl" and "dance" and the phrase "to fling" also impel the rhythm.

DISCUSSION WORKSHOP

Repetition and Rhythm (page 140)

In the Margaret Atwood poem "Variation on the Word *Sleep*," the phrase "I would like to" is repeated throughout. Other phrases and words are repeated in singular instances, such as "from the grief at the center / of your dream, from the grief / at the center" and the words "sleeping" and "sleep" in the first stanza. As in Roethke's "The Waking," the repetitions herein give rise to lulling, incantation-like rhythms, which reinforce the themes of sleep, dreams, and realms beyond our normal waking senses. There is also a certain humility as well as persistence in the recurrence of "I would like to . . . [watch / sleep with / walk with / give / protect / follow / be the air that inhabits] . . . you," which underscores the loving, constant, devoted attention of the would-be guardian angel.

Unearth a Poem (page 142)

Discussions will vary.

What's in a Name? (page 142)

Responses will vary.

Metaphors, Similes, and Symbols

6

Suggestions for Teaching

The purposes of this chapter are to stimulate an appreciation of the enormous power of symbols, metaphors, and similes; to make students aware of the ubiquity of symbols and metaphors; and to inspire excitement about noticing them and watching how they work in life and in poetry.

You might start off discussion by posing some or all of the following questions: Is it true, as the *Toolkit* asserts, that we live by and through symbols to a large extent? What would life be like without symbols? Is life without symbols conceivable? What are some of the symbols in our own lives? How do we use them? How do they affect us? Is it true that we make comparisons all the time? How often do we employ comparison? How many comparisons did you make today?

Solicit examples of symbols and metaphors students have noticed in advertising or the media. Solicit examples of metaphors that recently appeared in their conversations. (Perhaps offer a few of your own observations here to get the ball rolling—to use a metaphor!)

This is an extraordinarily rich topic. It will probably take at least two class sessions to cover it well and to give students a fair chance to explore it. This topic should spark plenty of lively discussion, interest, and possibly fascination. It is, after all, a "bottomless" subject. It will require some sensitivity and alertness to be aware of when the discussion is bogging down into an impressionistic mire and to keep it moving along energetically. On the one hand, you want to allow students a chance to explore their thoughts thoroughly and to understand what a particular symbol or metaphor means for them; on the other hand, too much thinking aloud in this vein—as they're processing their impressions—will not hold the class's interest.

WRITING WORKSHOP:

Noticing Similes and Metaphors (page 149)

The simile in Rita Dove's "November for Beginners" is "that softening sky like a sigh of relief." The sigh, of course, would be the release of snow. "Cargo of zithers" is a metaphor for the sound of the wind in the rain. "Breeding mood" is also, arguably, a metaphor. A mood can be created and deepened, but not literally *bred*. Another possible metaphor is the ambiguous "music of decline," which could mean muted, listless conversation or any other manifestation of "winding down" for the season. It most likely does not refer to actual music.

Noticing Metaphors and Similes in Conversation (page 155)

Responses will vary.

Spotting Personification (page 159)

The personification in "Flock" by Lance Henson occurs in the phrase "ice huddles." Only people and animals can huddle. "Joyless valley" too could be considered a personification. Some students may feel that the "whisper of leaves" is also a personification. This is arguable because *whisper* is now a common word for any rustling sound; its meaning has been generalized and calling it a metaphor may be stretching it. Also "snow moves / like an ancient herd" is a personification.

Caged Bird Symbols (page 165)

Maya Angelou's "Caged Bird" can stand for any form of imprisonment: slavery, oppression, jail, poverty of body, mind, or spirit. "Orange sun rays" is a vibrant image of expansion and fulfillment. "Claim the sky" seems to represent making life one's own, pursuing ambitions, living to the fullest, and experiencing an infinity of possibility. The "fearful trill" of the caged bird is the imprisoned soul's expression of frustration, grief, rage, and sorrow. Other forms such an expression might take are various abusive behaviors to oneself and others. But whatever the expression, the oppressed soul "sings of freedom," for it is this instinctive desire that gives rise to the "song" in all its forms, however twisted or sad. The "tune is heard / on the distant hill" for when souls are suffering and incarcerated in prisons of limitation, cruelty, and injustice, the world must somehow hear their cries of pain, even if the hearing occurs on a subconscious level. Because Maya Angelou has often written specifically of the African-American experience, we might assume that the caged bird is African-American. This, however, is merely one feasible reading out of many.

WRITING WORKSHOP

Taking the Symbolic Measure of Simple Things (page 175)

The concrete details of Gary Soto's "Old House in My Fortieth Year" connote many themes, including time, nature, and history. The images of the snail's "single bubble," the chinaberry roots, the moist earth, and the weeds all call to mind the natural place whereupon the house is set, the life of the earth that existed there long before and will continue to be there long after the house and man perish, but which, in the meantime, play host to the artifacts of humanity. The "flesh with its laughter and fatherly scent / Flesh held up by a frayed belt on its last hole" connotes the weakness and ephemerality of the body, the inevitability of its decline and death. Yet there is a sentimentality in all these details as well; the body is, after all, a loyal and well-known friend, and the natural things of the earth are somehow inhuman yet not impersonal, especially in this familiar place. We can sense, through a careful reading, that the natural elements convey intimations of reassurance (as well as mortality) to this narrator; they affirm that he too has a rightful place in this arrangement, that he and his house are part of the natural scheme of things.

In the second stanza, "the man pushing a cart" and the "long row of cotton" probably represent other lives this narrator could just as easily have found himself leading, had he been born in another body, in another place. But "stars wheeled around an icy comet" and, just as inexorably and mysteriously, the hand of fate, or chance, or luck, decreed that he be made "at home in this body" and in this life, as opposed to another.

There is an overriding theme here of *home* and all that *home* can symbolize. Having "a place to call home," a "place to be in the world," is a marvelous and mysterious thing. How did we come to be rooted (or oriented) where we are? How did we come to inhabit these particular bodies? What divine chance made it such that we come from these particular roots and not others? Is there a reason for it, a master plan? Or did we just happen into our particular places?

DISCUSSION WORKSHOP

Mind-Healing Metaphors (page 179)

Kahlil Gibran's verse "On Death" contains a host of symbolic and metaphorical images, all of which promise a greater destiny and more expansive existence beyond life as we know it. We are compared to the owl "whose night-bound eyes are blind unto the day." So is our vision "night-bound" as well, though we don't know it? Is death in fact a "brighter day" than life? "For life and death are one, even as the river and the sea are one." The river, vast and grand as it may be, is but a small stream compared to the ocean. So is life as we know it but a tributary of the vast ocean that death has in store for us? "In the depth of your hopes and desires lies your silent knowledge of the beyond; / And like seeds dreaming beneath the snow your heart dreams of spring." Here again, we are dreaming, yearning for something as yet inaccessible to us; we are "beneath the snow." Death, it seems, holds out a great promise to us of our inarticulate heart's desire. Like the shepherd "more mindful of his trembling" than of the honor about to be bestowed when he stands before the king, our fear of death is but a reflexive flinching from the new and unknown, even as we sense deeply that we are about to undergo an exalted transformation.

The metaphorical images that follow in the last two stanzas are still more dramatic and affirmative and exciting. To "stand naked in the wind and melt into the sun" and to "free the breath from its restless tides," are images that suggest tremendous peace, power, and liberation. The final three lines (last stanza) are paradoxes, just as death itself is allegedly a paradox, the very opposite of what it seems; actually a birth, an opening into a new life.

Both Whitman and Gibran are very optimistic about death, but their views are somewhat different in emphasis. Whitman envisions the ceaseless continuation of nature, of which we are necessarily a part. In Whitman there is no explicit reassurance that we continue to exist as individual souls after our deaths, whereas Gibran emphatically affirms that we do, in his repeated use of the word "you" and in his emphasis on transcendent states of being. While Whitman extols the glory of grass and "the smallest sprout," Gibran speaks of the opportunity to "rise and expand and seek God unencumbered." Whitman is earthly; Gibran ethereal. What they have in common is a vision of death as an *opening* into a greater, more expansive identity, a union with some all-encompassing source.

DISCUSSION WORKSHOP

Visions in the Darkness (page 180)

Concerning Robert Frost's "Acquainted with the Night," words such as "night" and "rain" will naturally call forth a plethora of connotations. Some students will also perceive the "luminary clock" to be the moon, in its aspect as an indicator of the passage of time. "Furthest city light" and "saddest city lane" may represent the extremes of one's soul, the desolate areas in one's internal universe. "Time was neither wrong nor right" could indicate the absence of bearings in a dark, uncharted place, where normal points of reference—including night and day—have been forsaken. The "watchman" could be a conscience, or a last vestige of normalcy and civilization. The "interrupted cry" could signify fear, terror, perhaps even a murder or some other dark crime. In any case, there is apparently a strong suggestion of danger here. "Acquainted with the night" could mean familiarity with danger, dark places, the obscure recesses of the soul. There are an infinite number of ways to "interpret" the symbolic resonances in this poem, and no doubt students will come up with several.

WRITING WORKSHOP

A Radiant Poem (page 182)

There are also many ways to view "The Sick Rose" by William Blake. In a general sense, this poem speaks of some insidious agency "worming" its way to the core of that which is healthy and vibrant, wreaking destruction and ruin. Students may see the worm as a metaphor for cancer or some other degenerative disease that sabotages the body. The "bed of crimson joy" may be the blood cells. Others may perceive a theme that all good, healthy, and living things are ultimately undone and disintegrate; the "invisible worm" is but the force of destiny and time. But perhaps the most provocative phrase in the poem is "dark secret love." Why use the word *love* for a destructive element? When, in life, is "love" actually dark and destructive? What does "love" do? Well, sometimes love, like the worm, clings, nests, sets in, does not let go, devours. That which is loved is inevitably changed as well; love leaves its mark. The rose may bloom with independent beauty for a little while in its "bed of crimson joy," but once it has attracted the "worm" of love, things can never be the same. Arguably, loss of innocence is also a theme here.

The "night" is dark, and the powers of destruction often move and thrive within the darkness. The "howling storm" is fierce and fearsome—and an expression of nature, just like the rose. A sense of inevitability pervades this poem, for some readers, as if all of the elements and agencies involved, and the dynamics between them, are all of one piece.

WRITING WORKSHOP

Unearth a Poem (page 183)

Responses will vary.

WRITING WORKSHOP

A Symbolic Object (page 183)

Responses will vary.

A Grab Bag of Devices

7

Suggestions for Teaching

The objectives of this chapter are to increase students' awareness of various poetic devices and to draw their attention closer to the details of how poems are constructed, line by line and word by word.

You might begin discussion by asking these questions: Which of the devices covered in this chapter of the *Toolkit* were of particular interest, and why? Were there any that people had never heard of before? Which ones? How does awareness of the existence of these devices—and other ones examined in previous chapters—affect the overall experience of reading poetry? Does it cause us to look more closely at poems? Does it distract from the immediate, intuitive, emotional apprehension of poetry? Or does this awareness work in tandem with intuition? Ask if anyone knows of any other poetic devices, aside from those which have been covered in the *Toolkit*.

You may want to stress that this catalog of poetic elements should not cause students to feel overwhelmed. They should consider it a bank of interesting items to notice in poems, not a list of terms to memorize.

Remember to emphasize what the devices *do,* as well as what they *are.* Especially with instances of allusion, provocative line breaks, or thematic recurrence, the primary focus should be on their *purpose* or *effect,* and this should spark some good, reflective discussion.

Connecting with Line Breaks (page 189)

In William Carlos Williams's "The Last Words of My English Grandmother," the third line of the third stanza ends with "I won't go" and the sentence is completed in the next line: "to the hospital." In the following stanza, second line, the narrator says "Let me take you" and this sentence also breaks before the concluding words "to the hospital." There may be a subtle intimation here that the hospital is somehow unmentionable, that going there implies a terrible fate.

The final line of the fourth stanza, "and after you are well," is left hanging, as it were, before the next stanza begins. It is a lie; the narrator knows his grandmother will not get well again, and so does she. There is hypocrisy in these words, and it is "poetic justice" that it should linger glaringly in the pause between the stanzas.

The last two lines of the eighth stanza, "Then we started. / On the way," could be one syntactically complete sentence. In fact, "Then we started." is a complete sentence onto itself, and "On the way" begins the following sentence. But this ambiguity is also portentous: "On the way," unspecified, suspended between the stanzas, has symbolic connotations of a final journey.

The second-to-last line of the poem ends with the words "Well, I'm tired" and then, in the final line, this sentence is concluded: "of them." The surface meaning of this statement is that she is tired of trees (a curious statement in itself!). However, "Well, I'm tired" by itself, before the line break, indicates a more general, all-inclusive tiredness, perhaps a state of being tired of life itself. One plausible reading of the poem is that when she "rolled her head away" she also died that same moment.

WRITING WORKSHOP

Extracting the Motif (page 196)

The motif of snow in Kenneth Patchen's "The Snow Is Deep on the Ground" seems to represent purity, goodness, and holiness. Perhaps it also represents cleansing and renewal. Just as "rain washes clean," so also must the snow, and this is why "war shall fail" ultimately. "Whiteness" in this poem seems equated to godliness and spiritual majesty. This is one classical symbolic interpretation of "white light," just as "old king" is one of the classic images of God.

DISCUSSION WORKSHOP

Hyperbole, Homelessness, and You (page 201)

People may disagree as to whether Julia Vinograd is actually blaming passersby for stinginess in her poem "Sparechangers." There are indications of blame ("you couldn't spare a quarter?") and also indications of sympathy ("You have a right to the self you were / before you walked down the block"). In any case, she is calling attention to a dilemma. Passersby may wish to deny that there *is* a dilemma when they are faced with a block of bereft panhandlers, but Vinograd denies them their denial. Perhaps the accusations in the poem are ironic, perhaps the sense of guilt is overblown and unjust, but what is plain is that *a sense of responsibility* is a natural and rightful response to the sight of other humans in a destitute condition (especially when these destitute ones are begging for help). The question is, where does one's responsibility begin and end? What is a passerby to do, after all? One cannot feed or clothe or give money to each and every homeless person. There are certainly no easy answers; Vinograd herself provides none, but she affirms that *the dilemma is real,* and that the dilemma is *shared* by the homeless as well: "And the homeless want their homes back / they have a right to the selves they were before." We are all in this together, there is no ignoring it.

Students will have diverse reactions to this poem. Some may become defensive; others righteous. Some may "agree" with Vinograd. This poem is a kind of mirror for how one feels about oneself in these kinds of situations, presuming one has been in such a situation. Many readers may feel called upon to justify themselves after reading this poem, rationalizing why they do not and should not ever give change to panhandlers. It is important to try and keep the focus on the poem, not on the issue of panhandling. Do you feel accused by Vinograd? Where? Why? Do you think she's altogether serious here?

WRITING WORKSHOP

Synesthetic Synergy (page 204)

"The Blindman" by May Swenson is replete with instances of synesthesia: "purple's taste," "fragrances of the rainbow," "crimson's flute," "Trumpets tell me yellow," "Only ebony is mute." Also the blindman's excitement is green (the feeling of the grass against his cheek), and he "feels" the red color in the thread of the scarf. Metaphors include "fallen beads of sight," "vectors to its thread that dance down from the sun," "orange hair of flames," and the notion of grass as "little whips." This poem is largely about colors, tastes, textures, smells, and sounds, all of which broadcast the vibrancy of the blindman's world of sensation. The symbolic import of the various colors may be entirely subjective; in fact, they are entirely subjective—to the blindman. For many of us, green is a calm color and crimson is loud and dramatic, not subtle and delicate like a flute. To many readers, ebony is quite eloquent and sea-blue and white are joyous colors (as opposed to a "basin of tears"). The key here is that symbolic resonances rely on context and also on our individual sets of associations; this blindman's associations may necessarily differ from ours. Still, what we have in common with the blindman is that all touches and tastes and sensations reverberate symbolically and associatively in our psyches, though we may not often be as keenly awake to these resonances as the blindman is.

WRITING WORKSHOP

Unearth a Poem (page 207)

Responses will vary.

WRITING WORKSHOP

Unearth Another Poem (page 207)

Responses will vary.

Creating a Quilt (page 207)

Answers will vary.

Irrationality, Dreams, and Paradox

8

Suggestions for Teaching

In a sense, this is a fairly challenging chapter, and in another sense, this should be one of the easiest. The purpose here is to allow students to move away, temporarily, from rigorous analysis and to let go of all "explanations." Another objective is to induce students to consider the limitations of ordinary thinking habits and the possible practical uses of irrationality.

Ask: What are the uses of irrationality? How does irrationality play a part in our lives? When is it expedient to be irrational, to employ irrational thinking or behavior? (Examples could include falling in love, listening to music, or rooting for a sports team.) How does irrationality *serve* us?

Some people may resist this topic; they may feel threatened by the idea of taking the irrational seriously. Reassure them that this is merely an optional avenue of exploration, a diversion even, and most certainly not a prescription for how we should normally live or think. If one is generally rational, an occasional small dose of irrationality will not endanger one's mental health.

At this point in the course, students will be used to analyzing poems in a rational manner, and they will probably employ their accustomed methods of articulating the impact of poetic devices to this chapter's poems. By all means, permit this; this may be the only language available with which to discuss irrational material, and this is perfectly appropriate.

Ask what people know, or have heard, of Zen. Perhaps bring in a few Zen stories to share, or some Zen koans. You might also bring in a print of a painting by a surrealist artist like Salvador Dalí. In discussing dreams, you might also explain, in broad strokes, the aboriginal concept of dreamtime and the value that aboriginal cultures place on dreams.

What does it mean to have expanded perception? In what ways, if any, do our habitual modes of thought limit what we perceive? (Perhaps solicit examples of moments of expanded awareness, but beware that some people may wax rhapsodic.)

In preparation for this class session, you might ask everyone in the class to write down five of their favorite words. Stipulate that at least two of these words should be concrete nouns. Then type each of these favorite words onto a sheet of paper and make photocopies for every three to four students in the class. Cut these lists so that each word appears on its own separate scrap of paper, or better yet, ask the students to do this for you in small groups.

Instruct your students to create, in a small group, a poem from this set of words. Instruct them to spread the words out on their desks, shuffle them around, and order and reorder them until they have made, to their minds, a poem. Also explain that they are not required to use all of the words.

Give them at least fifteen to twenty minutes for this exercise. Tell them that they can add whatever conjunctions, prepositions, or articles they need, but otherwise they may utilize only the words they have at hand. (Perhaps you may also permit them to alter verb tenses.) You might encourage them to create poems that seem to make intuitive, meta-rational sense. In the end, allow each group to share its brand new poem with the entire class.

This entire discussion may give rise to a good deal of laughter. If so, that's great. There is certainly no need to be excessively serious about that which is, by definition, unserious.

Anything There? (page 214)

There are many conceivable symbolic implications in the stanzas of Roger McGough's "What You Are." The theme of iconoclasm seems present throughout, and in particular, a certain antiwar/military/retribution sentiment seems intimated in the first, second, fifth, and sixth stanzas. The third and fourth stanzas connote themes of vulnerability and fallibility ("turned into flesh," "closed their eyes," "burst into tears," "picked their noses") in counterpoint to the themes of violent force and catastrophe in surrounding stanzas.

There is a motif of some sort in the repetition of "you are the moment." There is unquestionably a momentous, portentous quality to this phrase, as if one is standing at the brink of some cataclysmic event, possibly one of cosmic proportion. Stanza by stanza, by and large, the lines that follow this phrase do not disappoint such expectations.

Some of this, of course, seems purely fantastical, particularly the last stanza ("You are the moment / before the clouds became locomotives / and hurtled headlong into the sun"). But even this, with its themes of ascension and transcendence, follows thematically from intimations of Armageddon in previous stanzas.

Some students may choose to analyze this poem in terms of the individual stanzas. This is fine, but it may be useful to point out that these stanzas could bear some relationship to each other.

Grasping the Ungraspable (page 216)

In Antonio Machado's poem, the statement "We know nothing of our own souls / that are ununderstandable and say nothing" is a compound of negatives. There may be something Zenlike in so much negation. It strains the limits of rationality to even contemplate the existence of something so unknowable and inconceivable, and yet this particular something is the essence of what we *are,* our souls. So how can we know anything at all, if our own core is so obscure to us?

In the second stanza, Machado states that the sounds of wind and water have as much to "teach" us as the wisest of words. Here again, this is not irrational per se; it is merely unfathomable. In trying to fathom how it could be so, we are, in a sense, up against a kind of Zen koan. To grasp the truth, such as it is, in what he is saying here, we cannot use rationality; we have to think in an altogether different way.

Plumbing the Paradox (page 222)

Concerning the paradoxes in Gary Snyder's "As for Poets," the Fire Poets who "burn at absolute zero" are clearly more powerful and "explosive" in their activity than propane gas or fuel oil. Subfreezing temperatures may still the gaseous elements, but the inspiration of the poet is irrepressible and it flows impervious to temperature. The Space Poet dwells in the infinity of space; there is no end to his sky, but there may be an "edge" past which things can no longer be perceived or articulated. His poems fly headlong into a deep mystery, beyond the horizon of what may constitute, for us, the "edge" of our understanding and knowledge. The house of the Mind

Poet is, of course, his mind, which has no walls and is empty of furniture and other such clutter; it is entirely open to the "elements," and it is illuminated from all directions at once.

Looking at the other stanzas, the Earth Poets are genuinely humble; they write poems that reflect their understanding of their place and proportion; they are securely oriented and require no "help" for they are firmly supported by the very ground. The Air Poets ride the winds; they leave the ground and their words give expression to the rhythms of the air. The Water Poets are primeval; they delve deep, they get muddy and "covered with seaweed," and they come into contact with the organismic precursors of complex life.

DISCUSSION WORKSHOP

Who Might She Be? (page 225)

Karynn Fish's turtlewoman can be many things. She may be another aspect of the speaker's personality. She may represent some primitive identity or deeper self that the addressee of the poem is looking for in other people, instead of seeking within. In this poem, there is a distinct yearning in the direction of a more primitive, less conscious state of being: ". . . she's some wisewoman / Who can tell you why you've wasted so much time / with ribs, and thumbs, and wombs. . . " Ribs and thumbs and wombs are definitions we evolved as mammals, after much time spent out of the water. Perhaps, in some deep recess of our being, we all long for our primordial home. Perhaps there is even a certain wisdom attendant to the purely instinctive mind, which is subsequently lost to cognitive animals and becomes farther and farther removed with the advent of rationality and more sophisticated brain functions. Fish makes skillful and deliberate use of line breaks in this poem. Twice she ends her lines with the word *think:* "I used to think," "You think." Both of these, at a glance, stand as statements unto themselves, and this echoes the theme of rationality as a kind of evolutionary culprit.

Other "loaded" line breaks include "hatched in the corpse-glow," "your fingers were searching," "you were the one," and, most especially, "I know the turtlewoman kept your number." All of these contain possible double meanings and symbolic implications.

There is a tension in this poem between the primordial and youth. Youth and newness are qualities in this poem that are as inescapable and inexorable as evolution itself. Hence one may go searching for "a more primitive water" and instead find oneself following "pennyspun ellipses" around the moon. The turtlewoman may have a "birdnosed face" and "scuffed-leather eyes," but she is also young and rich. Oddly, this poem turns on its head the common theme of youth denying or ignoring history, ancestry, and mortality—youth always feeling itself to be "something new under the sun" with no debt of obligation or acknowledgment to that which came before. Instead, this poem identifies an impulse to cleave to biological origins, to embrace the enormity of history at the expense of that which is new and fresh.

In a sense, we can be said to possess two essential dimensions: a contemporary, forward-looking, self-creating dimension and an historic, preconscious, biologically determined dimension. Each is as real as the other; both are powerful and utterly intrinsic to our being. There is no escaping either one, no denying one for sake of the other.

WRITING WORKSHOP

Articulating the Sense That You Impose (page 230)

Wallace Stevens's "Thirteen Ways of Looking at a Blackbird" stanzas lend themselves to an extremely broad and subjective array of interpretation. The common theme, however, is that

blackbirds are portentous and powerful. They are also pierc-
ingly conscious and knowing. The blackbird in stanza III has
a "part of the pantomime." In stanza V the blackbird is
implicitly capable of creating "innuendoes." Blackbirds inspire
fear in stanza XI and, even more significantly, the narrator
in stanza VIII declares that "the blackbird is involved / in
what I know."

WRITING WORKSHOP

Your Own Dreamy Nonsense (page 230)

Responses will vary.

WRITING WORKSHOP

Unearth a Poem (page 231)

Responses will vary.

WELDING IT TOGETHER

9

Suggestions for Teaching

The object of this chapter is to give students a chance to express what they feel they have gained from this course and what they now think about poetry in general. This is an especially appropriate time to allow students to share poems they like or have written themselves, as a way of concluding the term on a celebratory note.

Ask: Does poetry make a difference in our lives? In what ways is poetry like life, and life like poetry? Allow students, if they like, to give short presentations about particular poets they have discovered for themselves.

This final class should be light and enjoyable, perhaps as much a forum for "show and tell" as a unit of classroom instruction. This is primarily an opportunity for students to look back and reflect on what they have learned and felt throughout the course. As such, it will amplify and reinforce their cumulative experience.

Concerning the poem "I Know I'm Not Sufficiently Obscure," it may be worth noting that Roy Durem employs distinctly poetic techniques in quite a few instances that are not specified in the text. There are several alliterative phrases, including "pale poets," "black boy, blacker," "a little whine, a little whimper," and "finer feelings." Also, "clothe the carnage" contains both alliteration and metaphor.

DISCUSSION WORKSHOP

How about Us? (page 238)

There is a danger that small group discussions about *meaning* and *being* could slip into amorphous abstraction, particularly if any alert individuals should introduce *doing* into the discussion as a third dimension or as an aspect of *meaning*. The best thing to do is to try and clarify distinctions (such as they are) early on, perhaps before breaking the class into small groups. Ask: What is the *difference* between *meaning* and *being*? What is the relationship between the two? This preliminary discussion could and probably should be brief; still, arriving at consensual definitions in a large group may provide some useful scaffolding for the small group discussions that follow.

You may want to encourage students to come up with some concrete examples of *meaning* and *being* in their small group discussions, in addition to their explanations. In a large-group preliminary discussion, you might want to pose questions such as, "When you're asleep, are you *being* or are you *meaning*? Which are you doing *more* of? How about when you watch TV? When you write an English paper? When you're reading? Driving? How about right now? *Why?*"

Should anyone object that these conceptual distinctions are ultimately artificial and meaningless, you might point out that, whether or not this is true, they are nonetheless useful tools with which we may examine ourselves and our condition and with which we can investigate the mystery of who and what and why we are. The ultimate answers to these questions may be forever inaccessible, but they are relevant to us all the same. Therefore, the activity of pursuing these answers is worthwhile. This pursuit of mystery—the drive to articulate the inexpressible—is also a primary function of poetry.